The
Pleasure of
Your Company

Also by Molly O'Neill

New York Cookbook
A Well-Seasoned Appetite

The
Pleasure of
Your Company

How to Give a Dinner Party
Without Losing Your Mind

Molly O'Neill

Recipes tested by
Lee Ann Cox

VIKING

VIKING
Published by the Penguin Group
Penguin Books USA Inc., 375 Hudson Street, New York, New York 10014, U.S.A.
Penguin Books Ltd, 27 Wrights Lane, London W8 5TZ, England
Penguin Books Australia Ltd, Ringwood, Victoria, Australia
Penguin Books Canada Ltd, 10 Alcorn Avenue, Toronto, Ontario, Canada M4V 3B2
Penguin Books (N.Z.) Ltd, 182-190 Wairau Road, Auckland 10, New Zealand

Penguin Books Ltd, Registered Offices:
Harmondsworth, Middlesex, England

First published in 1997 by Viking Penguin, a division of Penguin Books USA Inc.

1 2 3 4 5 6 7 8 9 10

LIBRARY OF CONGRESS CATALOGING IN PUBLICATION DATA
O'Neill, Molly
The pleasure of your company : how to give a dinner party
without losing your mind / Molly O'Neill.
p. cm.
Includes index.
ISBN 0-670-87226-0 (alk. paper)
1. Dinners and dining. 2. Entertaining. I. Title.
TX737.044   1997
642'.4—dc20   96-43710

This book is printed on acid-free paper.

∞

Printed in the United States of America
Set in Bernhardt Modern
Designed by Richard Oriolo

For Adair Miller Burlingham,
    who has never feared company for dinner,

And R. Scott Bromley,
    who can turn any place into a party with three yards of ribbon, two
    candles, six long-stemmed roses, and ten yards of gauze,

and Peter W. Prestcott,
    who always knows what to say,

       with thanks

The author wishes to thank the editing, fact-checking, and art departments of *The New York Times Magazine*, who work together every week to produce the food column. Especially Andy Port, my thoughtful and irascible editor, and Sarah Harbutt, the imaginative and dogged photo editor.

Thank you, too, Dawn Drzal, senior editor at Viking, whose unflagging enthusiasm remains invaluable.

And finally, Arthur H. Samuelson, who hates to entertain but loves me enough to do so with alarming frequency.

A Note from the Author

Over the past three years, it has been my privilege to listen to a group of hostesses as well as a caterer discuss entertaining in the age of dietary health concerns and the two-income household. I was a fly-on-the-wall as this group sought to reconcile its Martha Stewart impulse with the reality of the time pressure in their daily lives.

While none of them intended to accomplish anything more than figure out how to cook for company without losing their minds, it occurred to me that the issues they grappled with and the menus with which they resolved these issues actually constituted a blueprint for rational entertaining in an irrational world. Therefore, the group has generously allowed me to record their conversations, expound on the basic concepts they created and developed, and test their recipes for publication. They asked to remain anonymous. I remain in their debt.

While writing a weekly column for *The New York Times Magazine* and speaking about cooking across the country, I hear the same questions that this group asked themselves: How can I cook a memorable meal for company while working full-time and caring for my family? What sorts of dishes can be prepared ahead of time? What do guests really want? How can I give a party and enjoy my company at the same time?

As I researched the eating habits of Americans for several months in the past year, the paradox between what people say they want and what they actually eat became clear to me. At no other time in recent American history have people said they wanted to eat more healthfully—and in fact eaten quite as unhealthfully as they do today. In researching entertaining styles, another paradox emerged: Hostesses clamor for simplicity, but they dream—and often produce—grand schemes. Indeed, as the time available for leisurely cooking has shrunk, the expectation for the sorts of meals that require lengthy preparation time, as well as significant skill, has skyrocketed.

The questions I hear from readers tell me that cooking for company became the crux of the paradox between what people say they want, what they fantasize, and what, in the end, they finally do. The impulses are so conflicting that many people simply give up entertaining altogether. Others overcompensate and produce overwhelming fêtes that exhaust them and strain their budgets. Still others try scheme after scheme—simpler menus, buffets, catered affairs, buying certain dishes fully cooked and preparing others from scratch—in an attempt to strike a reasonable, and convivial, balance.

Entertaining is not easy. Even the simplest-looking affair takes time and money and skill. The hostess juggles these commodities, exchanging one for the other. Reading memoirs and household diaries from the nineteenth and twentieth centuries has convinced me that this has always been true. Cooking for company is either a challenge or a chore; it depends on how you look at it.

Imaginative concepts and stylish, reliable recipes can help turn the chore into a challenge. Clear forethought can turn the challenge into a pleasure. In nearly a hundred conversations, the group got to the pleasure part. That is why I am telling their story.

Contents

Part One **The Group**

Part Two **A Program for Rational Entertaining in an Irrational Age**
The Process, the Concepts, the Menus, and the Recipes of Five People Who Care

The
Pleasure of
Your Company

Part One

The Group

The Day
the Party Died

Mr. D., the famous if not infamous Manhattan caterer, caught a glimpse of himself in the double glass doors of Mrs. J.'s Traulsen refrigerator. In his Armani tuxedo and Nicole Miller bow tie, he looked perfect, of course. But he was disturbed by his hair. Thinning, it had to be combed just so. The reflection showed the hair falling at a rakish angle to be sure, but there it was: the hint of a pate.

Even as he caressed the errant strands back into place, Mr. D. knew that something more than a hair crisis was pulling his signature smile into a troubled frown.

"Is something the matter with the caviar?" he asked Lance, the captain. Mr. D. knew full well that the caviar was perfect, each gray egg luminously fresh, flawless in crunch and brine.

"Haven't you heard, darling?" replied Lance, who had just returned from the dining room with four Limoges plates on which the mounds of beluga lay virtually untouched. "The rich prefer potatoes." He licked his fingers and winked meaningfully, as if he'd just shared some secret of the universe.

Too weak to push through the swinging door and survey the softly lighted dining room, Mr. D. imagined instead the delicately dappled scene recast in the dark, cruel strokes of van Gogh's *Potato Eaters*. Suddenly, he felt very tired, bonetired, tired in the soul, the sort of tired he hadn't known since the days he waited tables and scrambled from acting class to dance class, from voice class to auditions. In the end, he'd chosen to be a one-trick pony; no one played consort to and coddler of the rich better than Mr. D.

He'd never doubted his decision until tonight, as each of the five waiters pushed through the dining-room door bearing Limoges smudged with scorned caviar.

"Mrs. Kaplan brought her own baked potato," said Lance. "Can we steam vegetables for her?"

Mr. D. felt a cold sweat spread across his brow. It was over. The days of grilled fish and celery and pasta and mesclun salad had come to an end. Potatoes were the signal that the rich meant to eat—or at least to appear to eat—wholeheartedly again.

The caterer was not sure why this realization made him tremble. No one understood the fickle tide of tastes and appetites better than he. Once he had gotten over envying the rich—that is, as soon as he himself began to make money—he understood the essence of their eating habits, which, in a democracy, is all about perversity.

This recognition was the key to his prodigious career. The day he saw frozen quiche at the A&P in East Hampton, he knew that the rich would lose their taste for it, and before you could say beef Wellington, he had ushered in Nouvelle Cuisine—not invented, of course, no; Mr. D. had minted the dishes for high-class dinner parties.

And while he remains justly proud of his raspberry vinaigrette and his chicken breast poached with dried apricots and Sauternes, he'd known, even before the kiwi hit, that the time was propitious for the New American Cuisine.

For a moment, his troubled expression softened and he allowed himself to smile. Underneath all that venison and regional this and that, the New American Cuisine was all about lettuce and celery. Guests wanted the picture of a pretty plate, the allure of creativity, tinged with a hint of Americana. But they only ate cellulose, just as they always had.

Maybe the money had distracted him. In retrospect, Mr. D. realized that he had missed a cue. Now that obesity, diabetes, hypertension, and heart disease were recognized as public-health hazards, now that the general public had become aware of its nutritional deficiencies and excesses, now that lean, stylized dishes appeared on the covers of women's magazines, and mainstream supermarkets sold organic mesclun, of course the rich would require a change of menu.

A wave of relief washed over the caterer. He had seen the future and it was brown (in contrast to the vividly colored, low-fat dishes), communal (unlike the à la carte entrées shown in the magazines), and peasant-like (yes, the mood is definitely moving toward Marie Antoinette in her dairy). The future was stew.

It's Life, Not
Potatoes, Not Stew

Johanna lifted the large, brightly glazed mug she had purchased in the "seconds" shop at Deruta, in Umbria, toward her lips. She inhaled the aroma of the first morning cappuccino and luxuriated as the dense foam that topped the beverage tickled her upper lip. Two-percent milk. How the threshold of indulgence changes! Her slurp seemed to echo through the rambling apartment at Seventy-fifth and Central Park West. Mark and the children were still asleep, the traffic that later in the day would beetle noisily between her window and the park was languid, almost still. For this reason, along with caffeine and morning papers, the forty-five-year-old documentary filmmaker was always up at 5:00 A.M. It was, she supposed, a holdover from the years when the children were young and sleep was no longer an option. But now that they were in school, the hour between 5:00 A.M. and 6:00 A.M. was the only time she had the chance to respond to nothing but herself. And her coffee.

She scanned the headlines and flipped, automatically, to Page 6 in the *New*

York Post. She told herself, as well as anyone who noted her morning habit, that gossip columns were research. She documented popular culture. Her most recent film, *A Day at a Time*, a ninety-minute report on the recovery movement in America, had won an Emmy and found an audience both among academics and in art cinemas across the United States. And in fact, she'd first noticed the increased talk about twelve-step programs and recovery in the raw gush of tattletale on that page in the latter part of the 1980s. It was like Le Tout Society was recovering from a bender, each confronting (or at least claiming to confront) his or her own peculiar manifestation. It took three years of research and interviews for Johanna to place this phenomenon in its cultural context. Jaded critics suggested that she'd actually timed the release of *Getting Better* with the sixtieth anniversary of Alcoholics Anonymous. But they were wrong. Johanna had read the newspapers and followed her hunch.

"Park Avenue Potato Eaters," announced the headline that caught her eye.

"The cream, or should we say the no-fat yogurt, of Manhattan Society boycotted caviar and staged a sit-in for potatoes at the Park Avenue Penthouse of society poohbahs Eliza and Kenneth (Mr. Arbitrage) Jameson last evening. They sat in Biedermeier chairs, of course. And presumably demanded exclusive fingerling potatoes.

"'I heard no call for Idahos,' sniffed Danny Delight, owner of the oh-so-posh Fabulous Food catering company. Insiders say that Mr. D. did hear the roar of a culinary sea change, however. 'Conspicuous Consumption is passé,' said one-who-was-there. 'Too much guilt, too much arterial plaque.'

"What happens when they just can't eat cake? Stay tuned."

Johanna gazed out through the gray February morning. The skeletal trees looked, for a moment, vascular and vulnerable to her. She was almost as well known for her dinner parties as she was for her films; she noticed that the glue that holds a party together had been loosening for several years. It wasn't, she thought, entirely a result of the psychic change from the go-go-go eighties to the deep and meaningful nineties.

Sure, the narcissism of the eighties had promoted health concerns; fitness and health, she thought, were two of the gifts of excess. And as those concerns escalated, she'd noticed increasing numbers of her dinner guests requesting special meals for their very special diets. She accommodated them, but felt what she called "the me-me dinner guest" (*my* Program, *my* Diet, *my* Concerns are more important than *your* menu) eroding the communal nature of the dinners she cooked.

There was a growing "à la carte" mentality that Johanna found both annoying and, for reasons she couldn't quite express, sad. This happened in the eighties; well, the rich are always a decade behind, she thought smugly. Johanna rarely missed an opportunity to assert herself as a "scholarship student," particularly now that her pictures were making, well, quite a tidy sum. She didn't mention that her "scholarships" and "work-study" were courtesy of Barnard.

Individual health concerns had decimated dinner parties. But only because the form of parties had not changed rapidly enough to accommodate the change in how people ate. The form, in fact, was a dinosaur. The traditional dinner party was predicated on a woman's remaining at home, with lots of help. Women hadn't been at home for nearly thirty years! And who had "help," other than baby-sitters and cleaning ladies? No one she knew, certainly.

Guilt? Mrs. J.'s guests feel guilty? About the homeless? About the unemployed? About those who can't afford to seek medical advice (and, presumably, more up-to-date diets) outside their own HMOs? They should try being a working woman if they want a little taste of guilt!

Being a listener, Johanna had heard plenty of murmuring about how the mothers of her generation were "indulging" their children, what a disgrace it was that they couldn't just-say-no to their children. Well, you try dropping your ten-month-old off at a day-care center for nine hours a day and see how easy it is to tell them they can't have a cookie before dinner, sweetheart!

She'd heard women of her mother's generation talk about how they'd spent thirty years "building" a home, while their daughters just dashed out to Bloomingdale's or ABC Carpet and Home Furnishings and *bought* the stuff that turns a house into a home. Well, ladies, you try thinking in terms of thirty years when you don't have thirty minutes to call your own! You were *home*. We buy interior designs because we haven't got time for an inner life! We buy hominess because we aren't at home. Get it?

And she'd seen plenty of raised eyebrows over the drama her generation made about cooking and entertaining and fussing and obsessing. Sure, it's expensive and takes tons of time. But guess what? That's the price of guilt.

Besides, food and style had been a wedge between her generation, self-anointed enlightened epicures, and her mother's, the casserole queens, since the former had come home from college and demanded vegetarian Thanksgivings. And we kept distinguishing ourselves: Nouvelle Cuisine, New American Cuisine, California Cuisine, Lean Cuisine.

No single force had turned Mrs. J.'s guests against caviar, she thought. No, there were dozens of tributaries—health, the two-income household, the residual need to distinguish oneself from and do better than Mom, the madness of maintaining the appearance of hospitality and grace when one barely has the time to, well, go to the bathroom, if you'd like to know the truth.

The fact that all of this had to do with social stature did not escape Johanna, nor was she unaware of the fact that women, in her opinion, were, as usual, carrying the burden of showing the world that everything is fine, just great, grand.

The dinner party, she thought, had always been a pageantry of image in which a hostess delineates precisely how she wishes her family and self to be perceived by the world. What sort of self-portrait did she paint? Bountiful and capable. Johanna suddenly felt teary. The trees in the park, all those naked branches, like vessels around hearts, all feeding from the same ground, up against the same air, each reaching for the light in a different way.

Nan, the serious young medical researcher who had worked as a consultant on *Getting Better All the Time*, often called her in a panic about the parties she and her husband gave. It occurred to Johanna that the sixteen-year difference in their ages played a large role in the confidence that she herself had about her cooking and the lack of confidence from which Nan suffered.

It didn't have to do with age: Johanna had always been a self-assured hostess. Rather, having grown up in the 1950s, she had a memory of meals that were not so much about food as they were about being together. She had fragments of memories about the feel of food as she stood on a stool, "helping" her mother, of smells, of sounds. Johanna could remember visceral hate for certain tastes— Brussels sprouts, for instance—and unmitigated love for others, such as the crack-lings from the fried chicken that would be left in the pan, the thrill of licking German Chocolate Cake batter from the spatula.

These experiences, she thought, gave her both an emotional and a physio-logical relationship with food. However cockeyed and back-of-the-box-gourmet her mother's cooking had been, dinner had been about time and care. Sure, she rebelled against her mother's Foley food mill and Jell-O molds. But even the rebel-lion was about feeling and taste—the rebellion, in fact, showed her where she stood in this world. All this added up to a certain sort of self-knowledge, which in Johanna's book is the essence of self-confidence.

At twenty-nine, Nan was a member of the microwave and Cuisinart genera-tion. Her mother had worked. Her first experiences in the kitchen were of the typical latchkey-kid variety. When she got home from school, she attempted to assiduously follow the notes that her mother had left her: "Turn on the Crock-Pot at 4:00 P.M.," "Put the chicken in the oven at 350 degrees at 4:30." When the little girl fell short, dinner was misery. Nan once confided that following recipes and instructions had been fine training for a young scientist. But, thought Johanna, it made Nan a nervous cook. The poor thing had never had a visceral relationship with food; rather, she had had an intellectual relationship with following directions.

Nan's intellectual approach to cooking had eventually received further

It's Life,
Not Potatoes,
Not Stew

grooming from newspapers and magazines. When she set up her household, celebrating food in print was passé. By then, all you could read about was the danger: salt would kill you, eggs would clot you, alar would deform your children. The worry-a-day school of journalism, if you asked Johanna. And look what the approach bred: a generation scared of their own shadows in the kitchen.

Johanna had eaten at Nan's several times and had the feeling that there was a good cook beneath all the younger woman's worry. Frankly, if you asked Johanna, Nan's insecurity was still being fed by the food magazines, the women's magazines, the blueprints for doing the impossible.

"How can you please twenty different people in one party when they all want different things?" she'd asked the young woman, just the week before, in an effort to make her stop worrying. But the question nearly convinced Nan to cancel a party she'd planned.

And really, who was Johanna to talk? She simply wowed people out of their individual concerns, her parties were that fierce and that grand. She tried to envision *not* killing herself to impress her guests. It was unimaginable.

Weakly, not unlike a wino grasping the bottle for the first morning nip, she reached for her Filofax and began flipping through, looking for a page where the evening was not yet claimed. The dinner party might well be her next subject. Meanwhile, there were some people she'd been meaning to invite.

Elizabeth was well aware of Mr. D.'s enthusiasms. About the time she made her debut in Manhattan, he'd been messianic about quiche. When she and Peter were married, his fervor for chicken and apricots poached in Sauternes had been unquenchable. Nevertheless, she was unprepared for the fascination her mother's caterer showed when she called to engage his services.

"I have a rather untraditional request," she'd said. After explaining that she was planning a dinner for thirty business associates and was, of course, making her rather famous beef stew with garlic and orange but felt that she needed help in designing a first course and a dessert that could provide an elegant frame for so plebeian a main course, she heard the caterer gasp through the telephone. She imagined that he was insulted to be asked to, well, subcontract. But she'd been mistaken.

"My dear child," he'd said. "What an absolutely brilliant concept. Always on the cutting edge, Libby," he said. Mr. D. was known for his flattery as well as for his perfectionism, so Elizabeth was neither moved nor perplexed by his compliment. To her, subcontracting some froufrou to frame her famous stew was a sensible plan. It gave the meal a personal stamp, reined in the budget, and saved her precious time. If Mr. D. wanted to consider it brilliant, that was his business, after all.

She was, however, surprised when Eliza J., the great gray lady of Park Avenue entertaining, invited her to lunch at Restaurant Daniel several days later.

"I'm worried about dear old D.," Mrs. J. said. "He's been quite down about the direction dinner parties have been moving in for some time—almost depressed, I'd say—and I suppose it's not all ideological. I doubt the nineties have been kind to his bottom line.

"Now he's gotten some bee in his bonnet about stew. And he's crediting you, my dear."

Mrs. J. surveyed the younger woman, crisp and quite practical in her Calvin Klein suit, an attorney, she'd heard, about her daughter's age. Elizabeth did not appear to be the sort of person who would deliberately overthrow social convention. Cool, calculated, and probably wound a little tight, surmised Mrs. J., but clearly a woman of breeding and education, not some lunatic flacking the culinary version of Radical Chic.

Although Elizabeth smiled, the faint knit of her brow did not disappear. Yes, clearly she understood that Mrs. J. was not simply addressing the mental health of her caterer, she was questioning, and indirectly defending, a social order.

"Of course, I was raised on the six-course company meal," said Elizabeth briskly. "But frankly, I can't eat that way and get into my clothes. I can't cook that way and get in to my office on time. I can't entertain that way and afford the co-op fees."

Mrs. J. arched her brow ever so slightly above her half-frame tortoiseshell glasses. She studied her menu, closed it, and nodded toward the waiter. "So it's not your worldview, per se, but the world itself?" she asked Elizabeth.

Elizabeth was fascinated by the question. But before she could acknowledge that, well, it was a little of both, Mrs. J. had ordered foie gras and lobster meat in a sherry vinaigrette on a pyramid of haricot vert, a little filet mignon, medium-rare, with herb butter, and a soufflé, Grand Marnier, for dessert.

Elizabeth ordered salmon à la nage, in a ginger court bouillon, no butter, no oil, a little salad to start, dressing on the side, the berries will be fine for dessert. For the rest, and for once, Elizabeth was at a loss for words.

"You'd think I was serving stone soup and Jonestown Kool-Aid, the way she looked at me," Elizabeth later told Johanna, a client but a woman whom she barely knew. Elizabeth was, in fact, merely making small talk, telling a funny story, before telling Johanna that quarter's bad tax news. Johanna produced documentary films, which her husband, Mark, sold very well indeed; their business, however, posed challenging tax issues.

"Was it difficult for you to streamline your dinner parties?" Johanna asked Elizabeth. And when her tax lawyer regarded her blankly, she continued, "I mean, doesn't part of you want to impress people? Doesn't part of you want to kill yourself making a party that will knock them dead?"

Elizabeth opened the file on her desk and exhaled, blowing the wisp of honey-colored hair that had escaped her blown-dry coif off her forehead. "What could be more impressive than efficiency and competence?" she asked.

Pushing the file toward her client, she added, "Here's the bad news."

Recovering the Heart

Johanna was well prepared for her meeting with the infamous Mr. D. and his favorite client, Mrs. J., doyenne of the Park Avenue fête. She'd read *Distinction: A Social Critique of the Judgment of Taste*, by Pierre Bourdieu; *The Civilizing Process*, by Norbert Elias; and *The Rituals of Dinner*, by Margaret Visser. She had purchased and perused every pretty book about entertaining offered at Kitchen Arts & Letters on Manhattan's Upper East Side (thirty-six volumes, more than a thousand dollars). She had acquired a sense of the evolution of the dinner party, and that had given her some insight into the current fantasy surrounding dinner parties.

She leafed through every issue of *Martha Stewart Living*. Subsequently, she was compelled to reread *Perfection Salad: Women & Cooking at the Turn of the Century*, by Laura Shapiro; and *More Work for Mother: The Ironies of Household Technology from the Open Hearth to the Microwave*, by Ruth Schwartz-Cowan.

She'd conducted preliminary interviews with nine caterers across the country and had attended twenty-three dinner parties in fifteen cities. None of this "background" glowed as luminously as her own awakening, however. Confronting the stacks of dirty dishes and wine-stained linen the morning after her last dinner party, Johanna admitted that she had a hostessing disorder.

To a certain extent, she realized, she was the product of an era. Curled in the corner of any Baby Boomer's psyche is a Donna Reed waiting to be born. From the mid-1970s through the 1980s, the national obsession for finer and finer food had provided a trendy pretext for her compulsion, had, in fact, fed her denial. Her mother had washed windows and polished silver for dinner parties. She, the "liberated" one, pored over cookbooks and conducted endless culinary experiments.

In retrospect, she saw that she'd been in the maw of a mania as smooth and stealthy as crème anglaise. Eventually, she'd found more comfort in the kitchen, in the flowers, in tying napkins in filigreed gold ribbon, than she'd found with her guests. Buoyed by her own proficiency, she was insulated from company. There was this false sense of security: if they love the meal they'll love me. She had labored—oh, how she had labored—under the delusion that the conflicts of a working woman could be reconciled and all the mistakes and second thoughts redeemed in a flawless dinner-party performance.

Johanna's need to be the brunette Martha Stewart lifted. She wanted to surrender herself to simplicity, as well as the occasional hired hand and loaf of store-bought bread. But she needed help.

Ostensibly, she called Mr. D. because she was, in fact, considering a documentary on the shift in entertaining styles in America. She saw this as a vehicle to discuss not only the drift toward informality, but also a poignant image for how the culture had drifted from one of conspicuous consumption to what Margaret Visser called "conspicuous competence."

Johanna saw that she herself embodied competence in one rather grand and showy way, while her tax lawyer, Elizabeth, was conspicuously competent in a brisk and austere sort of way. Nan, on the other hand, affirmed the importance of competence by bemoaning her lack of it, at least when it came to cooking and entertaining.

The dinner party had become a way to show one's awareness of the relationship between diet and health, one's knowledge of cooking (which, as ever, implies having had the leisure and privilege that becoming a good cook requires), and perhaps most important in a world in which time (particularly leisure time) has become more precious than money, one's efficiency.

Johanna suspected that something important and very human had gotten lost. She suspected that when one person was a slave to conspicuous competence, everybody at the party was robbed of the comfort of human company. No wonder people wanted to eat baked potatoes! It wasn't guilt that trimmed the caviar from hoity-toity menus. Competence was a cold fish that, she suggested, might dim the appetite for cold fish eggs.

Mr. D. found it amusing that Johanna offered this analysis over lunch at Le Bernardin, the posh Manhattan fish restaurant. Mrs. J. insisted that the younger generation was responsible for the confusion and growing lack of coherence in company meals. Johanna, who had, after all, heard as much from Elizabeth with regard to Mrs. J.'s conviction, was prepared.

"I think that every generation distinguishes itself from the previous one with food and entertaining," she said. "Do you recall that marvelous passage in Mary McCarthy when the group makes a case for casseroles and canned food?" she asked. "Harald convinced them that this kind of food was 'ever so much better and imaginative than the tired old roasts that mother had ordered up from the caterer.'"

Pulling a Xerox of the page from her small Prada knapsack, Johanna read:

"'He began to talk, very learnedly, about the prejudice that existed in conservative circles against canned goods; it went back, he said, to an old fear of poisoning that derived from home canning, where spoilage was common. Modern machinery and factory process, of course, had eliminated all danger of bacteria, and yet the prejudice lingered, which was a pity, since many canned products, like vegetables picked at their peak and some of the Campbell soups, were better than anything the home cook could achieve. "Have you tasted the new corn niblets?" asked Kay. Dottie shook her head. "You ought to tell your mother about them. It's the whole-kernel corn. Delicious. Almost like corn on the cob. Harald discovered them." She considered. "Does your mother know about iceberg lettuce? It's a new variety, very crisp, with wonderful keeping powers. After you've tried it, you'll never want to see the old Boston lettuce again. Simpson lettuce, they call it."'"

Mrs. J., who had listened closely, smiled. "McCarthy was at Vassar when I was at Smith," she said. She meant to assert a certain superiority, which was not altogether lost on Johanna, given her own Seven Sisters alma mater.

"So with the dream of improving humanity through technology, your generation eschews mother's fresh corn and lettuce. Then along comes your daughter, idealistic, back-to-the-earth, not completely conscious that by ridiculing iceberg lettuce she ridicules the idealistic foundation of her mother's life, but not completely unconscious, either, that mesclun causes some consternation at Christmas dinner!" said Johanna.

"Indeed!" cried Mr. D.

"Interesting," murmured Mrs. J. "I do recall that my mother found me insufferably casual. Perhaps it is more a slow deterioration than a sudden destruction of social mores that concerns me."

Johanna watched as the waiter boned the turbot the party had ordered, deftly and gently surrounding each fillet with tiny vegetables and turned potatoes and napping it with a basil-infused jus.

"Were you casual in order to defy your mother?" she asked.

"Not at all," said Mrs. J. "I'd had the benefit of more education, I had a concern for humanity, I didn't have the household staff she had." As the waiter settled a plate in front of her, she smiled and admired its composition. Free-form and modern as it was, it still showed care and infinite respect.

"It's the respect for humanity that I worry about. I suppose you are right, my dear. It doesn't truly matter what you serve, but serving company in my day was a gift of respect, for their humanity. And yes, I know what you are thinking, there was a certain one-upmanship involved, and you are right in a limited way. What I see happening today in all this slop and hurry, however, is a fundamental disregard. I've certainly stroked my own ego through entertaining, but I have also learned a great deal about giving. My daughters don't *give*, they *provide*; it's a different thing altogether, and, I would presume, not as satisfying."

"Stew!" exclaimed Mr. D. "I'm convinced of it. Stew is the solution!"

"Stew is ugly, it's sloppy, it's globby, it's brown," sniffed Mrs. J. "There is no freshness, no spontaneity, no sense of timeliness, no festivity, no indulgence. Stew is nothing special; that is what is meant by the word 'stew.'"

"Indeed," said Mr. D., "stew is not without problems, aesthetic and otherwise. But I am quite taken with Elizabeth's notion of framing a stew, or a one-pot sort of dish, with other, more elaborate courses. What we are seeing is a crisis of time constraints, not of concern, darling. From my perspective, it seems possible to streamline company meals, parcel out the preparations over the course of several days, and *give* rather than *provide* a dinner party."

Over small green salads and very rich fallen chocolate cake, the three discussed how different people reacted to modern life, how some overcompensated and overproduced ("That's me, the recovering hostess with the mostest," said Johanna), how others "played dead," in Mrs. J.'s words, and didn't entertain at all, and of the myriad adaptations in between.

Egged on by Mr. D., they discussed culinary sleight of hand—adding, for instance, the fresh herbs at the last minute to a pre-made dish to infuse it with newness, using dramatic temperature variations and exotic seasonings to distract from the leanness of a dish, relying on food served at room temperature so that the risks of overcooking and of blowing a company meal at the last minute were minimized.

They began to consider the different sorts of ingredients each season offers, to project what sorts of dishes would be flattered by those ingredients. They talked about how the seasons affected social moods, as well, making one type of party perfect for winter but a logy disaster for summer. They talked until the first dinner guest arrived at Le Bernardin.

Mr. D. was flushed with enthusiasm, Mrs. J., unflaggingly intrigued. For her part, Johanna suspected she had tapped a vital source for her own recovery. To say nothing of a brain trust for the documentary that, in her mind, bore the working title *The Pleasure of Your Company*.

Several weeks later, in mid-March of 1993, Mr. D. and Mrs. J., Johanna and Elizabeth and Nan began to meet for tea on Tuesday afternoons in Mrs. J.'s apartment. Their stated mission was to provide one another with support for the hospitality impulse.

Mr. D., the caterer, was primarily worried about remaining relevant (and solvent). Mrs. J. was increasingly concerned that convenience would deracinate the dinner party and steal a rare manifestation of elegance and heart from society. Johanna was concerned with reining in her impulse to overwhelm guests, and exhausting herself in the process.

Nan, the youngest and least experienced hostess in the group, didn't come to break a hostessing habit but to acquire one, and everyone, except Elizabeth, envied the fact that her age—and their shared experience—meant that she could find a style that was comfortable and smart without relinquishing one that she'd already honed and held dear. Elizabeth felt that she had made her peace with where she came from and the world that she inhabited. She initially came to the group to share her concepts, her recipes, and her coolheaded resolve.

In thirteen months of meetings, the group used menus as a metaphor. They planned menus to ease the idiosyncratic concerns of each, to accommodate the skill or deficiency of each. They planned menus to bring the best out of ingredients, to address the social moods of each season. They planned menus because, they found, having a clear concept and a game plan freed them from the tyrant of last-minute hustle. Imagination, like graciousness, flows freely when the clock ticks not.

The following snapshots and menus and recipes show the progress of each member of the group. It is their hope that these pages also provide a blueprint for doing the impossible in a time-driven world.

Part Two

A Program for
Rational Entertaining
in an Irrational Age

*The Process, the Concepts,
the Menus, and the Recipes
of Five People Who Care*

Salving the
Moods and the
Appetite of Spring

For the recovering hostess with the mostest, spring is the cruelest season. Neither the weather nor the season's ingredients nor the ambient mood of the weeks between the final thaw and the first blast of summer heat lends itself easily to simple entertaining.

The weather is unreliable. Balmy evenings require soft flavors and crunchy textures that gently surprise guests. A cool and damp evening, on the other hand, begs for a reassuring meal. Since one cannot predict vernal moods, one has to construct a menu that hedges bets.

Nan had no problem asking the group for help. The group had no problem sharing their experience, strength, and hope—as well as their menus.

In late March, for instance, Johanna said that she could not risk planning any cold dishes. Her progression of warm courses relied on lighter techniques than would be employed in cold-weather cooking. She chose ingredients that summon spring—wild mushrooms, for instance, and a bird—and combined them with winter produce.

Only a month later, Elizabeth shared that the traditional progression of a chilled first course followed by a warm main course freed her of the tyrant weather. There could be a sweet breeze or it could spit and drizzle; in either case, her bases were covered. Her reliance on exotic seasoning, however, distracted both from the traditional construction of her menu and from the old-fashioned ingredients she used. Elizabeth's ode to spring is basically a meat-and-potatoes affair. Beneath its unusual flavors, it is a familiar and reassuring menu.

The fresh, fragile nature of spring ingredients requires the sort of last-minute cooking that is anathema to easy entertaining. An asparagus, a soft-shell crab, even wild salmon are not happily stewed, nor are they easily prepared ahead of time. When cooking for company in the spring, the season's ingredients must be used judiciously. Elizabeth, for instance, showcased the vegetables of spring in her first course, knowing that the rest of her menu required virtually no last-minute attention.

Spring ingredients are somewhat opposed to the social mood of the season. After a hunkered-down winter, there is a certain optimism among people, as well as a need to reconnect. Taken literally, this would seem to mandate a meal that is a joint effort, such as the one that Mrs. J. served in late April. Though any sit-down meal with a set menu provides the sort of community that the social mood of spring yearns for.

Although each has her particular demons and dilemmas, the members of the group, through trial and error, produced spring menus that mirrored the mood of the season within the limits of modern life. Their meals were spare, clever, and idiosyncratic. The dishes were designed for the dedicated amateur. The recipes were within the reach of a cook who has not attended culinary school. Organization—shopping and pacing the preparation over several days—was in order.

Overstated planning is the backbone of understated elegance.

22

A Program
for Rational
Entertaining
in an
Irrational
Age

The Caterer's
Apprentice

Nan Bromley was raised on Crock-Pots, self-timing and self-cleaning ovens, and microwaves. "Fancy" in her house meant Fanny Merritt Farmer. Long before she studied biological psychiatry, before she rose within the ranks of a major research hospital, her mother had made quite certain that she understood that Mrs. Farmer had transformed the impressionistic cooking descriptions of the nineteenth century into formulas with precise measurements and scientific instructions.

Mrs. Farmer's precision appeals to Nan, who is twenty-nine years old. But as she and her husband considered giving the occasional dinner party for family and friends, Mrs. Farmer's definition of elegance gave Nan pause.

Exactly when are the working parents of two young children with no household help and a limited budget going to prepare the six courses that Mrs. Farmer decreed necessary for a proper company dinner? In their dreams, if you ask Nan.

She joined the hostess-recovery group with no hostessing to recover from.

She was a neophyte with a dream of hospitality and little cooking experience beyond the daily exercise of getting dinner on the table by 6:00 P.M. She did, however, have a palpable need to do things correctly. So stymied was she by the traditional prescription for correct entertaining that she had simply not entertained.

Daunted by the expertise of the other members, Nan initially offered little beyond her perpetually perplexed expression. Gradually, she began to see her dilemma in its proper historical context. In short order, she understood that entertaining used to entail a feast of epic proportions, but that the constraints of the two-income household have turned dinner for company into culinary haiku.

Fortified by the knowledge that a mere three courses can make a proper dinner party, Nan assiduously researched recipes, and with Mr. D.'s help, composed both a menu and a strategy for her first "grown-up dinner party." She and her husband, Ted, were no strangers to backyard barbecues. It was the sitting-down thing that had given them pause.

Nan was intrigued by the ingredients of spring. Intimidated by Mr. D.'s dire warnings about the fragility of the produce and the significant risk that an inexperienced hostess ran of overcooking them, she took his advice and adapted a recipe for a warm mélange of vegetables. She might have attempted to prepare the warm salad right beforehand for a small group—her family, for instance—but with guests expected, she steamed the vegetables the evening before her party and stored them, well covered, in the refrigerator. After the guests arrived, she brought the vegetables to room temperature and combined them with the warm vinaigrette after the guests had been seated.

Given her profession, Nan is aware of health concerns. It is fair to say that she was obsessed with current dietary data when the group first began meeting. Working with one of Mr. D.'s cooks, she concocted a vinaigrette that uses leeks in place of some of the oil. It's serendipitous that the contrast of the cool vegetables and the warm vinaigrette brings out the flavor of the leeks, which, in turn, lend a subtle, sweet note to the more herbaceous vegetables in the mélange.

While Nan could easily have used a delicate store-bought bread, she thought herbed popovers would add a certain panache to the course. She prepared the batter several hours before the guests arrived, stored it in the refrigerator, and then ladled it into warmed muffin tins. When the final guest had arrived, she baked them in a hot oven, leaving time for cocktails and assuring a warm and lofty complement to her first course.

Unwilling to risk a main course that required last-minute attention, she chose to prepare a light fish stew several hours before the party and gently reheat it after the guests had arrived. "The professional chef has the time to spend on the

24
A Program
for Rational
Entertaining
in an
Irrational
Age

artistic arrangement of food," announced Mr. D. "A working woman might want to use the time fluffing up herself."

Nan, who was painfully aware that her eternal-student appearance—the chinos, the Lacoste shirts, the thick-soled Doc Martens that she found comfortable in the laboratory—was not quite up to the standard set by the other members of the group, wondered if this remark was a hint. Like, would her guests have a better time if she got a $150 haircut and a few streaks?

Her self-consciousness, however, evaporated as Mr. D. held forth about the fine line between a dowdy, one-pot dish and a suave, modernist one. Exotic seasonings and unusual combinations, he said, differentiate the two. Clearly, reasoned Nan, Mr. D. was talking fashions in food, not fashion à la Ann Taylor—a store, by the way, that Nan herself was beginning to notice with more regularity.

On the weekend before their dinner party, Nan and Ted shopped for the meal, purchasing everything but the seafood, which Ted picked up on his way home on the day of the party to ensure maximum freshness. Over the weekend, the couple made a tomato broth infused with lemon grass, garlic, and jalapeño peppers. The bold Indochinese flavors, they found, made up for the fat that the recipe eschewed.

Yes, agreed Mr. D., who stopped by to taste the broth, "an easy way to replace the old-fashioned comfort of rich food is to suggest an adventure. Your stew will look familiar, not unlike a classic bouillabaisse, but the flavor is startling." He suggested topping each serving with a fresh soft-shell crab—"to conjure the spring's tides and temperatures and possibilities," he said.

Nan reheated the broth and added the fish to it an hour before her guests arrived, plenty of time for the flavors to mingle and deepen. Though he may have been serving his own business interests, Mr. D. did point out that few one-pot dishes suffer from being made ahead and reheated, which makes them excellent candidates for purchasing from a gourmet shop or ordering from a caterer.

This sort of "component" catering, he said, is becoming more popular as a time- and money-saving device, particularly for large dinner parties. Mixing the store-bought and the homemade allows the cook to put his or her imprimatur on the meal.

Whether store-bought or homemade, he decreed, dessert is a time for a fanciful presentation. Nan had planned to make a fallen angel food cake that was light and nearly fat-free. Mr. D. suggested embellishing the cake with lemon curd and raspberries to make a more dramatic presentation. The components of the dessert—making the cake and the curd, and cleaning the berries—were done the evening before the dinner party, though Nan was careful to cover the cake well and store it at room temperature and to keep both the berries and the lemon curd very,

very cold to ensure a contrast in temperatures between the different parts of her meal's end.

Knowing little about wine, the couple chose both an inexpensive white wine (in their case a crisp California blend) and an inexpensive light red (this time, a Spanish blend), both of which they chilled and placed on the table, along with mineral water, allowing guests to serve themselves. They offered coffee after the meal, but found no takers. It was 10:30 P.M. Modern guests, they found, are as worried about work and the morning after as modern hosts and hostesses are.

26

A Program
for Rational
Entertaining
in an
Irrational
Age

Pepper-Chive Popovers

The flavor of this batter can be altered simply by changing the herbs that are added to it. Fresh thyme leaves can be substituted for the chives, for instance, and lemon zest for the pepper; parsley and grated Parmesan cheese make a wonderful popover, as do fresh rosemary and pepper. To avoid fallen popovers, do not open the oven door for the first 15 minutes of their baking time.

1 cup all-purpose flour
¾ teaspoon salt
¼ teaspoon freshly ground pepper
⅓ cup chopped chives
2 large eggs, lightly beaten
1 cup low-fat milk
1 tablespoon unsalted butter, melted, plus more for greasing the pan

1. Preheat the oven to 450° F. Stir together the flour, salt, pepper, and chives in a medium-size mixing bowl until well combined. Add the eggs, milk, and butter and stir with a fork just until mixed.

2. Grease a 12-cup muffin tin and divide the batter among the cups. Bake for 15 minutes. Lower the heat to 350° F. and continue baking until the popovers are browned and cooked through, about 20 minutes longer. Serve immediately.

Makes 12 small popovers

Steamed Spring Vegetables in
Warm Leek Vinaigrette

The vegetables for this recipe can be cooked, cooled completely under cold, running water, and stored, well covered, in separate containers in the refrigerator for up to two days before a dinner party.

Shiitake or even white domestic mushrooms can be substituted for the morels; fiddlehead ferns or tender young pea pods can be added, should they be available. The leek vinaigrette lends a lovely sweetness and depth to this recipe, but those with more traditional tastes might prefer to use a warmed version of the Lemon Vinaigrette on page 68.

½ cup dry white wine
1 cup chicken broth, homemade or low-sodium canned
6 leeks, white and light green parts only, washed well
3 artichokes, stems removed, halved lengthwise, cut surfaces rubbed with
    lemon juice
18 small red potatoes (about 1 inch in diameter)
4 large carrots, peeled and cut on an extreme diagonal into ¼-inch-thick
    slices
1 bunch thin asparagus, ends snapped off
2 cups fresh morels, cleaned
1 teaspoon fresh lemon juice
1 teaspoon extra-virgin olive oil
Salt and freshly ground pepper to taste
1 scallion, trimmed and chopped
2 tablespoons chopped fresh mint

1. Place the wine, chicken broth, and leeks in a medium-size saucepan. Bring to a boil over medium-high heat. Reduce heat and simmer until the leeks are soft, about 30 minutes. Remove the leeks from the liquid and set aside. Increase the heat slightly and cook until the liquid is reduced to ¼ cup, about 5 minutes. Set aside in the pan.

2. Steam the artichokes until the hearts are tender and the leaves pull out easily, about 40 minutes. Scrape out the chokes. Steam the potatoes until tender, about

28
A Program
for Rational
Entertaining
in an
Irrational
Age

25 minutes. Steam the carrots until tender, about 12 minutes. Steam the aspara-gus until crisp-tender, about 5 minutes. Steam the morels until softened, about 3 minutes. As the vegetables are done, set them aside. When cooled to room temper-ature, arrange on 6 plates.

3. Just before serving, warm the leek liquid over low heat. Whisk in the lemon juice, olive oil, salt, pepper, and scallion. Drizzle the vinaigrette over the vegetables and sprinkle with the mint. Serve immediately with Pepper-Chive Popovers (page 27).

Serves 6

Light Tomato and Seafood Stew with Lemon Grass and Jalapeño

The lobsters add a sweetness to the flavor of this stew and also a note of extravagance to the dish. However, other varieties of fish and shellfish can be substituted for those suggested in this recipe. Shrimp can take the place of lobster; any firm white-fleshed fish such as halibut, scrod, even orange roughy, can be used instead of the red snapper or the scallops; and clams can be substituted for the mussels.

15 medium-size plum tomatoes, quartered
4 teaspoons olive oil
2 cloves garlic, coarsely chopped
4 large shallots, coarsely chopped
4 stalks lemon grass, cut into 2-inch lengths
1 large jalapeño, seeded and coarsely chopped
½ cup dry vermouth
1½ teaspoons grated lime zest
2½ teaspoons kosher salt
3 lobsters, 1¼ pounds each
24 small mussels, cleaned and debearded
3 medium-size carrots, peeled and cut into a fine julienne
1 cup snow peas, cut into a fine julienne
3 red snapper fillets, cut into 1-inch pieces
24 sea scallops
⅓ cup all-purpose flour
1 teaspoon freshly ground pepper to taste
6 soft-shell crabs, cleaned

1. Working in batches, place the tomatoes in a food processor and process until pureed. Strain through a fine sieve.

2. Heat 2 teaspoons of the olive oil in a large pot over medium-high heat. Add the garlic, shallots, lemon grass, and jalapeño. Sauté for 5 minutes. Add the vermouth and cook, stirring often, for 3 minutes. Stir in the tomato liquid and bring to a boil. Reduce the heat and simmer for 30 minutes. Strain through a fine sieve.

30
A Program
for Rational
Entertaining
in an
Irrational
Age

Clean the pot and return the liquid to it. Stir in the lime zest and 1½ teaspoons of the salt.

3. Meanwhile, steam the lobsters for 10 minutes. When cool enough to handle, remove the meat from the claws. Twist the tails off the bodies and cut them in half lengthwise; do not remove the tail meat from the shells. Steam open the mussels. Set the lobster meat and mussels aside.

4. Bring a medium-size pot of water to a boil. Add the carrots and cook for 30 seconds. Add the snow peas and cook for 5 seconds longer. Drain well and set aside.

5. Bring the tomato mixture to a boil. Reduce to a simmer and add the red snapper to the pot. Simmer gently for 2 minutes. Add the scallops and simmer until just cooked through, about 1 minute.

6. Shortly before serving, place the flour, 1 teaspoon each of salt and pepper in a paper bag. Add the soft-shell crabs and shake the bag to coat them in flour. Heat the remaining 2 teaspoons oil in a large skillet. Add the crabs, in batches if necessary, and sauté until browned and cooked through, about 2 minutes on the top and 1 minute on the bottom.

7. Add the lobster and mussels to the stew and cook just until heated, about 1 minute. Taste and add more salt if needed. Ladle the stew into 6 large bowls, dividing the seafood evenly. Top each bowl with a soft-shell crab and surround with the carrots and snow peas. Serve immediately.

Serves 6 as a main course

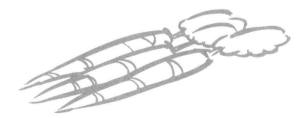

Fallen Angel Cake with Lemon Curd and Raspberries

So little fat and flour is used in proportion to the egg whites in this recipe that the cake rises and then gently settles, leaving it slightly more dense than typical angel food cakes.

The cake and the lemon curd can be made the day before a party. In fact, high-quality lemon curd is available in many supermarkets. The cake can also be served with strawberries, blueberries, or peaches, or a puree of one of these fruits, should raspberries be unavailable.

THE CAKE

2 teaspoons unsalted butter, melted
½ cup ground almonds
8 large egg whites
½ teaspoon kosher salt
1 teaspoon cream of tartar
2 teaspoons almond extract
1¼ cups sugar
1 cup cake flour, sifted
½ cup sliced almonds
Confectioners' sugar, for garnish

THE LEMON CURD

3 large eggs
¾ cup, plus 2 tablespoons sugar
2 teaspoons grated lemon zest
½ cup fresh lemon juice
3 tablespoons unsalted butter
2 cups fresh raspberries

32

A Program
for Rational
Entertaining
in an
Irrational
Age

1. To make the cake: Preheat the oven to 325° F. Brush a 10-inch tube pan with the butter and coat the bottom and sides with the ground almonds. Set aside. In a large, clean bowl, beat the egg whites with an electric mixer on low speed until foamy. Add the salt and the cream of tartar, increase the speed, and beat until soft

peaks form. Add the almond extract. Continue beating the egg whites while gradually adding the sugar. Beat until stiff peaks form. With a large spatula, carefully fold the flour into the whites. Spoon the batter into the prepared pan and smooth out the top. Sprinkle the sliced almonds evenly over the top. Bake until a tester inserted into the center of the cake comes out clean, about 45 minutes. Immediately turn the cake out of the pan and place on a cake plate, with the sliced almonds on top. Let cool.

2. To make the lemon curd: Place the eggs and the sugar in a medium-size, nonreactive saucepan and whisk until thickened and light in color. Whisk in the lemon zest and juice. Place over low heat and cook, whisking constantly, until thick, about 6 minutes; do not let the mixture come to a simmer. Remove from the heat and whisk in the butter. Place plastic wrap directly over the curd and refrigerate until cold.

3. When ready to serve, sift the confectioners' sugar lightly over the top of the cake and cut into slices. Pass the lemon curd and the raspberries in separate bowls.

Serves 8

The Woman Who
Wowed Too Much

Johanna had a strong and persistent desire to entertain in the style to which she was trying to become unaccustomed. For months, she had attended meetings faithfully, always saying, "My name is Johanna and I am addicted to giving dinner parties." In the sanctuary of the meetings, she had admitted to being powerless over her need to wow and seduce her guests. She had explored the possibility that the Herculean nature of her efforts was, in fact, affecting the rest of her life in a negative fashion.

She discovered a pattern of peaks and valleys in her productivity professionally; the valleys at work coincided with her peaks as a hostess. Her husband had begun to get headaches during the mildest, most preliminary discussions of guest lists. Her children, with the exception of the youngest, moaned like a Greek chorus, *"Not again!"* The four-year-old, for reasons that Johanna in fact understood, continued to think it possible that her mother would one day hire elephants and clowns to entertain her dinner guests.

Johanna had summoned the courage to curtail her hostessing. She had, in recent months, served stew to guests on several occasions. She'd even *bought,* rather than baked, dessert. And she had found, much to her surprise, that she had not melted like the Wicked Witch of the West under the stream of conversation that she was, when the preoccupation with cooking had been lifted, hit with. Rather, she'd found herself affable and relaxed to the point that later she and her husband had actually flirted as they did the dishes. It was surprisingly invigorating.

Nevertheless, Johanna began to experience a familiar itch as the snow melted and the days began to lengthen. She came to believe that it was the weather that made her long for a fling in the kitchen, the later setting of the sun that made her hanker for a purpose, and that these elements combined to make her want to give a dinner party in the very worst way. She shared this at her meeting and was warned to proceed cautiously.

"It's not that you *can't* entertain," said Eliza J., "it's that you don't *want* to entertain in a way that exhausts you, taxes the other parts of your life, costs you an arm and a leg, and cuts you off from your guests."

Johanna, therefore, planned her menu carefully. In searching her soul, she discovered that she didn't wish to wow her guests as much as she wished to give them the gift of style and substance and surprise—give them, in other words, a frisson of excitement on a breezy, suggestive night. This, to Johanna, meant moving beyond stew. It meant finding distinctive dishes whose components could be prepared on the weekend before the party, when she had leisure time, and assembled at the last minute.

She decided on a wild mushroom timbale for several reasons. It is a luxurious dish. It is an old-fashioned, comforting dish, and it would not compromise her recovery. The timbale could be cooked up to two days in advance, reheated in the microwave, and given a daring garnish, such as crumbled bacon and arugula, that she could manage to prepare while guests sipped their drinks.

She decided to serve Cornish hens because they are cute on the plate and forgiving in the oven—which is to say that a Cornish hen will bear a bit of over-cooking, particularly if it is larded with a compound butter. The butter, a mixture of sun-dried tomatoes and rosemary, Johanna could make on the weekend, wrap in plastic, and freeze until she was ready to slice it and push it under the skin of the little birds. Thus insulated, the birds could roast unminded while she devoted herself to making a soft polenta.

The polenta, Johanna realized, might pose a bit of a threat. Even enriched with soft mascarpone cheese, the cornmeal could not be simmered ahead of time. At the outside, if the polenta was slightly undercooked, it would tolerate 15 minutes, covered well, over a double boiler before the creamy stuff became a sodden mass. On the other hand, soft polenta is a cinch to serve. Rice or potatoes would be less trouble, but Johanna found it impossible to resist the charm and comfort she imagined in a creamy, warm cornmeal. To say nothing of what a delicious counterpoint it would be to the small, buttery bird.

Johanna realized, with some satisfaction, that she had thrown dietary caution to the wind. "It's just *one meal*," she explained at the meeting. "Am I the *only* one hungry for a rich meal?"

No, in fact, she was not, although she was the only one who had not considered the last-minute assembly that her dessert, Apple and Fig Napoleons with Red Wine Sauce and Sour Cream Ice Cream, would require. Clearly, she could make the sour cream ice cream any time she wished—"or buy some damned ice cream, for that matter," said Elizabeth.

She could also make—or, as Elizabeth was quick to point out, buy—the fig jam ahead of time, and the red wine sauce would keep up to two days refrigerated. Both could be brought to room temperature and then warmed over the slowest of flames during dinner. The phyllo squares that she planned as a foundation for the dessert could be baked up to an hour before the guests arrived, as could the apple compote, as long as it was kept warm. Nevertheless, she would, at some point, have to excuse herself from the table and become the Frank Lloyd Wright of desserts. "I think you might be better off with a pie," said Mr. D.

This warning continued to ring in the mind of Johanna L. But it was merely a leitmotif in the early-spring meal she managed to create, a day at a time, in the days preceding the appointed hour, much to the delight of her guests.

36
A Program
for Rational
Entertaining
in an
Irrational
Age

Cornish Hens Roasted with Sun-Dried Tomato-Rosemary Butter

The compound butter used in this recipe can be made up to a month ahead of time and stored, well wrapped, in the freezer. It need not be thawed prior to use; simply hack off the amount needed. The butter can also be melted over sautéed, grilled, or baked chicken breasts or used to flavor pasta or rice.

8 tablespoons (1 stick) unsalted butter, softened
½ cup oil-packed sun-dried tomatoes, drained and finely chopped
5 tablespoons fresh rosemary, finely chopped
5 teaspoons kosher salt
¼ teaspoon freshly ground pepper plus more for seasoning cavities and skins
　　of hens
1 tablespoon fresh lemon juice
4 Cornish hens, 1½ pounds each

1. Preheat the oven to 425° F. Stir together the butter, tomatoes, rosemary, 1 teaspoon salt, ¼ teaspoon pepper, and lemon juice. Using 1 teaspoon of salt for each, salt and pepper the hens inside the cavity and over the skin. Loosen the skin over the breasts and thighs to make pockets. Using 2 tablespoons of butter for each hen, place the butter in the pockets between the skin and meat. Rub any remaining butter over the outside of the hens.

2. Place the hens in a large roasting pan, breast side down. Roast for 20 minutes. Lower the oven temperature to 375° F. Roast until just cooked through, about 30 minutes longer. Split the hens in half lengthwise. Place a half hen on each of 8 plates along with Braised Escarole (page 41), Creamy Mascarpone Polenta (page 40), and Roast Garlic (page 44).

Serves 8

Wild Mushroom Timbales with Bacon and Arugula

These individual mushroom timbales can be prepared up to two hours in advance and reheated in a slow oven or in a microwave prior to serving. The wider the variety of mushrooms used, the more intense the flavor will be. Either shiitake or white domestic mushrooms can be substituted, however, should fresh wild mushrooms not be available. Likewise, watercress or a mixture of spicy greens can be used in place of, or in addition to, arugula.

THE TIMBALES

3 tablespoons unsalted butter
1 small onion, peeled and chopped
4 cloves garlic, finely chopped
1½ pounds mixed wild mushrooms, stemmed and cut into ½-inch dice
1½ teaspoons kosher salt
Freshly ground pepper to taste
1 teaspoon grated lemon zest
¼ cup finely chopped Italian parsley
1 teaspoon finely chopped fresh thyme
½ cup freshly grated Parmesan
½ cup heavy cream
½ cup milk
3 large eggs
Vegetable oil spray

THE GARNISHES

8 strips thick-sliced bacon
¼ cup balsamic vinegar
1 cup beef, veal, or duck-and-veal demi-glace (see Mail-Order Sources, page 275)
8 cups arugula, tough stems removed

1. Preheat the oven to 325° F. Heat the butter in a large skillet over medium heat. Add the onion and cook for 5 minutes. Add the garlic and cook for 1 minute. Add the mushrooms and cook for 10 minutes. Set aside to cool.

38
A Program
for Rational
Entertaining
in an
Irrational
Age

2. Stir the salt, pepper, lemon zest, parsley, thyme, and Parmesan into the cooled mushrooms. In a large bowl, whisk together the cream, milk, and eggs. Stir in the mushroom mixture. Spray eight 6-ounce ramekins with vegetable oil. Fill each with the custard and set in a large roasting pan.

3. Pour enough hot water into the roasting pan to come halfway up the sides of the ramekins. Bake until set, about 55 minutes.

4. Meanwhile, cook the bacon in a heavy skillet over medium heat until crisp. Drain on paper towels, crumble, and set aside. Pour the fat from the skillet. Add the vinegar and demi-glace and simmer over medium heat for 2 minutes, scraping up any bacon bits stuck to the pan.

5. To serve, run the tip of a small knife around the edge of the ramekins to loosen the custards. Spoon 2 tablespoons of the sauce onto the center of 8 plates. Mound 1 cup of arugula in the center of each plate. Unmold the timbales onto the center of the arugula. Scatter the bacon around the timbales and serve immediately.

Serves 8

Creamy Mascarpone Polenta

If mascarpone, the creamy Italian dessert cheese, is not available, a facsimile can be made by beating 2 tablespoons heavy cream into ¾ cup ricotta cheese, or see page 275 for mail-order sources. This combination will provide the creaminess for the cornmeal but will not have the same depth of flavor the traditional Italian cheese does.

8 cups water
4 teaspoons kosher salt
2 cups yellow cornmeal
1 cup mascarpone
Freshly ground pepper to taste

Bring the water to a boil in a large saucepan. Add the salt. Whisking constantly, add the cornmeal in a very thin, steady stream. Turn the heat as low as possible. Cook for 1 hour, stirring vigorously every 10 minutes. Add the mascarpone, season to taste with pepper, and beat until smooth and creamy. Serve hot.

Serves 8

40
A Program
for Rational
Entertaining
in an
Irrational
Age

Braised Escarole

This dish, which makes a marvelous companion for roast Cornish hens, can be made days ahead of time, stored in the refrigerator, and warmed before serving. The recipe is a good candidate for doubling, or even tripling, as the escarole keeps well. It makes a fine accompaniment to pork, chicken, or beef and can be tossed with pasta and Parmesan cheese or combined with chicken broth and white beans to make a hearty soup.

2 teaspoons olive oil
18 cloves garlic, lightly crushed
32 cups escarole, cut into 2-inch pieces, washed but not dried
Kosher salt and freshly ground pepper to taste

1. Heat the olive oil in a large, wide pot for 1 minute over high heat. Add the garlic and cook, stirring frequently, until fragrant, about 45 seconds. Add 8 cups of escarole and cover immediately. Cook for 2 minutes. Continue adding the escarole in batches and letting it wilt until there is room to add more.

2. When all of the escarole is in the pot, stir, turn heat to low, re-cover, and cook for 1 hour. Season with salt and pepper to taste. The escarole can be made ahead and reheated.

Serves 8

Apple and Fig Napoleons with
Red Wine Sauce and Sour Cream Ice Cream

A high-quality vanilla ice cream can be substituted for the homemade sour cream version, and a commercial fig jam could also be used instead of the fig spread. For a simpler dessert, the prepared fruit can be combined with the red wine sauce to make a compote that can be garnished with ice cream, crème fraîche, or mascarpone cheese.

THE ICE CREAM

2 cups whole milk
1 vanilla bean, split lengthwise
6 large egg yolks
¾ cup sugar
2 pounds sour cream
Zest of 1 lemon, removed in fine strips with a zester

THE PHYLLO

6 sheets phyllo (keep covered with a damp cloth)
3 tablespoons unsalted butter, melted
6 tablespoons sugar

THE SAUCE

2 bottles fruity red wine (like Beaujolais)
1½ cups sugar
1 tablespoon black peppercorns
1 (2-inch) cinnamon stick

THE APPLES

8 McIntosh apples, peeled, cored, and cut into ¾-inch chunks
¼ cup sugar
3 (2×¼-inch) strips lemon zest
1 vanilla bean, split lengthwise
1 teaspoon fresh lemon juice

42

A Program
for Rational
Entertaining
in an
Irrational
Age

8 ounces dried black mission figs, stemmed

½ cup heavy cream

1 tablespoon Armagnac

1 teaspoon fresh lemon juice

1. To make the ice cream, place the milk and vanilla bean in a medium saucepan over medium heat and bring just to a simmer. Meanwhile, whisk together the egg yolks and sugar. Whisking rapidly, pour the milk into the yolk mixture. Pour the mixture back in the saucepan, place over low heat, and stir constantly until thick enough to coat the back of a spoon; do not let mixture simmer. Pour into a bowl, cover, and refrigerate until cold. Remove the vanilla bean and whisk in the sour cream. Freeze in an ice cream machine according to the manufacturer's instructions. Store in freezer until shortly before serving.

2. To make the phyllo, preheat the oven to 375° F. Lay 1 sheet of phyllo on a work surface, brush lightly with butter and sprinkle with 1 tablespoon of sugar. Top with another sheet of phyllo, brush with butter and sprinkle with sugar. Repeat once more. Trim the edges to make a 10×14-inch rectangle. Cut into eight 3½×5-inch rectangles. Place on a baking sheet lined with parchment paper. Repeat with the remaining phyllo, butter, and sugar. Bake until lightly browned and crisp, about 5 minutes. Set aside.

3. To make the sauce, combine the wine, sugar, peppercorns, and cinnamon stick in a large saucepan and simmer until liquid has been reduced to 1⅓ cups, about 40 minutes. Strain and set aside.

4. To make the apples, combine the apples, sugar, lemon zest, vanilla bean, and lemon juice in a medium saucepan over low heat. Cook, covered, for 8 minutes, stirring once. Uncover and simmer until apples are soft but not mushy, and some liquid has evaporated, about 5 minutes more. Remove the lemon zest and vanilla bean and set aside.

5. To make the fig spread, puree the figs in a food processor. Add the cream, Armagnac, and lemon juice and puree until smooth. Set aside.

6. To assemble, on each of 8 plates place 1 piece of phyllo, cover the pastry with some of the fig spread, and spoon the apple mixture over it. Spoon a pool of the sauce beside the pastry on each plate. Lean 1 piece of phyllo over the sauce and against 1 of the longer edges of the plated phyllo. Repeat with all the plates. Place a scoop of ice cream beside the napoleons and sprinkle with a few strands of lemon zest. Serve immediately.

Serves 8

Roast Garlic

This sweet, pungent garlic can be used to season meat, fish, or vegetables, can be pureed into soups, sauces, mayonnaise, or vinaigrette, or can be added to butter or olive oil to dress bread. It keeps up to four days if wrapped well and refrigerated. It makes a wonderful garnish for Cornish game hens served with braised escarole.

8 medium heads garlic
4 teaspoons olive oil
Kosher salt and freshly ground pepper to taste

Smash the heads of garlic lightly to loosen but not completely separate the cloves. Place in a casserole with a lid, in a single layer. Drizzle with the olive oil and season with salt and pepper. Cover and roast in a 300° F. oven until the garlic is soft, about 1 hour.

Serves 8

44
A Program
for Rational
Entertaining
in an
Irrational
Age

A Hostess
Calculated and Cool

Elizabeth tends to be pragmatic, unsentimental, and very, very clear. In her efficient way, she accepts the fact that the image she has of herself as a hostess, the graciousness nurtured by her mother and grandmother, the competence honed by the assiduous study of lifestyle magazines, is basically like her appendix. A residual entity rendered purposeless by human evolution and social change.

Unlike some of her girlhood friends, Elizabeth still possesses her appendix. Though she thinks about that organ only when she looks at the twenty sterling place settings that she inherited. Butter knives and fish knives, sauce spoons, demitasse spoons, and marrow spoons—the appendixes of the table.

The tasks—in fact, the whole sort of life—that such cutlery bespeaks ended the day she graduated from law school. At least they ended in the Kittridge household. In the rest of the country, the same change came earlier to some and later to others. People who could afford help clung to the grand-hospitality impulse longer than Elizabeth; those who counted their pennies gave the whole thing up sooner.

Elizabeth views entertaining as an interplay of commodities. Time. Money. And know-how.

If you have time—time to shop carefully and knowledgeably, time to cook wisely and creatively—entertaining requires less money. If you have money—to buy the sorts of precious ingredients that shine with minimal effort in the kitchen, to order wine casually over the telephone, to hire waiters and florists and someone to wash up afterward—you need less time. If you have the smarts to know what can be prepared ahead in minimal time at a budget-pleasing cost, the experience to know inexpensive wines that make for pleasant and interesting quaffing, the touch of artistry that allows you to arrange a few perfect stems and make a beautiful table, you need less time and less money.

Elizabeth specializes in tax law. In her mind, life is composed of assets and liabilities. The fact that she and her husband, Peter, must entertain with some regularity and the fact that she was bred to entertain in a certain way are, in her view, both financial and temporal liabilities. She seeks to minimize the damage.

For many years, Elizabeth was in denial about the time it took to entertain frugally. Not anymore. At forty-five, with college-bound children, she is more realistic. She has made peace with spending more money in order to save time.

If she is cooking, she has no qualms about spending money on glistening lump crabmeat or shucked lobster: they are the stuff of a first course that she can make in fifteen minutes. Nor does she balk at purchasing expensive cuts of meat, such as veal, if it means she can put the thing in the oven and forget about it for an hour or two.

If, on the other hand, she is hiring a caterer to prepare the main course, she chooses less precious ingredients and pays somebody else for the time and skill it takes to make the humble soar.

These decisions, of course, are predicated on the fact that the Kittridges are relatively affluent people and that Elizabeth herself is no dummy when it comes to taste and style. She has found that unexpected flavors tend to create interesting table talk. Surprise, she believes, is the great social leveler.

In addition to her intact appendix, this insight is the main thing that distinguishes Elizabeth from the buttoned-down men and women with whom she works.

The complete lack of sentimentality shown in the streamlined tables she lays—no frivolous flatware, not a single superfluous flower or candle—would be expected of a woman of her education and professional interests. Likewise, a seemingly simple and opulent meal could be predicted. But exotic flavors provoke either

A Program
for Rational
Entertaining
in an
Irrational
Age

antipathy or adoration, and they are not the sort of social risk one would expect to see in a home like the Kittridges'.

That risk, along with the tally of business deductions possible in each meal, tickles the couple to such an extent that they tend, these days, to do the dishes together in order to prolong their analysis of the evening's proceedings.

Spicy Crab Salad with Carrots and Jícama

It is important to use large lump crabmeat in this recipe; shredded crabmeat will make a mushy and unappetizing dish. Served with bread and surrounded by a green salad, this dish would make a fine light meal, as well.

1 pound lump crabmeat, picked over for shells
3 hot green chilies, seeded and minced
½ teaspoon salt
⅛ teaspoon freshly ground pepper
2 tablespoons fresh lime juice
½ medium-size jícama, peeled and coarsely shredded
2 medium-size carrots, coarsely shredded
3 tablespoons fresh lemon juice
2 tablespoons chopped fresh mint
2 tablespoons chopped fresh cilantro
2 cups stemmed watercress

1. Put the crabmeat in a mixing bowl, add the chilies, salt, pepper, and lime juice and toss gently, being careful to break up the crabmeat as little as possible.

2. In another bowl, toss together the jícama, carrots, and lemon juice. The salad can be prepared to this point up to an hour ahead. Add the mint and cilantro to the jícama mixture and toss to combine.

3. Divide the crab mixture among 6 plates, mounding it in the center. Surround the crab with watercress. Scatter the jícama mixture over the crab and serve immediately.

Serves 6

48

A Program
for Rational
Entertaining
in an
Irrational
Age

Braised Veal with Cardamom-Spinach Puree

While not as sprightly or as intensely flavored, frozen spinach can be used instead of fresh in this recipe. The dish can be completed up to one hour before serving. Reduce the cooking time on the veal by five minutes and store it in a 150-degree oven under a damp cloth; puree the spinach and reheat the puree over a low flame or in a microwave before serving.

2 teaspoons olive oil

1 (3¼-pound) boned loin of veal, rolled and tied

1 teaspoon kosher salt, plus more for seasoning spinach

½ teaspoon freshly ground pepper, plus more for seasoning spinach

5 cups milk

2½ teaspoons ground cardamom

1 jalapeño pepper, seeded and minced

1 clove garlic, minced

1 small onion, peeled and chopped

8 cups stemmed young spinach, washed

1. Heat the olive oil in a large Dutch oven over medium heat. Season the veal with the salt and pepper. Place the veal in the pot and brown on all sides, about 10 minutes. Take the veal out of the pot and set aside. Pour in the milk. Stir in the cardamom, jalapeño, garlic, and onion. Bring just to a simmer. Reduce heat, return the veal to the pot, and adjust the heat so that the milk stays just below a simmer. Cook, uncovered, for 1 hour 20 minutes, turning the roast once. Remove from heat and let the veal stand in the liquid for 20 minutes. Remove the veal from the pot, remove the strings, and cover with a warm, damp towel.

2. Place 1 cup of the cooking liquid in a large saucepan. Bring to a simmer over medium heat. Add the spinach and cook, stirring constantly, until the spinach is completely wilted. Transfer to a food processor and process until smooth. Season to taste with salt and pepper.

3. Trim the ends of the veal and slice across into 6 pieces. Divide the spinach puree among 6 plates, mounding it to one side. Place the veal over the puree. Serve immediately with Indian-Spiced Potato Gratin (page 52).

Serves 6

Pistachio-Crusted Cheesecake
with Orange-Caramel Sauce

The cheesecake and sauce can be made the day before a dinner party. Both should be wrapped well and stored in the refrigerator. The cake should be brought to room temperature three hours before the guests arrive and the sauce should be warmed over very low heat just before serving.

THE FILLING

3 (8-ounce) containers plain low-fat yogurt

1½ pounds cream cheese, softened

1 cup sugar

1 teaspoon grated lemon zest

4 large eggs

¼ teaspoon kosher salt

2 tablespoons all-purpose flour

2 tablespoons plus 1 teaspoon fresh lemon juice

2 teaspoons vanilla extract

1 tablespoon honey

THE CRUST

1 cup shelled pistachios

1½ teaspoons grated orange zest

⅛ teaspoon kosher salt

1 teaspoon ground cinnamon

5 tablespoons sugar

4 tablespoons unsalted butter, melted and allowed to cool, plus more for greasing pan

THE SAUCE

4 oranges

¼ cup fresh orange juice

1 cup sugar

3 tablespoons water

½ cup heavy cream

50
A Program
for Rational
Entertaining
in an
Irrational
Age

1. One day before serving, make the filling: Place a sieve over a bowl and line it with a double layer of paper towels. Spoon the yogurt into the sieve and let drain for 2 hours.

2. Meanwhile, to make the crust, place the pistachios, orange zest, salt, cinnamon, and sugar in a food processor and pulse until nuts are ground. Put in a bowl and stir in the melted butter.

3. Butter a 9-inch springform pan. Press the pistachio mixture into the bottom of the pan and set aside.

4. Preheat the oven to 325° F. Place the cream cheese in a large mixing bowl. Using an electric mixer, gradually add the sugar, beating until light. Mix in the lemon zest and the drained yogurt. Mix in the eggs one at a time. Mix in the salt and flour. Mix in the lemon juice, vanilla, and honey.

5. Pour the batter into the prepared pan. Place in a large roasting pan. Pour enough hot water into the roasting pan to come halfway up the sides of the pan. Bake until the cheesecake is set, about 1½ hours.

6. Remove the cake pan from the water and let cool completely. Cover with plastic wrap and refrigerate overnight.

7. To make the sauce, use a paring knife to remove all peel and pith from the oranges, working over a bowl to collect any juice. Cut the orange sections out from between the membranes and place in the bowl. Add the orange juice and set aside.

8. Stir the sugar and water together in a medium saucepan. Use a pastry brush dipped in water to wash down any sugar crystals from the sides of the pan. Place over medium-low heat and cook without stirring until the sugar turns a nice caramel color. Remove from the heat and immediately pour in the heavy cream—taking care, as the mixture will bubble up. Place back on the heat and stir until the caramel is dissolved. Remove from the heat and stir in the oranges and juice. Set aside. The sauce can be made ahead, refrigerated, and warmed slightly before serving.

9. To cut the cake, rinse a large, sharp knife with hot water and cut a slice of cake. Wipe off the knife and reheat with hot water between slices. Place on dessert plates and spoon a pool of sauce, with orange sections, beside each slice and serve.

Serves 12

Indian-Spiced Potato Gratin

This dish can be completed up to two hours before dinner and kept in a 150-degree oven, uncovered until serving. It can be served family-style or in individual portions.

1 tablespoon unsalted butter, plus more for greasing dish
2 large onions, peeled, halved lengthwise, and thinly sliced crosswise
1 tablespoon ground cumin
1 teaspoon ground turmeric
Large pinch cayenne
1½ teaspoons kosher salt
½ teaspoon freshly ground pepper to taste
2 cloves garlic, minced
3 large baking potatoes, peeled and cut across into ⅟₁₆-inch slices
1 cup heavy cream

1. Preheat the oven to 350° F. Melt the butter in a large skillet over medium-low heat. Add the onions and cook, stirring frequently, until onions are caramelized, about 30 minutes. Set aside.

2. In a small bowl, stir together the cumin, turmeric, cayenne, salt, and pepper. Stir in the garlic.

3. Butter a 13×9×2-inch baking dish. Layer half the potatoes in the dish, overlapping them slightly. Sprinkle with half of the spice mixture. Cover with the onions. Layer the remaining potatoes over the onions and sprinkle with the remaining spice mixture. Pour the cream over the top.

4. Cover with aluminum foil and bake until the potatoes are tender, about 1 hour. Let cool slightly, cut into rectangles, and serve. The potatoes can be made ahead and reheated in a low oven, covered with aluminum foil.

Serves 6

52

A Program
for Rational
Entertaining
in an
Irrational
Age

Eliza J. and
Mr. D. Conspire

As abstemiousness came of age, Mr. D. found it necessary to spend many hours in his office reading dietary studies. It was enervating. Studying statistics about the relationship of dietary fat to heart disease and some forms of cancer left him rather cold. In fact, he often remembered his Uncle Seamus, the notorious and poetic drunk, who would, the morning after a bender, sit at the D.s' breakfast table, drain a bottle of stout, and say, "Ah, the chill of consciousness returns." After a decade of Bacchanalian entertaining, Mr. D. found the decade of dietary data tantamount to Seamus's stout.

Granted, Mr. D., like most of those who engaged his services, was not getting any younger. On bad days, he actually thought he could feel arterial plaque building inexorably toward bypass surgery within his chest. Even so, even as he became conversant with and proficient at what he calls "lean and mean cuisine," Mr. D. missed naughty nights of indulgence. The medicalization of food, he thought, was not without significant negative side effects to the social psyche.

"We used to suffer dark nights of the soul," he complained to Eliza J. over lunch at Le Cirque. "Now we tremble over the daily tally of fat grams and cholesterol."

Existential angst made for more interesting conversation, agreed Mrs. J., who had always been too secure in her own style to be swayed by fads. Trends, she once told Mr. D., are the tyrants of the insecure soul. One must know and even perhaps incorporate them, but blind obeisance to trends was to society what cosmetic surgery was to the individual, at least as far as Mrs. J. was concerned. She was proud of every gray hair under her subdued platinum rinse. Wrinkles and creases were a statement of character to her.

"If you look around this room you see women who've spent their whole lives distinguishing themselves and then spent a goodly sum to have all traces erased in a week in Buenos Aires," she whispered. "No wonder depression is rising in retirement villages!"

Mrs. J. was a great chum. In addition, possessing equal and contradictory impulses, she was one of his more interesting clients. She was too elegant to brook ostentation without a blush. At the same time, she was innately generous and quite lavish with regard to her guests. Privately, she and her husband dined sensibly and lightly, but as a hostess, she was known to be indulgent.

Over lunch, she considered the fate of her style in the Age of Abstemiousness.

"It is my opinion that one should assume personal responsibility for personal dietary needs and attend to them privately, much as one would attend to the matter of dental flossing or insulin injections," she said. "With the exception of absolutely dire medical circumstance, I find it difficult to believe that one who minds his diet at home can't kick up his heels a bit in public."

She found nothing more dreary than a guest in bondage to her personal regimen. "Isolation and me-firstism is the Enemy of the Party," she said. "You get one at a table and there goes the conversation. The possibility of shared pleasure is trampled by the sharing of disparate hells. My God, it's boring."

She acknowledged that by flouting the current Spartan ethos she would probably end up encouraging dietary talk. Besides, Mrs. J. was not one to flout. Rather, she felt that trends, which she often called "current thought," could subtly inform a hostess's sensibility. Provided, of course, that the hostess was firmly grounded in her own exquisite taste.

She pondered the issue of a spring menu for company—a dinner for eight, to be exact—while nibbling at the Cambodian spring rolls that the executive sous-chef of Le Cirque, Sottha Khunn, had prepared for the caterer and the matron. The sprightliness of the appetizer seemed to sharpen her senses and to jog her imagination.

54

A Program
for Rational
Entertaining
in an
Irrational
Age

"I have to admit that eating with my fingers is quite satisfying in today's antiseptic world," she said, fashioning a sort of burrito by encasing the crisp hand roll in lettuce leaves and fresh mint and munching it with relish. "The flavors, of course, are a sort of wake-up call. But what I like is the naughtiness, the informality. . . ."

Within moments, the matron and the caterer had devised an eminently civilized menu that nonetheless shunned the finer points of civilization. It featured a Cambodian hot pot in which the guests chose the bites of food they desired and cooked them at the table by using small wire baskets or chopsticks to dip the ingredients into simmering broth and then into a tangy dipping sauce.

By the time Mr. Khunn had served them a vanilla-scented plate of sautéed fruit, they had enlisted his expertise. On the day of the party, he painstakingly fashioned the hand rolls and made two dipping sauces. He simmered a broth and carefully cut chunks of fish and lobster, vegetables, and even beef and arranged it all on heaping platters on Mrs. J.'s table.

The meal appeared to be the essence of simplicity. "Simple," said Mr. Khunn. "The company cooks." But lacking the skill of a highly trained Cambodian chef or access to the impeccable quality of ingredients that such a simple meal requires, a hostess would want to simplify the cooking and substitute the ingredients available to her. The recipe is infinitely accommodating.

In replicating the Cambodian dinner, Mrs. J., in fact, combined fresh and low-sodium canned chicken broth for cooking the food and used a less stately array of vegetables as well as fewer (and less expensive) varieties of fish and carpaccio-thin sliced beef and skewers of chicken. She set her table with dinner plates, provided small saucers for dipping sauces, and encouraged guests to use one set of chopsticks for cooking, and another for eating.

Had she lived closer to an Asian neighborhood, Mrs. J. would have found inexpensive wire dipping baskets cheap and would have found, as well, copper hot pots for the broth that can be fueled with Sterno. As it was, she used Crock-Pots and an old fondue dish for the broth. The electrical wires were unsightly. No one seemed to notice.

Such changes, of course, affect the quality of the meal. They do not, however, change the fact that the style of the dinner forces guests to interact with one another, infuses the room with a shared task, and in the end, when the cooking broth is poured into each guest's bowl for sipping, issues a powerful sense of community.

Cambodian Hot Pot
(Adapted from Sottha Khunn, Le Cirque, Manhattan)

The broth and the dipping sauce can be prepared up to three days before the dinner and stored, covered, in the refrigerator. A low-sodium broth, frozen or canned, can be used to simmer the lemon grass and coriander for a less arduous (though somewhat less delicious) sauce.

The idea of this recipe is to showcase the best and freshest ingredients that are available; no single ingredient is sacrosanct. Almost anything can be prepared and served for dipping. A mail-order source for Asian ingredients can be found on page 275.

THE BROTH

2 large chickens, cut into pieces
8 quarts water
6 stalks fresh lemon grass (bottom 5 inches only)
1 tablespoon coriander seeds
2 teaspoons kosher salt
3 grinds freshly ground pepper

THE DIPPING SAUCE

4 lemons
8 cloves garlic
½ cup sugar
½ cup nuac nam (Asian fish sauce)
½ cup chicken broth
1½ teaspoons chili-garlic sauce, plus more to taste

THE VEGETABLES

2 fennel bulbs, trimmed and cut into 6 wedges each
4 small zucchini, trimmed, halved lengthwise, and cut across into 2-inch pieces
8 medium carrots, peeled, halved lengthwise, and cut crosswise into 2-inch pieces
16 asparagus tips with 2 inches of stalk left on
16 shiitake or white mushrooms, stemmed

1 pound salmon fillet
1 pound tuna steak
1 pound sea bass fillet
1 pound large shrimp
1 pound squid
1 pound sea scallops

1. At least one day before serving, make the broth by placing the chickens in a large stockpot. Add the water and bring to a boil. Lower the heat and skim off the foam as it rises. Cook 10 minutes. Add the lemon grass, coriander, salt, and pepper. Simmer slowly for 4 hours.

2. Meanwhile, to make the dipping sauce, squeeze the juice from 2 of the lemons and discard the 2 squeezed-out lemons. Peel the other 2 lemons with a paring knife, removing all peel and pith. Cut the lemon sections out from between the membranes. Squeeze out the lemon remains to get all juice. Set aside. Chop the garlic in a food processor. Add the lemon sections and juice and pulse to make a coarse puree. Scrape into a bowl and stir in the sugar, nuac nam, chicken broth, and chili-garlic sauce. Store, covered, in the refrigerator. Let come to room temperature before serving.

3. Strain the broth through a fine mesh sieve. Refrigerate overnight and skim off the fat. Place in a large pot and bring to a boil. Lower to a simmer and blanch the vegetables in the broth one type at a time, removing them with a slotted spoon or skimmer before adding the next kind. Blanch the fennel until crisp-tender, about 5 minutes; zucchini until tender, about 3 minutes; carrots until tender, about 12 minutes; asparagus until crisp-tender, about 1 to 2 minutes; mushrooms until tender, about 3 minutes. The vegetables can be blanched a few hours ahead of time.

4. When you are ready to serve, strain the broth again and divide between 2 electric cook pots, large fondue pots, or large pots to be placed over electric hot plates. Cut the salmon, tuna, and sea bass into chunks about 2 inches by 1 inch by ½ inch. Peel and devein the shrimp. Cut the squid into rings. If the scallops are huge, cut them in half. Arrange the vegetables and the uncooked seafood on platters. Spoon the dipping sauce into 8 individual shallow bowls. Guests should also have long-handled forks, individual dipping baskets or chopsticks for dipping, soup spoons, chopsticks for eating, and soup bowls. At the table, heat the broth to simmering and let guests cook the seafood and reheat the vegetables in the broth, as well as ladle some of the broth into the bowls.

Serves 8

Vanilla-Scented Sautéed Fruit

High-quality vanilla beans are essential to this recipe, which can be prepared up to one hour before guests arrive and kept in a 150-degree oven until serving. Like the hot pot, this is a recipe meant to utilize the fruit that looks and tastes the best and the ripest, and varieties should be substituted accordingly.

1 to 2 tablespoons unsalted butter
1 vanilla bean, split lengthwise

THE FRUIT (CHOOSE 6 TO 8)

½ pineapple, peeled, cored, and cut into medium-size chunks
2 nectarines, pitted and cut into sixths
2 mangoes, peeled, pitted, and cut into ¼-inch-thick slices
2 star fruit, cut across into ¼-inch-thick slices
3 bananas, peeled and cut across into ¼-inch-thick slices
4 blood oranges, all peel and pith removed, cut into sections from between
      membranes
1 pint strawberries, hulled and halved
1 cup (½ pint) raspberries, blackberries, or blueberries, cleaned
About ½ cup sugar
¼ cup dark rum
2 pints high-quality vanilla ice cream

1. Melt 1 tablespoon of the butter in a large nonstick skillet over medium-high heat. Add the vanilla bean and sauté for 30 seconds. Add enough fruit to barely cover the bottom of the skillet (do not overcrowd), beginning with the sturdiest and least ripe fruits.

2. Sauté until the fruit begins to brown, sprinkle with 1 to 2 tablespoons of sugar (depending on the ripeness of fruit), and sauté until the fruit is nicely caramelized and tender but not too soft. Place in an oven or microwaveproof baking dish (keeping the vanilla bean in the skillet) and continue until all the fruit is cooked (add the berries last, and cook only to heat through), adding more butter as needed between batches.

A Program
for Rational
Entertaining
in an
Irrational
Age

3. With all the fruit in the baking dish, add the rum to the skillet and deglaze the pan. Add to the fruit mixture and toss very gently to combine. Before serving, warm the fruit in the oven or microwave, divide among 8 bowls, and top with ice cream.

Serves 8

Putting on the Dog in the Dog Days

Theoretically, summer entertaining is an easy, fluid, carefree proposition. The fair weather that ensures a steady supply of good produce also invites a certain playfulness. Guests seem not to expect a succession of sit-down courses with attendant linen, silver, and stemware, at least not all the time. There are moments, of course, when even the most restrained host or hostess seeks to set a quiet and elegant note, simply to distinguish the dinner hour from the day.

But for the most part, summer entertaining is easy. Guests are willing to be wooed in a more casual key, so long as they can be part of the fun.

Witness the backyard barbecue. Even those who skirt the radius of a smoking grill become, if only aromatically, part of the ambience. The same can be said for picnics and clambakes, even covered-dish suppers. Summer's informality is predicated on participation.

This informality can be achieved, in part, with food that is simple and accessible—dishes that are bold and uncomplicated in flavor, more tactile than cerebral, served in a way that enhances, rather than detracts from, the laid-back summer mood. The host, of course, must appear cool and unruffled, offhand in attitude, disposed to easy and amiable chat. That's where the theory of summer entertaining parts from its practice.

The days may be longer, but the workday doesn't shrink; it is a happy coincidence that summer's best ingredients lend themselves to being prepared ahead of time and that the summer weather is appropriate for chilled or room-temperature meals. This allows the hostess to prepare dishes well ahead of the dinner hour.

Prolonged daylight seems to enforce a lengthened cocktail hour, one that nervously spans an attendant dip in the ambient temperature and a growing realization of actual, physiological, even growling hunger. Because the tiny nibbles served to whet the appetite in cooler months can't even take the edge off the anticipation of a late-summer supper, inventive and bountiful and substantial appetizers become more important in the warm months. Variety and heft in the hors d'oeuvre department allow for lighter meals. Appetite and availability are rarely at odds.

Parties in a statelier mood, sit-down events with a set menu, can function as intimate punctuation points to summer's typically casual gatherings. Menus for such occasions are most successful when a touch of cerebral conceit and even evidence of a little fussing is apparent on the plate.

In any mood, the concerns for healthy meals and timely preparations abide. And these, along with the idiosyncratic concerns and style of each member of the group, informed the menus and recipes they designed for summer entertaining.

Entertaining
the Masses

The mere thought of a carefree fête fills Johanna with fear and dread. Much of the success of such a gathering depends upon the vicissitudes of people's mood and the weather, things even Johanna can neither foresee or control. It just racks her nerves.

Nevertheless, she was determined to be a guest at her summer gatherings, bound to be and to appear to be unburdened by the logistics of cooking for crowds, fixated on having fun. For this reason, she took the "salad-bar" approach to the large summer gatherings she planned. She figured that if she prepared the components of the salads ahead of time, guests could assemble their meals.

Logistically, the plan was a boon to her serenity. Socially, it leveled the playing field. The dinner party became a group effort, the particular appetite of each guest being wordlessly accommodated.

Despite the fact that her need to impress was diminishing, Johanna had not completely accepted that the destiny of a party might be beyond her control, but the salad-bar approach has freed her to some extent. Planning the array of dishes as well as a strategy helps exorcise her compulsion.

She begins with the concept. Johanna accepts that she is simply not the sort of person who can put out a bowl of lettuce, strips of meat, and a bowl of croutons and yell, "Come and get it!" No, the sorts of salads she envisions are variations of the French composed salad, mounds of interesting greens surrounded by marinated vegetables, fish, or meat, flanked with crusty bread. Unlike the tossed salad, the composed salad challenges the cook's creativity and ingenuity, a challenge that hostesses like Johanna relish.

Shortly after Memorial Day, she began dreaming of presenting similar and opposing flavors so that guests could create a unified whole. Since variety and bounty are the crux of a build-your-own-salad meal, a certain amount of careful deliberation is involved.

Johanna considered the different sorts of sunny foods she herself loved— sharp onion and feta from Greece, cold lamb and artichokes done in the Italian manner, the bright peppers, basil, and mint of southeast Asia. She couldn't combine aspects of each into a single salad buffet—her guests would feel as disoriented as they would on a seven-day world cruise. Nobody knows better than Johanna how a little dissonance can dampen a dinner party.

The components of each salad remain within a coherent range of flavors. In *Ethnic Cuisines*, Elizabeth Rozin delineates what she calls "the flavor principles" of thirty cooking regions around the world, enumerating what ingredients unify and distinguish them from one another. Johanna used these principles—the olive oil, thyme, rosemary, and tomatoes of Provence, the tomato, cinnamon, lemon, and parsley of the Middle East, the sour-orange, garlic, and achiote of Mexico— to integrate the components of the menus she served throughout the summer.

Fresh basil leaves tossed in with the salad greens, she found, transform a cold buffet of marinated mozzarella, roasted peppers, and smoked beef into something emphatically Italian. A splash of tamarind in the salad dressing, and the effect is Indian. A fruity raspberry vinegar and mung bean sprouts, and you're in Central Asia.

The possibilities kept Johanna up late with cookbooks and old magazines. She secretly saw herself as an artist, providing the supplies for a performance piece called "Summer Dinner." It was a satisfying fantasy. Sometimes she served the salads together on a large buffet; other times, she served the fixings of a single salad, passing the components around the table, family-style.

Sometimes, she offered guests a stand-up first course from the grill and used the salads to beckon them to the table. Other times, she served a first course and then composed the salads in the kitchen and served them to guests. The bounty of the array gave her some respite from her need to impress. She didn't fidget. She cast no apprehensive glances. At no time did she break a sweat.

An Arresting Salmon and Potato Salad

After something casual, such as grilled chicken wings, or cocktails and dips (pages 118–21), this salad is the sort of main course that can bring the guests to the table. The components for the salad can be presented separately, allowing guests to determine the particular tastes and proportions they desire; for a less casual lunch or dinner, the salad can be composed in the kitchen, plate by plate.

If the main course is not preceded by food from the grill or a long cocktail hour, a warm soup such as the Almond Buttermilk Soup (page 125) makes a comforting start for this salad meal. If the soup is served first, bread—a French-style baguette or a crusty peasant loaf—transforms this light salad into genteel sufficiency. The savory Tomato-Lemon Biscotti (page 69), however, are an even better match. On a cool night, if you are willing to risk some last-minute preparations, Pepper-Chive Popovers (page 27) would also make a fine companion to this salad meal.

Given the light character of the food, a tart such as Mr. D.'s Strawberry Almond Tart (page 84) or a toasted Blueberry Crumb Cake (page 100) topped with a compote of blueberries, strawberries, or peaches provides a sweet and satisfying finish.

THE SALMON

1¼ pounds salmon fillet
½ teaspoon kosher salt, or more to taste
Freshly ground pepper to taste
1½ teaspoons fresh lemon juice
1 tablespoon thinly sliced fresh mint

THE ASPARAGUS

24 asparagus spears, ends snapped off
¾ pound sugar snap peas, strung
1½ cups cooked fresh peas
3 tablespoons Lemon Vinaigrette (page 68)
Kosher salt and freshly ground pepper to taste

A Program
for Rational
Entertaining
in an
Irrational
Age

1½ pounds small red potatoes, cut into ⅛-inch slices

¼ cup mayonnaise

5 tablespoons plain low-fat yogurt

¾ teaspoon grated lime zest

1½ teaspoons fresh lime juice

¾ teaspoon kosher salt

¼ teaspoon freshly ground pepper

1 scallion, green part only, thinly sliced, for garnish

12 cups salad greens

3 tablespoons Lemon Vinaigrette

1. Preheat the oven to 350° F. Place the salmon on a baking sheet and season with the salt and a sprinkling of pepper. Bake until just cooked through, about 10 to 20 minutes, depending on the thickness of the fillets. Let cool, pull off the skin, and flake with a fork into large chunks. Place in a bowl and gently toss with the lemon juice and with salt and pepper to taste. Garnish with the mint.

2. Separate the asparagus tips from stalks. Peel the stalks and cut into 1-inch pieces. Blanch the stalks in boiling, salted water for 2 minutes. Add the tips and blanch 1 minute more. Drain and refresh under cold running water. Set aside. Blanch the sugar snaps until crisp-tender, about 4 minutes; drain and refresh. Place the asparagus, sugar snaps, peas, and vinaigrette in a bowl and toss. Season with salt and pepper to taste.

3. Place the potatoes in a saucepan, cover with cold water, and bring to a boil. Lower the heat, cover, and simmer until just tender, 5 to 10 minutes. Drain and let cool. Whisk together the mayonnaise, yogurt, lime zest and juice, salt, and pepper. Toss the potatoes with the dressing. Place in a bowl and garnish with the scallion.

4. Place the salad greens in a large bowl and toss with the vinaigrette. Pass the dishes separately, letting guests build their own salads.

Serves 6

Lamb, Artichoke, and Roasted Potato Salad

This salad, which can utilize leftover grilled lamb, can be presented in components on a buffet, or the individual platters can be passed around the table, family-style. As a way of saving time and effort, frozen artichoke hearts are used in addition to the fresh artichokes, but the purist may prefer using all fresh artichokes. The lamb salad can bring people to the table after a round of grilled shrimp or skewered scallops or other substantial nibbles.

For a more elegant presentation, each salad can be composed in the kitchen and served to guests for a light lunch or dinner, accompanied by the Tomato-Lemon Biscotti (page 69). If grilling or other hors d'oeuvres are not on the menu, the salad should be preceded by the Wild Herb Soup (page 74) or the Roasted Tomato Soup with a Savory Froth (page 92). Sour Cream Ice Cream (page 42) topped with Vinegared Berries (page 85) or Blackberry-Lemon Tart with Champagne-Mint Granité (page 136) makes a delicious dessert that complements the flavor and style of the meal.

THE POTATOES

2½ pounds small red potatoes, quartered
1 tablespoon olive oil
3 teaspoons chopped fresh rosemary
1 teaspoon kosher salt
Freshly ground pepper to taste

THE LAMB

1 teaspoon olive oil
8 loin lamb chops, boned and trimmed
2½ tablespoons Lemon Vinaigrette (page 68)
Kosher salt and freshly ground pepper to taste
1 teaspoon chopped Italian parsley

THE ARTICHOKES

2 (9-ounce) packages frozen artichoke hearts, cooked and cooled
4 large fresh artichoke hearts, raw, very thinly sliced
1 (10-ounce) package frozen baby lima beans, cooked and cooled
2 cloves garlic, minced

66

A Program
for Rational
Entertaining
in an
Irrational
Age

¼ cup Lemon Vinaigrette
2 teaspoons chopped Italian parsley
Kosher salt and freshly ground pepper to taste

THE GREENS

12 cups salad greens
3 tablespoons Lemon Vinaigrette
1½ cups imported black olives
1½ cups fresh-shaved Parmesan cheese

1. Preheat the oven to 425° F. Place the potatoes in a roasting pan and toss with the olive oil and 2 teaspoons of the rosemary. Roast until tender, stirring from time to time, about 30 minutes. Let cool. Place in a bowl and toss with the salt and freshly ground pepper to taste. Garnish with the remaining 1 teaspoon rosemary.

2. To make the lamb: Heat the olive oil in a large nonstick skillet over medium-high heat. Add the lamb and sear on all sides until medium-rare, about 4 minutes. Remove from the skillet and let cool. Thinly slice the lamb and toss with the 2½ tablespoons vinaigrette, adding additional salt and pepper to taste. Place on a platter and garnish with the parsley.

3. Place the cooked and raw artichokes, lima beans, and garlic in a bowl and toss with the ¼ cup vinaigrette. Toss in the parsley and season with salt and pepper to taste.

4. Place the salad greens in a large bowl and toss with the 3 tablespoons vinaigrette. Place the olives and Parmesan in separate bowls. Pass the dishes separately, letting guests build their own salads.

Serves 6

Lemon Vinaigrette

This vinaigrette can be used to dress greens, blanched green beans, or grilled vegetables. It's a fine dressing for steamed artichokes and also makes a lovely marinade for mushrooms that have been lightly blanched in salted water, drained, and then tossed with the vinaigrette while warm. A fresh herb such as thyme, minced chives, parsley, dill, or basil can be added to this vinaigrette as well, to add more flavor to green salads, or if used as a sauce for grilled food, to meat, vegetables, or fish. The vinaigrette can add a splash of newness to almost anything left over from a previous meal.

1 teaspoon Dijon mustard
¼ cup fresh lemon juice
½ teaspoon kosher salt
¼ teaspoon freshly ground pepper
½ cup extra-virgin olive oil

Whisk the mustard, lemon juice, salt, and pepper together. Whisking constantly, slowly drizzle in the olive oil.

Makes about ¾ cup

68
A Program
for Rational
Entertaining
in an
Irrational
Age

Tomato-Lemon Biscotti

These savory biscotti make an intriguing counterpoint to chicken, lamb, or beef and can be made in large quantities well ahead of time. They keep up to two weeks if stored in an airtight container, though they should not be refrigerated.

3 cups all-purpose flour
1 teaspoon baking powder
1 teaspoon kosher salt
½ teaspoon freshly ground pepper
2 teaspoons grated lemon zest
½ cup oil-packed sun-dried tomatoes, drained and chopped medium-fine
3 large eggs
½ cup plus 2 tablespoons water
Olive oil spray

1. Preheat the oven to 350° F. In a large bowl, stir together the flour, baking powder, salt, pepper, lemon zest, and tomatoes. Whisk together 2 of the eggs and the water. Make a well in the dry ingredients, pour in the egg mixture, and gradually combine.

2. Lightly flour your hands and a work surface. Turn out the dough and knead until smooth. Divide the dough in half and shape each piece into a 2½-inch-thick log. Coat a baking sheet with the olive oil spray and place the dough logs on it. Whisk the remaining egg and brush it over the dough. Bake for 35 minutes.

3. Let cool for a few minutes and then cut the biscotti on the diagonal into ¼-inch slices. Divide between 2 baking sheets and bake until biscotti are browned on the bottom, about 25 minutes. Remove biscotti from baking sheets and place on a rack to cool.

Makes about 24 biscotti

An Asian Summer Salad Buffet

Japanese Chicken Salad with Nori Rolls

This Japanese variation on the standard summer chicken salad makes a fine lunch or dinner. While the chicken can be prepared specifically for the salad, the recipe can also utilize leftover grilled chicken that has been chilled, skinned, and shredded.

Because it is such a light meal, it should be served after substantial hors d'oeuvres. For a more elegant, sit-down meal, serve a cold soup such as the Almond Buttermilk Soup (page 125) before the salad. Japanese crackers and rice crackers are available in many gourmet markets and make a more cohesive meal than European-style bread, but the ambitious cook may want to make Poppy Crackers (page 73) to accompany this salad.

A filling dessert is needed, such as the Pistachio-Crusted Cheesecake with Orange-Caramel Sauce (page 50), topped with fresh berries rather than caramelized fruit. Alternatively, a warm dessert such as the Vanilla-Scented Sautéed Fruit (page 58), using peaches, nectarines, and berries and served with ice cream, is a tasty and fitting finish to this light meal.

THE CHICKEN

Kosher salt and freshly ground pepper to taste
1 pound boneless skinless chicken breasts
2 teaspoons canola oil
6 cups cubed shiitake mushrooms

70
A Program
for Rational
Entertaining
in an
Irrational
Age

2 small tofu cakes, cut into ¼-inch cubes

¼ cup teriyaki sauce

¾ teaspoon toasted sesame oil

1½ cups stemmed watercress

THE NORI ROLLS

2 teaspoons wasabi powder

2 teaspoons water

1½ cups cooked sticky rice

1½ teaspoons rice vinegar

2 scallions, minced

½ teaspoon kosher salt

2 sheets nori

THE CUCUMBERS

2 medium cucumbers, peeled, halved lengthwise, seeded, and cut into ¼-inch
        dice

8 large red radishes, trimmed and julienned

1 teaspoon rice vinegar

¼ teaspoon kosher salt

12 cups salad greens

3 tablespoons Lemon Vinaigrette (page 68)

1. Preheat the oven to 350° F. Sprinkle salt lightly over the chicken and bake it until just cooked through, about 20 minutes. Let cool and slice on the diagonal. Meanwhile, heat the canola oil in a large nonstick skillet over medium-high heat. Add the shiitakes, season with salt and pepper, and cook until softened, about 5 minutes. Set aside.

2. In a bowl, toss the chicken and tofu together, add the teriyaki sauce, and let stand for 30 minutes. Toss in the shiitakes, sesame oil, and watercress and season with salt to taste.

3. Stir together the wasabi and water and let stand 10 minutes. Stir together the rice, vinegar, scallions, and salt. Lay 1 sheet of nori on a work surface with the longer side toward you. Spread half of the rice mixture over the nori, leaving a 1-inch border on the edge nearest you. Starting at one of the shorter ends, dab a line of the wasabi paste across the rice, using half of the paste. Starting with the edge nearest you, roll up the nori. Repeat with the remaining nori ingredients. Trim off the ends and cut the rolls into ¾-inch slices. Place on a platter.

4. In a bowl, toss together the cucumbers, radishes, vinegar, and salt. Place the salad greens in a large bowl and toss with the vinaigrette. Pass the dishes separately, letting guests build their own salads.

Serves 6

72

A Program
for Rational
Entertaining
in an
Irrational
Age

Poppy Crackers

These crackers are distinctive and yet can complement a wide range of summer meals; almost any Asian-inspired, Middle Eastern, or Eastern Mediterranean dish will be flattered by them. They can be made ahead and must be stored in an airtight container at room temperature. Crackers like these can also be purchased in many specialty grocery shops.

1 cup warm water
1 package (¼ ounce) active dry yeast
2 tablespoons olive oil
2¾ cups all-purpose flour
2½ teaspoons kosher salt
1 large egg, lightly beaten
2 tablespoons poppy seeds

1. Place the water and yeast in a food processor and pulse to combine. Let stand for 5 minutes. Add the olive oil and 1 cup of the flour and process until smooth. Add the remaining flour and 1½ teaspoons of the salt and process for 1 minute. Turn the dough out onto a lightly floured surface and knead until smooth. Place in a lightly oiled bowl, cover with plastic wrap, and set aside in a warm place until doubled in bulk, about 1 hour.

2. Punch the dough down, reshape, and let rise again until doubled, about 45 minutes. Preheat the oven to 400° F. Punch down the dough and divide in half. Roll 1 piece of the dough into a square of about 13 inches, stopping as necessary to let the dough rest. Place on an oiled baking sheet and crimp the dough heavily with a fork. Repeat with the remaining dough.

3. Brush both dough squares with the egg. Sprinkle with the poppy seeds and the remaining teaspoon of salt. Bake until browned and crisp, rotating the pans once, about 20 minutes. Place on a rack to cool. Break into irregular pieces.

Serves 6

An Eastern Mediterranean Salad Buffet

Wild Herb Soup

This is a variation on a soup made throughout the Mediterranean area and France, using whatever wild herbs and greens can be found. Here, herbs and greens that are available most widely throughout the United States are called for. If you have access to wild spinach or watercress, sorrel or ramps, spring onions, chives, or other wild greens, they will make a more intensely flavored soup. The key is the proportion of sour greens and milder ones: bitterness is possible and is the enemy of this soup. The cook must add and taste and judge. The portions listed yield a soup that is both mellow and sharp and deeply herbaceous.

The soup keeps well in the refrigerator for up to three days. It is tasty served hot or cold (garnished, perhaps, with yogurt or sour cream). For this meal, however, the warm soup could bring people to the table, take an edge off hunger, and set the stage for a meal of salads.

THE SOUP

1½ cups loosely packed young spinach leaves
1½ cups mâche
8 fresh sage leaves
3 tablespoons fresh chervil leaves
¾ cup dandelion greens
3 large baking potatoes, peeled and cut into ½-inch dice
Kosher salt and freshly ground pepper to taste
3 cloves garlic, chopped

74
A Program
for Rational
Entertaining
in an
Irrational
Age

6 cups chicken broth, homemade or low-sodium canned
3 teaspoons fresh lemon juice

5 tablespoons coarsely chopped mâche
3 teaspoons chopped fresh sage
3 teaspoons chopped fresh chervil
4½ teaspoons chopped fresh chives
1½ teaspoons finely chopped lemon zest

1. To make the soup, combine the spinach, mâche, sage, chervil, dandelion greens, and potatoes in a large saucepan; season lightly with salt and pepper. Stir in the garlic and chicken broth. Bring to a boil over medium-high heat. Lower the heat and simmer slowly until potatoes are tender, about 20 minutes.

2. Process the soup mixture in a food processor until smooth. Add additional salt and pepper to taste.

3. To make the garnish, toss together the mâche, sage, chervil, and chives. Just before serving, stir the lemon juice into the soup. Ladle into 4 bowls and sprinkle with the herb mixture and then the lemon zest. Serve immediately.

Serves 6

Spiced Pasta, Avocado, and Onion-Feta Salad

Most of the components of this salad can be prepared well in advance. It can be served as a buffet or as a family-style meal, before or after mildly seasoned, simple grilled chicken or fish. Poppy Crackers (page 73) make a lovely companion for the salad. The mood of this casual, rustic meal could be continued with a dessert such as Mr. D.'s Strawberry Almond Tart (page 84), or pushed up the elegance scale with a showier and more complex sweet course, such as the Caramelized Oranges with Chocolate Shortbread and Caramel Ice Cream (page 86).

THE PASTA

1 pound fusilli
2 jalapeño peppers, seeded and minced
2 teaspoons olive oil
3 tablespoons chopped fresh cilantro
1 teaspoon kosher salt
½ teaspoon freshly ground pepper

THE ONIONS

6 medium red onions, peeled and cut into ⅛-inch slices
1 tablespoon olive oil
½ cup crumbled feta
¾ teaspoon kosher salt
¼ teaspoon freshly ground pepper

THE PEPPERS

3 red and 3 yellow bell peppers, roasted, peeled, seeded, and cut into ¼-inch strips
1 tablespoon olive oil
1 tablespoon fresh lemon juice
1 teaspoon kosher salt
Freshly ground pepper to taste

76

A Program
for Rational
Entertaining
in an
Irrational
Age

3 avocados, peeled, pitted, and cubed
1 tablespoon fresh lime juice
3 cloves garlic, minced
¾ teaspoon Tabasco
Kosher salt to taste

THE GREENS

12 cups salad greens
2 tablespoons olive oil
1 tablespoon lime juice
1 teaspoon kosher salt
Freshly ground pepper to taste

1. Cook the fusilli in boiling salted water until al dente. Drain, rinse, and drain well again. Place in a bowl and toss with the jalapeños, olive oil, and cilantro and season with the salt and pepper.

2. Meanwhile, preheat the broiler. Place the onions on baking sheets and brush with the oil. Broil until browned, about 5 minutes. Let cool and coarsely chop. Place in a bowl and toss with the feta, salt, and pepper.

3. Place the roasted peppers in a bowl and toss with the olive oil, lemon juice, salt, and pepper. Place the avocados in a bowl and toss with the lime juice, garlic, Tabasco, and salt.

4. Place the salad greens in a large bowl and toss with the olive oil, lime juice, salt, and pepper. Pass the dishes separately, letting guests build their own salads.

Serves 6

Zucchini, Herb, Grilled Eggplant, and Tomato Salad

This salad can be served alone for a light lunch or dinner; for a more substantial meal, serve it as an accompaniment to grilled chicken, lamb, beef, or fish. The components of the salad can be combined (without the lettuce) and used as a topping for grilled country bread. It keeps up to one week, and, since the vegetable mélange is so versatile, is a good candidate for making in large quantities and using to perk up leftovers like cold pasta or rice.

THE ZUCCHINI

6 medium zucchini, halved lengthwise and cut across into ¼-inch slices
1½ tablespoons fresh lemon juice
1½ teaspoons olive oil
1 teaspoon kosher salt
½ teaspoon freshly ground pepper
2 tablespoons chopped fresh mint
2 tablespoons chopped fresh parsley

THE EGGPLANT

6 baby eggplants, halved lengthwise
4 teaspoons olive oil
Kosher salt and freshly ground pepper to taste

THE TOMATOES

9 large plum tomatoes, cut into large dice
6 tablespoons thinly sliced fresh basil
3 tablespoons olive oil
Kosher salt and freshly ground pepper to taste

THE MOZZARELLA

1 pound lightly salted fresh mozzarella, cut into ¼-inch slices, each slice halved
2 tablespoons thinly sliced fresh basil

78

A Program
for Rational
Entertaining
in an
Irrational
Age

9 cups salad greens
¾ cup torn fresh basil
¾ cup torn fresh mint
2 tablespoons fresh lemon juice
3 tablespoons olive oil
Kosher salt and freshly ground pepper to taste

1. Blanch the zucchini in boiling salted water for 30 seconds. Drain and refresh under cold running water. Drain again and pat dry. Place in a bowl and toss with the lemon juice, olive oil, salt, pepper, mint, and parsley.

2. Heat a grill or broiler. Brush the cut side of the eggplants with olive oil and sprinkle with salt and pepper. Grill or broil until browned and tender, about 5 to 10 minutes. Place on a platter.

3. Toss the tomatoes, basil, and olive oil together and season to taste with salt and pepper. Arrange the mozzarella on a platter and garnish with basil. Place the salad greens, basil, and mint in a large bowl, toss with the lemon juice and olive oil, and season to taste with salt and pepper. Pass the dishes separately, letting guests build their own salads.

Serves 6

Basil, Snap Pea, and Rice Salad with Creamy Yogurt Dressing

Served buffet-style or family-style, this salad makes a wonderful lunch. For a larger evening meal, it could be served after grilled chicken, fish, or seafood. It makes a marvelous meal if followed by the Mustard and Curry Roast Pork (page 99). Preceded by the Roasted Tomato Soup with a Savory Froth (page 92), the salad makes a satisfying main course. The Blackberry-Lemon Tart with Champagne-Mint Granité (page 136) or Mr. D.'s Strawberry Almond Tart (page 84) provides a lovely ending to the meal.

THE SNAP PEAS

1¼ pounds sugar snap peas, strung
2½ teaspoons olive oil
1 teaspoon kosher salt
Freshly ground pepper to taste

THE RICE

3 cups cooked white rice
½ cup thinly sliced fresh basil
2 teaspoons fresh lime juice
Kosher salt and freshly ground pepper to taste

THE CUCUMBERS

6 medium cucumbers, peeled, halved lengthwise, seeded, and cut across into
    ¼-inch slices
2 tablespoons fresh lemon juice
1 teaspoon kosher salt
6 tablespoons coarsely chopped fresh mint

THE GREENS

10 cups salad greens
2 cups torn basil

80
A Program
for Rational
Entertaining
in an
Irrational
Age

1 cup plain low-fat yogurt
1 tablespoon milk
4 teaspoons olive oil
1 small clove garlic, minced
Kosher salt and freshly ground pepper to taste
2 scallions, minced

1. Blanch the sugar snaps in boiling salted water until crisp-tender, about 4 minutes. Drain, refresh under cold running water, drain again, and pat dry. Place in a bowl and toss with the olive oil, salt, and freshly ground pepper to taste.

2. Place the rice in a bowl and toss in the basil, lime juice, salt, and pepper.

3. Place the cucumbers in a bowl and toss with the lemon juice, salt, and mint; set aside.

4. Place the salad greens in a large bowl and toss with the basil. Whisk together the yogurt, milk, olive oil, garlic, salt, and pepper. Stir in the scallions and place in a small bowl. Pass the dishes separately, letting guests build their own salads.

Serves 6

Sweet Endings
for a Summer Night

The following desserts are the sorts of things that can bring a sense of closure and community to an evening, as well as lending both elegance and substance to a light summer meal. Most can be made the morning of the party and, unless otherwise noted, should be stored at room temperature until serving.

Panna Cotta

(Adapted from Gramercy Tavern, New York City)

This tart, smooth dessert can be made up to a day in advance of serving, but it must be unmolded and brought nearly to room temperature before being placed in front of guests. Very lightly sweetened raspberries, blueberries, and strawberries make a wonderful foil. Chopped fresh peaches and nectarines do as well. Almost any combination of summer fruit will flatter this delicate and satisfying dessert.

1 cup plus 2 tablespoons heavy cream
½ cup sugar
3 tablespoons cold water
1 package powdered gelatin
1⅔ cups buttermilk
⅛ teaspoon kosher salt
Fresh fruit, for garnish

1. Place the cream and sugar in a medium saucepan over medium heat until the sugar dissolves, about 7 minutes. Meanwhile, place the water in a small bowl and sprinkle the gelatin over it; do not stir. Let stand for 5 minutes.

2. Stir the gelatin mixture into the warm cream until melted. Stir in the buttermilk, add the salt, and ladle the mixture into six 6-ounce ramekins. Refrigerate, loosely covered, until set, at least 2 hours.

3. To serve, run the tip of a small knife around the panna cotta and unmold onto individual plates. Let stand until almost at room temperature, about 1 hour. Serve surrounded by fresh fruit.

Serves 6

Mr. D.'s Strawberry Almond Tart

1¼ cups all-purpose flour
¼ teaspoon kosher salt
2 teaspoons sugar
½ cup (1 stick) cold unsalted butter, cut into pieces
¼ cup ice water

THE FILLING

4 ounces almond paste
4 tablespoons (½ stick) cold unsalted butter, cut into ½-inch pieces
¼ cup all-purpose flour
2 tablespoons sugar
⅛ teaspoon kosher salt
1 large egg
½ teaspoon vanilla extract

THE BERRIES

2 pints fresh strawberries, hulled and halved
Confectioners' sugar, for garnish

1. Place the flour, salt, and sugar in a food processor and pulse to combine. Add the butter and pulse until butter is the size of small peas. Add the water and pulse until dough barely begins to come together. Press the dough together with your hands, flatten into a disk, wrap in plastic wrap, and refrigerate for 30 minutes.

2. Preheat the oven to 350° F. Roll the dough out to a thickness of ⅛ inch. Fit it into a 9½-inch quiche dish. Line the dish with baking parchment, fill with pie weights or raw beans, and bake for 25 minutes. Remove the paper and the weights and bake for 2 minutes more. Set aside.

3. Place the almond paste and butter in a food processor and process until smooth. Mix in the flour, sugar, and salt. Add the egg and vanilla and process until smooth. Scrape the mixture into the tart shell, spread into an even layer, and bake until set, about 15 minutes. Let cool.

84

A Program
for Rational
Entertaining
in an
Irrational
Age

4. Make a ring of strawberries around the edge of the dish, leaning the cut side of the berries up against the edge. Repeat, making concentric circles until the tart is covered. Just before serving, sift confectioners' sugar over the top. Cut into wedges to serve.

Serves 6

Vinegared Berries

2 pints ripe strawberries
1 tablespoon balsamic vinegar
1 to 2 tablespoons sugar

Rinse and hull the berries and cut each in half. In a large bowl, toss the berries with the vinegar. For the best results, choose a high-quality, aged balsamico. Add 1 tablespoon of the sugar and toss the berries. Taste and add additional sugar if needed. Some favor adding several turns of freshly ground pepper or a pungent herb such as bruised rosemary to the berries to intensify the flavors. The berries should rest, covered, in the refrigerator for at least 1 hour before serving. They can be served alone, with a berry sorbet, or simply with a butter cookie.

Serves 6

Caramelized Oranges with Chocolate Shortbread and Caramel Ice Cream

Each component of this dish can be prepared ahead of time. The oranges should be stored, well wrapped, in the refrigerator; the cookies should be stored in an airtight container and kept at room temperature.

THE ICE CREAM

1¼ cups sugar

¼ cup water

2½ cups milk

1½ cups heavy cream

6 large egg yolks

2 teaspoons vanilla extract

THE SHORTBREAD

2 cups all-purpose flour

½ cup confectioners' sugar

½ teaspoon kosher salt

6 tablespoons unsweetened cocoa powder

1 large egg, lightly beaten

THE ORANGES

6 oranges, peeled, sections cut from between membranes

6 tablespoons sugar

1. Place 1 cup of the sugar in a medium saucepan and stir in the water. Use a pastry brush dipped in water to wash down any sugar crystals on the side of the pan. Place over medium heat and cook without stirring until mixture turns a deep caramel color. Remove from heat and carefully add the milk and cream. Return the pan to the heat and stir until caramel is dissolved. Bring to a simmer. Meanwhile, in a large bowl, whisk the egg yolks and the remaining ¼ cup sugar together.

2. Whisking rapidly, add the caramel mixture to the yolks. Pour the mixture back into the pan and place over low heat. Cook, stirring constantly, until mixture is thick enough to coat the back of a spoon, about 15 minutes; do not let it come

86

A Program
for Rational
Entertaining
in an
Irrational
Age

to a simmer. Pour into a bowl, let cool, and refrigerate until cold. Stir in the vanilla. Freeze in an ice cream machine according to the manufacturer's directions.

3. Meanwhile, make the shortbread: Preheat the oven to 350° F. Place the flour, confectioners' sugar, salt, and cocoa in a food processor and pulse to combine. Add the egg and pulse just until mixture begins to come together. Press the dough together. On a lightly floured surface, roll the dough out to a thickness of ¼ inch. Cut the dough into rounds using a 2-inch cookie cutter. Gather and reroll scraps and cut out cookies until all the dough is used. Place cookies on baking sheets lined with baking parchment and bake until set, about 20 to 25 minutes. Let cool.

4. Preheat the broiler. Place the orange sections in a baking dish in a single layer and sprinkle with the sugar. Broil until the sugar begins to brown, about 4 minutes. Place a scoop of ice cream in 6 dishes. Top with the oranges and serve immediately with the shortbread.

Serves 6

Orange-Scented Flan

⅔ cup sugar
3 tablespoons water

3 cups milk
1 teaspoon grated orange zest
3 large eggs
2 large egg yolks
½ cup sugar
¼ teaspoon kosher salt

1. Preheat the oven to 325° F. To make the caramel, combine the sugar and water in a medium saucepan. Use a pastry brush dipped in water to wash down any sugar crystals on the side of the pan. Cook over medium-low heat, without stirring, until the mixture is a light amber color. Remove immediately. Pour into an 8-cup soufflé dish and set aside.

2. To make the custard, place the milk and orange zest in a medium saucepan. Bring the milk to a boil over medium heat, cover, remove from the heat, and allow to stand for 10 minutes. Meanwhile, in a large bowl, whisk together the eggs, yolks, and sugar. Whisking constantly, pour the milk into the eggs. Add the salt and strain the custard into the soufflé dish. Let stand 2 to 3 minutes and skim the foam from the top.

3. Place the soufflé dish in a deep baking pan and pour enough hot water into the pan to reach halfway up the sides of the soufflé dish. Bake until the flan is just set (it will tremble slightly in the center when shaken) and a small knife inserted into the center comes out clean, about 1½ hours. Remove from the oven and take the soufflé dish from the water. Let stand at least 30 minutes before serving, or refrigerate, loosely covered, and serve chilled.

4. To serve, run a small knife around the edge of the dish to loosen the flan. Turn out onto a rimmed serving dish. Slice into wedges and spoon caramel over each piece.

Serves 8

88

A Program
for Rational
Entertaining
in an
Irrational
Age

The Woman Who
Wants to Please

One can never underestimate the pressure that a simple summer fête can exert on the hearts and minds of people who need to please people. For Nan, even after several months of meetings, the initial flush of generosity—"Ah, a weekend supper," she thinks—inevitably becomes a palpable tension beneath her sternum before she has even begun to compose a guest list.

Before she knows whom she will have the chance to please, in other words, Nan is worried about pleasing them. Unlike Johanna's entertainment motive, Nan's is not precisely the urge to impress. Rather, she is driven by a compulsion to coax acceptance, if not affection, from her guests. Mostly, she wants everyone to be happy.

The era of the sit-down dinner party with a fixed menu would have been hell for Nan, with its seemingly intractable progression of courses offering only four to six opportunities to recognize and court the individual tastes of her guests. Fortunately, she didn't begin to entertain until the early 1990s.

"*Nobody* gives four-course meals anymore, honey," said Johanna. As is her habit when feeling slightly anxious, she expounded in an intellectual fashion. "Social mores," Johanna said, "have always lagged behind social reality. In a world in which personal dietary habits and tastes are, at least temporarily, more important than collective communion, the four-course set piece is an impossible form."

Nan was somewhat relieved to hear that only a professional caterer with a doctorate in human behavior as well as possibly a medical degree and a higher-than-average dose of intuition could possibly address the dietary concerns and conceits, the personal preferences and political convictions of a large party of guests in a mere four courses. If you need to please people as much as Nan does, serving four courses would be a little like playing Russian roulette.

There might be hostesses capable of not noticing uneaten morsels on their guests' plates. There might, as well, be those who would not take umbrage at the guest who, faced with an extravagant meal, pats his stomach and asks for salad, dressing on the side. Nan is not there yet. For this reason, the fashion of serving a buffet at room temperature—presented as an array of appetizers before a meal, or as the meal itself—sounded like just the ticket to her.

Call it tapas, call it antipasti—in any case, call it hedging your bets and relax. An assortment of dishes to satisfy the vegetarian and the low-fat acolyte, those with adventuresome tastes and those who favor traditional cooking, is the most a well-meaning hostess can do to accommodate the me-me dinner guest.

Such a menu can be prepared well ahead of party time and begs for a minimum of attention once guests have arrived. The recipes below constitute the sort of menu elastic enough to serve a crowd; increase or decrease the quantity as your guest list requires. The recipes are also well suited to being given to a cook or a caterer to prepare.

Should the nature of your party include weekend guests, these are the sorts of mix-and-match dishes that can be prepared ahead and used in various combinations throughout the weekend.

Elizabeth advised Nan to build a menu the way she would build a wardrobe. But she quickly corrected herself. "Well, as some would build a wardrobe," she said. "What I am trying to say is that whether you are planning an assortment of dishes for a buffet or a procession of do-ahead dishes meant to last a weekend, create a collection that can be mixed and matched. Dishes that can be served in different incarnations at different meals."

Planning a menu that can be made in large quantities—particularly sturdy, one-pot dishes that can compose a buffet—is essential. For Nan, who cooks in the evenings before a party, the keeping qualities of a given dish are important. For

90

A Program
for Rational
Entertaining
in an
Irrational
Age

Elizabeth, who views recycling as a form of "amortizing," the possibility of expanding a given recipe to serve a crowd looms large.

The two women collaborated on a strategy that works for either a large summer dinner or for cooking ahead for weekend guests.

Begin as early as Thursday night, with baking. Most cakes remain fresh for several days, and the cookies below are made for keeping. Choose a confection like crumb cake or cobbler, which can play dessert as well as breakfast, and a recipe that is easily doubled or tripled. As with all do-ahead dishes, the cook should err on the side of generosity.

On Friday, large grain or bean salads can be made, meat or fish can be marinated for later barbecues, and other food that needs to be cooked and chilled can be prepared. Only lighter salads require last-minute attention. Knowing that the pasta served Friday night can become a salad for Saturday lunch, or that cold grilled vegetables can become sandwich fixes, part of a salad, or a garnish for grilled meat, gives a cook a Zen-like calm.

Cooks with a larder and a plan are imperturbable people, even if temperatures suddenly shoot up and five unexpected guests arrive for dinner. The longer days of summer grant the leisure for such cooking. The season also issues a challenge of balancing kitchen work with the charms of an endless afternoon. Summer weekends are a rare opportunity to have it all—if, at the outset, there is a plan.

Used in almost any combination, doubled or tripled as the size of the crowd calls for, the following recipes can be the backbone of a weekend's meals.

Roasted Tomato Soup
with a Savory Froth

This simple soup can be served warm or cold. It is a versatile and soulful summer dish that seems to offset the lightness of most of the season's cooking.

FOR THE SOUP

12 ripe plum tomatoes
2 teaspoons kosher salt, plus more to taste
4 cups chicken broth, homemade or low-sodium canned
¼ teaspoon freshly ground black pepper, plus more to taste
Bread crumbs for thickening soup, as needed
½ teaspoon fresh lemon zest

FOR THE FROTH

4 cloves garlic, unpeeled
½ cup plain yogurt
1 tablespoon minced red onion
2 tablespoons minced fresh cucumber
½ cup heavy cream
Salt and freshly ground pepper to taste
2 teaspoons minced fresh parsley

1. To make the soup, preheat the oven to 325° F. Slice the tomatoes in half lengthwise, place them on a baking sheet and sprinkle lightly with salt, and bake in the oven for 2 hours. Place the unpeeled 4 cloves of garlic for the froth on the same baking sheet and roast until tender, 1½ to 2 hours, along with the tomatoes.

2. Remove the tomatoes and garlic, set the garlic aside, and place the tomatoes in a soup pot with the chicken broth, the remaining salt and the pepper, and simmer over low heat for 45 minutes. Pass the mixture through a food mill. If the tomatoes are particularly juicy, you may find that several tablespoons of fresh bread crumbs are necessary to correct the texture of the soup. Therefore, add bread crumbs as necessary, season with additional salt and pepper to taste, stir in the lemon zest, and chill the mixture.

92
A Program
for Rational
Entertaining
in an
Irrational
Age

3. Place the yogurt in a fine mesh strainer and drain out excess liquid for 1 hour. When the yogurt has drained, place it along with the roasted garlic, the red onion, and the fresh cucumber in the bowl of a food processor and process until smooth. Remove to a medium-size mixing bowl.

4. Using a wire whisk, beat the heavy cream to stiff peaks. Gently fold the whipped cream into the yogurt mixture and season with salt and pepper. Fold in the minced parsley. Serve the soup warm or cold, garnished with a dollop of the froth.

Serves 4

Farfalle, Arugula, and Tomato Salad

The pasta for this salad can be boiled in salted water until tender, rinsed under cold water, and tossed with a tablespoon of additional olive oil up to 3 hours before the salad is assembled. Served with a fresh cheese such as mozzarella or goat cheese, along with grilled bread topped with chopped tomatoes and basil, it can make a meal. It is also a foundation upon which a sprawling, Mediterranean-style buffet can be built.

½ pound farfalle, cooked, drained, and rinsed
3 cups stemmed and torn arugula
½ cup chopped fresh basil
2 large tomatoes, cut into ½-inch dice
1 teaspoon grated lemon zest
3 tablespoons extra-virgin olive oil
1 tablespoon fresh lemon juice
Salt and freshly ground pepper to taste

Place the farfalle in a large bowl. Add the remaining ingredients and toss until well combined, seasoning with salt and pepper to taste.

Serves 8

94
A Program
for Rational
Entertaining
in an
Irrational
Age

Couscous-Stuffed Eggplant

This eggplant can be made up to two days ahead. It can be served alongside grilled fish or chicken as a main course, surrounded by greens for a first course, or become part of a large buffet. This dish also makes a wonderful first course if it is served warm on a bed of lightly dressed bitter greens and surrounded by grilled shrimp.

4 small eggplants, about 10 ounces each
4½ cups cooked couscous
8 plum tomatoes, cut into small dice
6 cloves roasted garlic
½ cup toasted pine nuts
⅓ cup chopped fresh cilantro
1 large jalapeño pepper, seeded and minced
1 tablespoon fresh lemon juice
2 teaspoons ground cumin
Kosher salt and freshly ground pepper to taste

1. Preheat the oven to 400° F. Prick the eggplants a few times with a fork, place them on a baking sheet, and bake until soft, about 45 minutes. When cool enough to handle, cut the eggplants in half lengthwise. Scoop the flesh into a large bowl carefully to avoid tearing the skins. Set the shells aside.

2. Place the remaining ingredients in the bowl with the eggplant and stir to combine. Taste and adjust seasoning with salt and pepper. Mound the mixture in the eggplant shells. Either serve the stuffed eggplants whole or cut them in half crosswise. Place on a platter and serve.

Serves 8

Summer Wheat Salad

Faro, the cereal grain grown in northern Italy, is tough enough to tolerate the anchovies, chilies, and raisins in this lightly sweet, sour, and salty grain-and-vegetable salad, and tender enough to make a toothsome dish. The grain is available in specialty and Italian groceries. It is also sold as "spelt" in some health food stores. The flavor of this salad improves if it is made a day before serving and the flavors are allowed to intensify.

12 ounces faro
4 plum tomatoes
⅔ cup olive oil
2 cloves garlic, minced
6 anchovy fillets, patted dry and minced
¼ teaspoon chili pepper flakes
3 zucchini cut into bite-size chunks
1 cup water
½ cup golden raisins
1 tablespoon balsamic vinegar
1 tablespoon white wine vinegar
½ cup pine nuts, toasted
½ cup minced flat-leaf parsley
Kosher salt and freshly ground pepper to taste

1. Place the faro in a large bowl, cover with cold water, and soak overnight. Drain the faro well. Slice the tomatoes in half lengthwise, place on a baking tray, season lightly with salt and dry in a 200° F. oven for 1½ hours. Remove, cool, cut the tomatoes into bite-size chunks and set aside.

2. Place 2 tablespoons of the olive oil in a large skillet over medium heat. Add the garlic and cook until golden, about 2 minutes. Add 4 of the minced anchovy fillets and the chili pepper flakes, and continue cooking, shaking the pan to avoid sticking, until warm, about 1 minute. Add the zucchini to the skillet and sauté for 2 minutes, shaking the pan. Add the faro, 1 cup of water, and the raisins. Reduce the heat to low and continue cooking for 5 minutes or until the grain is tender. Add more water if necessary to keep the mixture from sticking.

A Program
for Rational
Entertaining
in an
Irrational
Age

3. In a large bowl, combine the 2 remaining minced anchovy fillets with the vinegars. Whisk in the remaining olive oil. Add the grain mixture and stir well to combine. Add the tomatoes, pine nuts, and parsley. Taste and adjust seasoning with salt and pepper if necessary. Serve warm or cold.

Makes 8 appetizers

Oven-Braised Salmon with Fennel

This salmon can be served hot from the oven as a main course, preceded perhaps by the Wild Herb Soup (page 74) or by the Roasted Tomato Soup with a Savory Froth (page 92). Warm or cold, it can be the centerpiece of a buffet.

The leftover salmon and fennel can be combined with cooked rice and a light vinaigrette such as the Lemon Vinaigrette (page 68), possibly seasoned with additional dill, to make a light lunch.

2 (2½ pound) whole salmon fillets
2½ cups white wine
2 tablespoons Pernod
1 large fennel bulb, trimmed, cored, and very thinly sliced, feathery greens
    reserved
Kosher salt and freshly ground pepper to taste
12 cups stemmed watercress, blanched briefly, refreshed in cold water and
    drained
3 tablespoons fresh lemon juice

1. Preheat the oven to 350° F. Place the salmon in 2 large roasting pans. Pour half of the wine and half of the Pernod around the salmon in each pan. Scatter half of the sliced fennel over each fillet. Braise until the salmon is just cooked through, about 30 minutes, basting from time to time.

2. Using 2 long spatulas, carefully transfer the salmon to platters. Season with salt and pepper. Toss the watercress with the lemon juice and season with salt and pepper. Arrange the watercress around the salmon. Chop the fennel greens and sprinkle them over the top.

Serves 8

98

A Program
for Rational
Entertaining
in an
Irrational
Age

Mustard and Curry Roast Pork

This pork can be oven-roasted or grilled, served hot along with the Indian-Spiced Potato Gratin (page 52) as a main course, or surrounded by salad. The Almond Buttermilk Soup (page 125) or the Roasted Tomato Soup with a Savory Froth (page 92) makes a fine first course for this pork; Sour Cream Ice Cream (page 42) topped with berries or the Caramel Orange Fool (page 128) makes a delicious dessert after the spicy meal.

The dish can also stand—hot, cold, or at room temperature—as part of a buffet, particularly one with green salads, rice salads, and marinated vegetables. Leftovers make a terrific sandwich.

½ cup Dijon mustard
¾ teaspoon curry powder
½ teaspoon coarsely ground pepper
2 boned and rolled pork loins, 2½ pounds each
2 bunches fresh spinach, wilted

1. Stir together the mustard, curry powder, and pepper. Rub the mixture all over both pork loins and let stand until the pork comes to room temperature.

2. Preheat the oven to 350° F. Place the pork loins in a large roasting pan and roast until they reach an internal temperature of 160°, about 1 hour 10 minutes. Let stand 10 minutes. Remove the string.

3. Cut a few slices from one of the pork loins and place the slices and remaining uncut loin on a platter. Surround the platter with the wilted spinach and serve, cutting more slices as needed or allowing guests to cut their own.

Serves 8, with leftovers

Blueberry Crumb Cake

This cake can be served as a dessert for lunch or dinner. It can be served alone, with heavy cream, with ice cream, or even with whipped and lightly sweetened mascarpone cheese (see page 275 for mail-order sources). It can also be served for breakfast. The cake keeps well, but as time passes, slices are better toasted and served instead of biscuits in a blueberry or peach shortcake.

THE TOPPING

¾ cup all-purpose flour

1 cup sugar

½ teaspoon ground cinnamon

½ teaspoon kosher salt

¼ pound (1 stick) cold unsalted butter, cut into ½-inch pieces

1 large egg white

THE CAKE

¼ pound (1 stick) unsalted butter, softened, plus additional for greasing pan

1 cup sugar

2 large eggs

1 teaspoon vanilla extract

½ cup milk

1½ cups plus 2 tablespoons all-purpose flour

2 teaspoons baking powder

½ teaspoon kosher salt

1 cup blueberries, cleaned

1. Preheat the oven to 350° F. To make the topping, combine the flour, sugar, cinnamon, and salt in a bowl. Add the butter and rub it in with your fingers until the mixture resembles coarse meal. Set aside.

2. To make the cake, generously butter a 9-inch springform pan. Set aside. Using an electric mixer, cream the butter and sugar until very light and fluffy. Add the eggs, one at a time, and beat well, stopping to scrape the sides of the bowl. Add the vanilla to the milk. Sift 1½ cups of the flour with the baking powder and salt. Add the flour mixture to the egg mixture alternately with the milk, beginning and

100

A Program

for Rational

Entertaining

in an

Irrational

Age

ending with flour. Mix just until combined. Toss the blueberries with the remaining 2 tablespoons flour and stir into the batter.

3. Scrape the batter into the prepared pan and smooth the top. Brush a little of the egg white lightly over the top and sprinkle with the topping. Bake until the cake springs back when touched in the center, about 1 hour. Place on a rack to cool for a few minutes. Run a small knife around the edge of the pan to loosen and remove the sides of the pan. Let cool.

Serves 8 to 10

Almond Shortbread Rounds

These cookies keep very well in an airtight container and make lovely companions to ice cream or sorbet, to a dessert wine, or to a summer fruit salad.

1 cup slivered almonds
4 cups all-purpose flour
1 cup confectioners' sugar
1 teaspoon kosher salt
1 pound cold unsalted butter, cut into ½-inch pieces
4 teaspoons grated lemon zest
1 teaspoon almond extract

1. Place the almonds in a food processor with ¼ cup of the flour. Process until the almonds are coarsely ground. Add the remaining flour, the sugar, and the salt and process until well combined. Add the butter, lemon zest, and almond extract. Process until the mixture begins to come together.

2. Divide the dough into 4 portions. Shape each portion into a log about 1¾ inches in diameter. Wrap in plastic wrap and refrigerate until cold.

3. Preheat the oven to 350° F. Working in batches or as needed, cut the dough into ¼-inch-thick slices. Place on a baking sheet lined with baking parchment and bake until cookies just begin to brown around the edges, about 10 minutes. Place on a rack to cool.

Makes about 120 cookies

102
A Program
for Rational
Entertaining
in an
Irrational
Age

Mr. D. Grows Tired
of Time Constraints

Occasionally, Mr. D. became impatient with the working couples' mantra, "No time, no time!" They screeched it, they whined it, they said it ruefully. Whatever their tone, they sang it like the theme song of a long-running soap opera, and really, it was becoming tedious.

And they all seemed so tentative about their own abilities in the kitchen. After nearly a hundred years of recipes and their tyranny, common sense with regard to cooking had given way to a sad sort of dependence on formulas as well as a sorry fear of one's own taste. But lack of confidence and lack of time, it seemed to Mr. D., were more a perception than a reality. The perception curtailed imagination and made mundane dinners a reality.

This was not acceptable to Mr. D. In thirty years of catering, he had certainly seen time as the enemy: too much time over cocktails meant a sloppy party and possibly a wizened entrée. Too little time between courses had, on one occasion early in his career, meant that a certain Chicken Divan was served raw in the center. My God, it was awful.

But had he designed his menus to be invulnerable to the effects of time, he'd probably be catering for an airline, not Manhattan's upper crust. And if hostesses surrender themselves to today's No Time song, they might as well just order Chinese food and call it a night, in his opinion. Time-use studies had convinced Mr. D. that, in fact, people have only a few minutes less time in any given week than they'd ever had, but the free time they have comes in dribs and drabs; few working people have unbroken hours of leisure.

By midsummer, he'd begun to think of himself as a sort of White Knight, selflessly liberating hostesses from the twin tyrants of No Time and No Confidence.

"Think backwards," he would say. "Imagine what you would like to cook and eat and then discard the patently impossible; no dancing girls, no à la carte cooking for parties of twelve or more, please, and develop a strategy for the rest. But imagine, imagine. Don't let life kill you!" Mr. D. sounded a little bit like a motivational speaker, if he did say so himself.

But under his tutelage the hosts and hostesses, particularly Nan, began to bridle under the harness of their perceptions and to question the public conviction that a working person has no time. They began to think beyond buffets and barbecue. They began to consider stylish, composed dishes that could augment and elevate a simple meal from the backyard grill.

This line of thought led to the notion of what Mr. D. called "savory semifreddo dishes" (not a totally accurate application of the term, simply his way of giving mystique to dishes that combine hot and cold ingredients): dishes that could be served as a main course or as a first course, but dishes in which the cook's taste and style, rather than the cook's accommodation to a crowd, triumphed.

The semifreddo dishes will bring guests to the table after a round of food from the barbecue or before an antipasti buffet. They can be served as main courses or as first courses. Either way, they add a certain panache to a simple summer supper for company.

104

A Program
for Rational
Entertaining
in an
Irrational
Age

Summer Vegetable Salad with Orzo

The salad can, and should, be made several hours in advance, as the flavor will deepen when it is stored, tightly wrapped and chilled; for longer storage, add everything but the arugula, which will wilt. Orzo, the rice-shaped pasta, should be cooked right before serving, so that the difference in the temperature of the two elements is distinct.

This salad can be served as a first course. As an entrée, it calls for a starter such as fresh mozzarella cheese, with basil, olive oil, and cracked black pepper, Roasted Tomato Soup with a Savory Froth (page 92), or Wild Herb Soup (page 74). The Tomato-Lemon Biscotti (page 69) or a crusty bread is a delicious accompaniment. Berries, perhaps macerated in balsamic vinegar (page 85) and served with a cookie such as Almond Shortbread Rounds or Chocolate Shortbread (pages 102 and 86) are in keeping with the light nature of the meal.

4 medium zucchini, cut into ½-inch dice

12 medium tomatoes, cut into ½-inch dice

4 medium yellow bell peppers, seeded and cut into ½-inch dice

8 cups stemmed arugula, coarsely chopped

2 tablespoons grated lemon zest

1 pound orzo

¼ cup fresh lemon juice

6 tablespoons extra-virgin olive oil

1 tablespoon kosher salt

1 teaspoon freshly ground pepper

1. Blanch the zucchini in salted boiling water for 20 seconds. Drain and refresh under cold running water and drain well again.

2. Put the zucchini in a large bowl and toss with the tomatoes, bell peppers, arugula, and lemon zest. Refrigerate until cold.

3. Just before serving, cook the orzo until al dente. Meanwhile, toss the salad with the lemon juice, olive oil, salt, and pepper. Drain the orzo, toss with the salad, divide among 4 plates, and serve immediately.

Serves 8

Panzanella with Grilled Chicken

The bread salad can be made up to two days in advance for this meal and should be served very, very cold. Topped with the hot chicken, it makes a lovely lunch. For dinner, the dish needs a predecessor, such as the Roasted Tomato Soup with a Savory Froth (page 92) or simply a large arugula salad garnished with shaved Parmesan cheese. The meal is light enough to be followed by a rich dessert, such as the Pistachio-Crusted Cheesecake with Orange-Caramel Sauce (page 50); or serve with Vinegared Berries (page 85), embellished with ice cream, sweetened whipped ricotta, or crème fraîche.

THE CHICKEN

½ cup fresh lemon juice
¼ cup olive oil
4 cloves garlic, coarsely chopped
1 teaspoon freshly ground pepper
1½ pounds boneless and skinless chicken breasts
½ cup fresh basil leaves, cut crosswise into thin strips

THE SALAD

8 cups crustless 1-inch bread cubes from good, firm, country-style bread
About 1¼ cups water
9 large tomatoes, cut into medium dice
1 large red onion, peeled and cut into small dice
4 large cloves garlic, minced
1 cup chopped Italian parsley
1½ tablespoons chopped fresh rosemary
3 tablespoons extra-virgin olive oil
1½ tablespoons red wine vinegar
1 teaspoon kosher salt
¼ teaspoon freshly ground pepper

1. To make the chicken, combine the lemon juice, olive oil, garlic, and pepper in a large, shallow dish. Add the chicken and turn to coat on both sides. Marinate in the refrigerator at least 2 hours.

106

A Program
for Rational
Entertaining
in an
Irrational
Age

2. To make the salad, toss the bread with enough water to moisten it completely. Let stand for 10 minutes. Squeeze out the excess water and coarsely chop the bread. Place in a bowl and toss with the tomatoes, onion, garlic, parsley, and rosemary. Mix in the olive oil, vinegar, salt, and pepper. Set aside.

3. Start a charcoal grill. Grill the chicken until just cooked through, about 3 to 4 minutes per side. Season with salt and pepper to taste. Slice the chicken on the diagonal into thin strips.

4. Divide the salad among 6 plates. Fan the chicken over the salad and garnish with the basil. Serve immediately.

Serves 6

Warm Scallop Puddings with Spinach and Cold Tomato-Basil Juice

Alone, these delicate warm puddings make a stunning first course, capable of turning a simple grilled meal into something in a more elegant key. They are also delicious served before or after the Lamb, Artichoke, and Roasted Potato Salad (page 66). If preceded by a green salad, garnished with sliced cold beef or the Basil, Snap Pea, and Rice Salad with Creamy Yogurt Dressing (page 80), the scallop puddings are substantial enough to constitute a main course. Mr. D.'s Strawberry Almond Tart (page 84) complements the mood of the meal.

THE JUICE

2 cups good-quality tomato juice
2 tablespoons chopped fresh basil

THE PUDDINGS

1 teaspoon olive oil
2 shallots, peeled and minced
2 cups stemmed spinach, washed but not dried
1 pound sea scallops
2 large eggs
1 cup crème fraîche
2 teaspoons kosher salt
½ teaspoon white pepper
5 fresh basil leaves, chopped
12 cooked shrimp, peeled and halved lengthwise

THE SPINACH

1 teaspoon olive oil
2 cloves garlic, minced
12 cups spinach, stemmed and washed but not dried
2 tablespoons fresh lemon juice
Kosher salt and freshly ground pepper to taste

108
A Program
for Rational
Entertaining
in an
Irrational
Age

1. To make the tomato-basil juice, line a fine-mesh sieve with a paper towel and place over a bowl. Pour in the tomato juice and let it drip through; this will take about an hour. Add the basil and refrigerate until cold.

2. To make the puddings, preheat the oven to 350° F. Heat the oil in a medium nonstick skillet over medium-high heat. Add the shallots and sauté for 30 seconds. Add the spinach and sauté until wilted. Let cool.

3. Puree the scallops in a food processor. Add the eggs, crème fraîche, salt, and pepper. Puree just until smooth. Take out half the mixture and set aside in a bowl. Add the spinach and the basil to the food processor and puree.

4. Grease eight 6-ounce ramekins. Place 3 shrimp halves in each ramekin, cut side up. Divide the white scallop mixture evenly among the ramekins, smoothing the top of each. Top with the green scallop mixture and smooth the top.

5. Place the ramekins in a large roasting pan and pour in enough hot water to come halfway up the sides of the ramekins. Bake until the puddings are firm, about 20 minutes.

6. To make the spinach, heat the oil in a large nonstick skillet over medium-high heat. Add the garlic and sauté a few seconds. Add the spinach and sauté until wilted. Season with the lemon juice and salt and pepper.

7. To serve, place a mound of spinach in the center of 8 shallow bowls. Invert the puddings over the spinach. Spoon the cold tomato-basil juice around the spinach and serve immediately.

Serves 8

Warm Potato-Lettuce Soup with Cold Seafood

Both the warm soup and the seafood can be prepared well ahead of the arrival of company. The soup could be served as an appetizer, but it is also complex and substantial enough to be the main event of a summer meal. It seems to beg for something crispy, such as the Thai Crab Cakes (page 205) as a first course and warrants a substantial and complex dessert such as the Blackberry-Lemon Tart with Champagne-Mint Granité (page 136) or Mr. D.'s Strawberry Almond Tart (page 84).

THE SOUP

4 medium baking potatoes, peeled and cut into 1-inch cubes
2 teaspoons olive oil
2 cloves garlic, minced
1½ cups dry white wine
4 large heads Boston lettuce, cored
1½ cups heavy cream
1 tablespoon kosher salt
1 teaspoon freshly ground pepper

THE SEAFOOD

4 lobsters, about 4½ pounds each, steamed and shelled
1 pound cooked medium-size shrimp, shelled
1 pound lump crabmeat, picked over for shells
4 red snapper fillets, steamed and cut into 1-inch chunks
½ cup fresh lemon juice
2 tablespoons extra-virgin olive oil
1 teaspoon kosher salt
½ teaspoon freshly ground pepper
¼ cup chopped fresh chives

1. To make the soup, boil the potatoes until tender. Drain, reserving the liquid. Pass the potatoes through a ricer. Set aside the liquid and potatoes.

110

A Program
for Rational
Entertaining
in an
Irrational
Age

2. Heat the oil in a large saucepan over medium heat. Add the garlic and cook for 30 seconds. Add the wine and bring to a boil. Add the lettuce, lower the heat, cover, and cook until wilted, about 2 minutes. Place the mixture in a blender and blend until smooth.

3. Place the potatoes in a large saucepan and stir in the lettuce mixture, 1½ cups of potato cooking liquid, the cream, the salt, and the pepper. Warm the soup over low heat.

4. To make the seafood, cut the lobster tails across into ¼-inch slices and cut the claws into ½-inch chunks. Arrange all the seafood on a platter. Whisk together the lemon juice, oil, salt, and pepper and drizzle over the seafood. Sprinkle the chives over the top.

5. Ladle the soup into 8 bowls and serve, passing the seafood separately.

Serves 8

Poached Chicken with Mixed Greens and Rosemary-Walnut Pesto

The Wild Herb Soup (page 74) is a lovely starter for this husky-flavored and substantial salad meal. Because it has a casual, rustic feel, an elaborate dessert provides a nice contrast, as well as a touch of finesse.

THE PESTO

¾ cup shelled walnuts
½ cup freshly grated Parmesan cheese
2 tablespoons chopped fresh rosemary
1½ tablespoons extra-virgin olive oil
½ teaspoon grated lemon zest
½ teaspoon kosher salt
¼ teaspoon freshly ground pepper

THE CROUTONS

2 teaspoons unsalted butter
2 cups ½-inch bread cubes from good, country-style bread
Kosher salt and freshly ground pepper to taste

THE CHICKEN

2 cups chicken broth, homemade or low-sodium canned
2 pounds boneless, skinless chicken breasts
Kosher salt and freshly ground pepper to taste

THE SALAD

64 asparagus tips, steamed until crisp-tender
6 teaspoons fresh lemon juice
½ teaspoon kosher salt, plus more to taste
¼ teaspoon freshly ground pepper, plus more to taste
8 cups radicchio, torn into 2-inch pieces
8 cups arugula, stemmed
1 tablespoon extra-virgin olive oil

112

A Program
for Rational
Entertaining
in an
Irrational
Age

1. To make the pesto, put all the ingredients into a food processor. Pulse just until the mixture forms a paste, leaving the walnuts slightly coarse. Set aside.

2. To make the croutons, melt the butter in a medium cast-iron skillet over medium heat. Add the bread cubes and season with salt and pepper to taste. Turn the cubes and shake the pan frequently until lightly browned and crisp, about 3 minutes. Set aside.

3. To make the chicken, bring the broth to a boil in a pan just large enough to hold the chicken in a single layer. Add the chicken, lower the heat so the broth is at a slow simmer, cover, and poach until the chicken is just cooked through, about 15 minutes. Remove the chicken from the broth and cut on the diagonal into ¼-inch slices. Season lightly with salt and pepper, return it to the broth, and keep it warm.

4. To make the salad, toss the asparagus tips with 3 teaspoons of the lemon juice and the salt and pepper. Set aside. Toss together the radicchio, arugula, the remaining 3 teaspoons lemon juice, the olive oil, and more salt and pepper to taste.

5. To assemble, place a dollop of the pesto in the center of each of 8 large plates. Alternate the asparagus tips and slices of the chicken over the pesto. Surround with the greens, top the greens with the croutons, and serve immediately.

Serves 8

Indian-Spiced Cucumber-Squid Salad

Almond Buttermilk Soup (page 125) makes a lovely antecedent for this sprightly summer salad dinner. An Indian bread such as nan, which is sold in some markets, is the logical companion to the salad, though on a cold night, a bowl of steamed basmati rice, garnished with torn fresh mint leaves, would be satisfying. The Caramel Orange Fool (page 128) rounds out the bold flavors of the meal with a gentle, sweet finish.

2 teaspoons cumin seeds
2 teaspoons coriander seeds
6 tablespoons fresh lime juice
¼ cup plus 2 tablespoons extra-virgin olive oil
10 medium cucumbers, peeled
3 teaspoons kosher salt, plus more for seasoning squid
1 teaspoon freshly ground pepper, plus more for seasoning squid
1 jalapeño pepper, thinly sliced crosswise
2 cloves garlic, crushed
2 pounds cleaned squid, bodies cut across into thin slices
½ cup coarsely chopped fresh mint
½ cup coarsely chopped fresh cilantro

1. Combine the cumin and coriander seeds in a small heavy skillet over medium heat and stir until lightly browned and fragrant, about 5 minutes. Crack the seeds with a rolling pin or knife and place in a large bowl. Whisk in the lime juice and ¼ cup of the olive oil.

2. Cut the cucumbers in half lengthwise. Scrape out the seeds and cut across into ⅛-inch slices. Put in the bowl and toss with the dressing. Season with the salt and pepper. Refrigerate until cold.

3. Heat the remaining 2 tablespoons oil in a large skillet over medium-high heat. Add the jalapeño and garlic and sauté for 1 minute. Remove the jalapeño and garlic with a slotted spoon and discard. Working in batches to avoid overcrowding, sauté the squid just until opaque, about 1 to 1½ minutes.

4. Season the squid lightly with salt and pepper and quickly toss with the cucumbers. Toss in the mint and cilantro and serve immediately.

Serves 6

114

A Program
for Rational
Entertaining
in an
Irrational
Age

Nan Anticipates
Pre-Barbecue Pangs

(Or How to Feed and Not Fatten Guests)

As late spring melts into summer, the hours between lunch and dinner lengthen as surely as the day. So does the urge to nibble and pick. Nan finds this troubling. Long summer sunsets seem to encourage a terrible sort of snacking. Nan believes that snacking is dangerous.

She understands, of course, that the wrinkle in time between the end of a summer workday and the beginning of dinner is more than just the enemy of the healthful lifestyle she strives to maintain. It is designated decompression time, time to oil the conversational machine, to hone and cajole your appetite for the meal to come. It is a time when conviviality and appetite are piqued and held for a few long moments, while restraint battles deliciously with desire.

Be that as it may, Nan can feel demons dancing just below the surface of even the most civilized sipping-and-nibbling interlude, demons that can turn sips to gulps and even the daintiest nibbler into a human Hoover.

At the backyard barbecues that she and Ted often throw on the weekends, she has seen what happens after a few sips of a stylish cocktail. Guests remember that they had no lunch, they count the hours since breakfast, they check their watches. Oh, they resolve to be firm. But how many times has Ted fanned the coals in the Weber as guests raced out and bought pounds of cheese and chips and lethal dips?

Even the savviest diner, the one who knows the exquisite pleasure of fore-stalled gratification, is at great risk. Nan has found that it's easier to change the nature of the food than it is to change human nature.

It isn't difficult, she found, to substitute a lean and tangy low-fat yogurt cheese for a high-fat sour cream or cream cheese as the basis of a dip. Replacing some of the oil in salsas or other vegetable dips with fruit or vegetable juices lightens the hors d'oeuvre and lowers the dietary damage.

The following recipes can be made up to two days ahead of time and stored, well wrapped, in the refrigerator. One, two, or even three of them can serve as an hors d'oeuvre for a barbecue; a wider array can create the sort of substantial first course that a light meal mandates. Surrounded by mounds of briefly blanched crudités, especially carrot sticks or sugar snap peas, or by fresh-cut raw peppers, cucumbers, or zucchini, or by crackers, bread sticks, or even toasted rounds of French bread, the concoctions beckon like cool pools. Nan and Ted are free to fan flames and mind the grill. The guests are shielded from pre-dinner pangs.

"Breathe easy," thinks Nan, pleased with her common sense and forethought. "Take a dip."

116

A Program
for Rational
Entertaining
in an
Irrational
Age

Yogurt Cheese

By draining the water from low-fat yogurt, the cook creates a thick, tangy substance that makes a fine medium for dips. It can also be used in place of sour cream or crème fraîche to garnish cold soups. The yogurt cheese, however, cannot be heated—it breaks and curdles—and is therefore not a good choice for hot soups or sauces.

1 quart plain low-fat yogurt

1. Place the yogurt in a sieve or yogurt strainer lined with a double layer of paper towels and let stand in the refrigerator until the liquid drips out, several hours or overnight.

2. The yogurt cheese can be stored in the refrigerator in a closed container for up to 3 days. It can be served on toast points with fresh mint or used as a base for myriad dips (see following recipes) or salad dressings, and can replace sour cream or cream cheese in most recipes. (Nonfat yogurt can be used, but the resulting yogurt cheese will be chalkier and less acidic.)

Makes 2¼ cups

Yogurt Cheese with Horseradish and Chives

4 cups yogurt cheese (page 117)
⅔ cup freshly grated horseradish
½ cup minced fresh chives
1 cup minced Italian parsley
1 teaspoon kosher salt
2 teaspoons freshly ground pepper

Combine all the ingredients in a glass or ceramic bowl until well blended. The dip can be stored in the refrigerator for up to 2 days. Serve with crudités and crackers or smoked fish and grilled bread.

Serves 8

Smoked Salmon Dip

½ pound smoked salmon, skinned
2 cups yogurt cheese (page 117)
½ teaspoon kosher salt
1 teaspoon freshly ground pepper
2 teaspoons freshly grated horseradish
¼ cup minced fresh dill

Combine the smoked salmon and yogurt cheese in a blender or food processor. Puree until smooth. Season with the salt and pepper. Fold in the horseradish and dill. Serve with crackers.

Serves 8

118

A Program
for Rational
Entertaining
in an
Irrational
Age

Greek Artichoke and Garlic Dip

2 cloves garlic
12 cooked large artichoke hearts
4 to 6 tablespoons fresh lemon juice
2 cups yogurt cheese (page 117)
1 teaspoon kosher salt
½ teaspoon freshly ground pepper

Place the garlic, artichoke hearts, 4 tablespoons of lemon juice, and the yogurt cheese in a food processor or blender. Process until smooth. Season with the salt and pepper. Adjust the seasoning with additional lemon juice, if needed. Serve with crackers, crudités, or pita bread. The dip can also be used as a dressing for chicken salad when extended with additional lemon juice or with mayonnaise.

Serves 8

Tomatillo Salsa

3 pounds tomatillos, husked
4 medium poblano chilies, roasted, seeded, deveined, peeled, and chopped
2 small garlic cloves, minced
8 scallions, minced
1 cup fresh cilantro, minced
2 tablespoons minced fresh marjoram

1. Preheat the oven to 375° F. Place the tomatillos on a baking sheet. Roast them in the oven until their skins blister, about 20 to 25 minutes. Set aside to cool.

2. Place the tomatillos in a blender with the remaining ingredients. Puree until smooth. The salsa can be stored in the refrigerator in a closed container for up to 2 days. Serve with corn chips.

Serves 8

Orange-Scented Roasted Tomato and Garlic Dip

1½ teaspoons olive oil, plus additional for greasing pan

15 plum tomatoes, cored and halved lengthwise

⅛ teaspoon orange oil or 1 tablespoon fresh orange juice and 1 teaspoon
    grated orange zest

5 cloves roasted garlic, peeled

2 teaspoons fresh lemon juice

¼ teaspoon cayenne

½ teaspoon kosher salt

¼ teaspoon freshly ground pepper

¼ cup chopped Italian parsley

1. Preheat the oven to 450° F. Lightly oil a baking sheet and place the tomatoes on it, cut side down. Roast until soft and very lightly browned, about 20 minutes.

2. Place the tomatoes in a food processor with the olive oil, orange oil, garlic, lemon juice, cayenne, salt, and pepper. Place in a bowl and stir in the parsley. Serve with cut vegetables, bread, or crackers.

Makes 2 cups

120

A Program
for Rational
Entertaining
in an
Irrational
Age

Roasted Yellow Tomato Dip

4 pounds yellow tomatoes
8 threads saffron
2 tablespoons grated orange zest
2 tablespoons grated lemon zest
½ cup fresh orange juice
1 teaspoon apple cider vinegar
12 cloves roasted garlic, peeled
4 teaspoons Tabasco
1 teaspoon kosher salt
¼ teaspoon freshly ground pepper
2 cups yogurt cheese (page 117)
½ cup minced Italian parsley
¼ cup minced fresh mint
¼ cup minced fresh basil

1. Preheat the oven to 375° F. Place the tomatoes on a baking sheet. Roast in the oven until the skins blister and split, about 15 minutes. Set aside to cool. Peel, core, and seed the tomatoes.

2. Put the tomatoes in a nonstick skillet. Add the saffron, orange and lemon zests, orange juice, vinegar, garlic, Tabasco, salt, and pepper. Cook slowly over medium-low heat until the tomatoes thicken into a dense paste, about 20 minutes. Taste and adjust seasoning if needed.

3. Put the tomato mixture in a bowl. Fold in the yogurt cheese. Transfer mixture to a clean bowl and garnish with the fresh herbs. This dip can be stored in the refrigerator in a closed container for up to 3 days. Serve with nuggets of grilled lobster, shrimp, or corn chips.

Serves 8

Barbecued Shrimp

These shrimp, which can be served straight from the grill or prepared ahead of time and served cold, are an addictive appetizer. Accompanied by lightly dressed bitter greens, they make a great first course.

1 tablespoon freshly ground pepper
½ teaspoon crushed red pepper
¼ teaspoon cayenne
Dash of Tabasco
1 teaspoon kosher salt
1 tablespoon extra-virgin olive oil
¼ cup fresh lemon juice
2 pounds medium-size shrimp in the shell

1. In a bowl, combine the black pepper, crushed red pepper, cayenne, Tabasco, and salt; whisk in the olive oil and lemon juice. Add the shrimp and toss to coat. Cover the bowl and refrigerate for at least 3 hours and up to 24 hours.

2. Heat a charcoal grill or the broiler. Cook the shrimp in their shells until pink, about 3 to 4 minutes on each side. Serve in the shell, or allow them to cool and shell them before serving.

Serves 4

122

A Program
for Rational
Entertaining
in an
Irrational
Age

Elizabeth Serves a Summer Lunch

Do-ahead dishes and buffets are the backbone of the entertaining that Elizabeth and Peter do in the summer. The efficiency, cost-effectiveness, and recycling possibilities inherent in such dishes appeal to Elizabeth; Peter, an inveterate jogger, cyclist, and tennis player who views food as fuel, likes the bounty and variety of buffets. To guests, they espouse the ease and flexibility of a buffet. To each other, they acknowledge that a groaning board accommodates a crowd and caters to the individual appetites of both adults and children.

There are, however, occasions that demand the intimacy of a sit-down meal and a small menu. On very rare occasions, they host events of the heart rather than fêtes to fulfill social, familial, or professional obligations. The annual visit of Peter's law school roommate and his wife is one such occasion, and the week that Elizabeth's mother spends with them each July generally mandates at least one meal in which adults gather around the table with a sense of occasion, without the children.

The Kittridges favor lunch. Their shaded porch creates an oasis on a hot day and a light, inventive menu can lend the sort of quiet diversion—a punctuation point—that alters the mood of the subsequent afternoon.

In a way, theirs is a sentimental choice. The couple spent a summer in Nantucket in their early courtship and still recall the magic of a lunch they once shared under the trellises of the Chanticleer Restaurant. The pop of a champagne cork, the delicate clink of the silver against the china set them apart from the steady plunk of tennis balls on the clay courts nearby, the cries and pounding of the surf from the beach in the distance. They were apart and very much together, and that sense lingered well past dusk.

Unexpected twists in the menu, they've found, enhance the secret adventure of a small summer lunch. In addition to the exotic seasoning that the couple enjoys, they've found that reversing the order of the courses served—presenting, for instance, a warm, substantial course and following it with a light, cold soup—adds a note of surprise. Sharing the surprise fosters kinship.

One of their favorite menus was inspired by a trip they made to Mexico—and adaptations they made, upon their return, to lighten and elevate several of the dishes they'd enjoyed there. They are unwilling to admit that serving the meal also provides them with an opportunity to discuss their travels. Beneath the far-flung flavors they love, the Kittridges are proper and traditional people. That the nature of the food they serve could guarantee them the conversational spotlight is not conceivable to them. They think that their guests' curiosity is a polite response to the gentle repose that invades one's bones during a summer lunch in the shade.

124

A Program
for Rational
Entertaining
in an
Irrational
Age

Almond Buttermilk Soup

This soup can be made up to three days in advance of serving, covered well and stored in the refrigerator. To make a more substantial dish, garnish the soup generously with lump crabmeat, chunks of fresh lobster meat, or chopped shrimp.

1 cup blanched slivered almonds, toasted
1½ cups crustless bread cubes, toasted
2 large cloves garlic, coarsely chopped
1½ teaspoons grated orange zest
6 cups buttermilk
2½ tablespoons fresh lemon juice
3 tablespoons fresh orange juice
2 teaspoons kosher salt, plus more to taste
½ teaspoon freshly ground pepper, plus more to taste
¼ cup whole cilantro leaves

1. Place the almonds, bread, garlic, and orange zest and 1 cup of the buttermilk in a blender and process until smooth. Pour into a bowl and stir in the remaining buttermilk. Stir in the lemon juice, orange juice, salt, and pepper. Refrigerate until cold.

2. Taste and adjust seasoning with additional salt and pepper if needed. Ladle soup into 6 bowls and float several cilantro leaves in each one.

Serves 6

Black Bean Quesadillas with Smoked Salmon, Goat Cheese, and Tomatillo Salsa

The salsa can be made up to one week before its use; equal parts of green and red tomatoes can be used if tomatillos are unavailable. For more convenience, a high-quality commercial salsa blend can be used instead of the homemade version. The black beans can also be made far in advance of serving. The final assembly of this recipe takes about ten minutes. It is a fine first course or, served after a large salad, a fine main course.

THE SALSA

1 pound fresh tomatillos (about 12), husked
2 tablespoons chopped fresh cilantro
1 jalapeño pepper, seeded and minced
2 teaspoons fresh lime juice
½ teaspoon kosher salt

THE QUESADILLAS

2 cups hot cooked black beans
2 teaspoons olive oil
4 teaspoons fresh lime juice
½ teaspoon kosher salt
1 clove garlic, minced
¼ cup chopped scallions
6 ounces soft goat cheese
6 small flour tortillas
6 large slices smoked salmon

THE SALAD

¼ cup fresh orange juice
2 teaspoons fresh lemon juice
1 teaspoon Dijon mustard
2 teaspoons walnut oil
½ teaspoon kosher salt

A Program
for Rational
Entertaining
in an
Irrational
Age

Dash of freshly ground pepper
10 cups stemmed arugula
2 yellow bell peppers, cut into thin strips

1. To make the salsa, pulse the tomatillos in a food processor until coarsely pureed. Add the cilantro, jalapeño, lime juice, and salt and pulse until well combined. Set aside.

2. To make the quesadillas, gently combine the hot beans, the olive oil, lime juice, salt, garlic, and scallions. Keep warm. Spread about 2 tablespoons goat cheese over half of each tortilla. Using a heaping ¼ cup of the bean mixture for each tortilla, press the beans into the goat cheese. Trim the salmon slices to fit half of the tortilla and lay the slices with the trimmings over the beans. Fold the tortilla in half and press the sides together. Set aside.

3. To make the salad, whisk together the orange juice, lemon juice, and mustard. Whisk in the walnut oil, salt, and pepper. Place the arugula in a large bowl and toss with the yellow peppers. Toss with the dressing.

4. Heat a large nonstick skillet over medium-high heat. Working in batches as necessary, place the quesadillas in the skillet and cook until browned and heated through, about 1 to 1½ minutes per side. Cut each quesadilla into 3 triangles.

5. Spoon a little of the salsa onto the center of 6 large plates. Place 3 quesadilla triangles around the salsa. Arrange the salad in a circle around the edge of the plates and serve immediately.

Serves 6

Caramel Orange Fool

This soft, fragrant dessert is a gentle ending to robust summer meals. It can be made up to two days in advance of company and should be covered very well and stored in the refrigerator.

THE PUDDING

2½ cups heavy cream
1 cup sugar
6 tablespoons cold water
2 packages powdered gelatin
3 cups buttermilk
½ teaspoon kosher salt

THE CARAMEL

1 cup sugar
6 tablespoons water
1 cup heavy cream
6 oranges

1. To make the pudding, place the cream and sugar in a large saucepan over medium heat just until the sugar dissolves. Meanwhile, place the water in a small bowl and sprinkle the gelatin over it (do not stir). Let stand for 5 minutes.

2. Stir the gelatin mixture into the warm cream until melted. Let cool slightly. Stir in the buttermilk and salt. Refrigerate until just set (the mixture should be neither liquid nor firm), about 2 hours.

3. Meanwhile, to make the caramel, place the sugar in a medium saucepan and stir in the water. Use a pastry brush dipped in water to wash down any sugar crystals on the side of the pan. Place over medium heat and cook without stirring until mixture turns a deep caramel color. Remove from heat and add the cream. Return the pan to the heat and stir until all the caramel is dissolved. Place in a bowl and let cool completely.

4. Use a paring knife to remove all peel and pith from the oranges. Working over a bowl to collect any orange juice, cut out the orange sections from between the membranes. Stir the juice into the caramel.

128

A Program
for Rational
Entertaining
in an
Irrational
Age

5. To assemble, whisk the pudding. Spoon about ¼ cup pudding into each of 6 large wineglasses. Top each with a scant 2 tablespoons of caramel sauce and a few orange slices, making sure both show around the edge of the glass. Repeat the layers. Top with the remaining pudding and drizzle with a little caramel sauce. Refrigerate for several hours before serving.

Serves 6

Powdered Sugar Pecan Cookies

These cookies are a crisp and delicious accompaniment to either ice cream or custard. They are also a nice addition to a selection of cookies served with a sweet dessert wine.

1 cup pecans, toasted
1 cup unsalted butter, softened slightly
6 tablespoons sugar
2 teaspoons vanilla extract
2 cups all-purpose flour
½ teaspoon kosher salt
½ cup confectioners' sugar

1. Put the pecans in a food processor and pulse until coarsely ground. Add the butter and pulse until combined. Mix in the sugar and vanilla. Add the flour and salt and pulse just to combine. Press the dough into a ball and wrap in plastic wrap. Refrigerate just until firm, or make up to 2 days ahead but let stand at room temperature until pliable but still cold.

2. Preheat the oven to 350° F. Using about 1 tablespoon of dough for each cookie, roll the dough into balls with your hands. Flatten with the palm of your hand to make mounds 1½ inches in diameter. Place on a baking sheet lined with baking parchment. Bake until browned on the bottom, about 12 minutes. Remove from baking sheet and let cool completely on rack. Sift the confectioners' sugar over the cookies.

Makes 32 cookies

130

A Program
for Rational
Entertaining
in an
Irrational
Age

A Summer Dinner
with Distinction in
a Lower Key

Like the Kittridges, Johanna experienced a certain unease whenever she ate with her fingers, a nagging sense of discontent after barbecues. She found herself humming "Is That All There Is?" after summer buffets, particularly when she was the hostess rather than a guest.

She was willing to concede that her own need to be the hostess with the mostest played some role in her post-party malaise. Along with the Kittridges, however, Johanna felt that summer needed moments of distinction—soft, quiet, intimate moments to stand in contrast to the season's brash, jocular mood. Call it sensitivity, but don't call it neurotic, thought Johanna. And Mr. D., of course, supported her itch to entertain in a somewhat more formal key.

She composed a menu for a sit-down summer dinner that was less ambitious than those she had attempted before joining the group. Her thought was that a warm appetizer that required some last-minute work in the kitchen could establish an elegant note and allow her to serve a main course that guests constructed, a salad of huge proportions and imaginative components. Given the light nature of the meal and the casualness of her main course, she concluded that a drop-dead dessert was in order.

Johanna was, however, far enough along in her recovery to design a salad whose components could easily be made ahead of time (even by a caterer, should the day in question prove too beautiful to while away in the kitchen), as well as a dessert that could be prepared and baked well in advance of dinner and that required little last-minute fuss.

Johanna was blissfully unaware of the fact that by showcasing the bounty of summer in breathtakingly simple guise, she was, in fact, displaying the success of her recovery. Rather, she was slightly concerned that the fuss she made over flowers would be cause for concern in the group.

But, honestly, how could a hostess bent on taming and restraining the bounty of summer, one striving for a somewhat sophisticated note, bear to set her table with vivid and sturdy zinnias or dahlias? Especially when there were delphinium and rambling roses, the paler shades of snapdragons, even branches of rosemary and the occasional peony for composing a sweet, Victorian-style bouquet?

132

A Program
for Rational
Entertaining
in an
Irrational
Age

Scallops with Fava Bean Puree and Shiitakes

Lima beans, or reconstituted dried beans boiled until tender, can be substituted if fresh fava beans are not available. In any case, the puree can be made up to two days before a dinner party and reheated slowly before serving. It's delicious with any firm, white fish, which can be used in place of scallops, should they not be available. The dish can be served as a first course before a light entrée, or it can follow a more substantial first course. It relies strictly on the flavor of the ingredients themselves, and therefore it can be surrounded by dishes with more exotic seasoning, though the feel of this dish is decidedly elegant and it asks for like-minded companions.

5 pounds fresh fava beans, shelled
½ cup chicken broth, homemade or low-sodium canned
¾ cup heavy cream
1½ teaspoons kosher salt, plus more to season shiitakes and scallops
1 teaspoon freshly ground pepper, plus more to season shiitakes and scallops
4 teaspoons olive oil
1 pound shiitake mushrooms, stemmed and thinly sliced
1½ pounds sea scallops
1 tablespoon fresh lemon juice
4 teaspoons coarsely chopped Italian parsley

1. Blanch the fava beans in boiling water until soft, about 8 minutes. Drain and let cool. Slip the skins off the beans, place in a food processor, and puree. Add the broth, cream, salt, and pepper and process until smooth. Scrape into a saucepan and warm gently over low heat.

2. Heat 2 teaspoons of the oil in a medium nonstick skillet over medium-high heat. Add the shiitakes and sauté until softened, about 5 minutes. Season lightly with salt and pepper. Keep warm.

3. Brush the remaining 2 teaspoons of oil over a large cast-iron skillet and place over medium-high heat. Pat the scallops dry with a paper towel. Place in the skillet and sear until browned and just cooked through, about 1 minute per side. Sprinkle with lemon juice and salt and pepper to taste.

4. Mound about ⅓ cup of fava bean puree onto the center of each of 8 plates. Top with scallops. Scatter the mushrooms over the scallops and sprinkle with parsley. Serve immediately.

Serves 8

Everything-Under-the-Sun Salad

Virtually all the components for this salad can be made ahead of time. The salad can be served as a buffet or family-style. For a more elegant mood, the individual salads can be composed in the kitchen and served to guests.

THE ZUCCHINI PICKLE

1 cup water
¾ cup white wine vinegar
⅓ cup sugar
1 clove garlic, crushed
½ jalapeño pepper, with seeds
10 black peppercorns
½ teaspoon kosher salt
5 medium zucchini, halved lengthwise and cut across into ¼-inch slices

THE SUGAR SNAPS

6 cups sugar snap peas, strung
2 tablespoons fresh lemon juice
1 teaspoon extra-virgin olive oil
½ teaspoon kosher salt
¼ cup chopped fresh mint

THE GREENS

6 tablespoons fresh lemon juice
2 teaspoons Dijon mustard
¼ cup extra-virgin olive oil
2 teaspoons kosher salt

134
A Program
for Rational
Entertaining
in an
Irrational
Age

½ teaspooon freshly ground pepper

¼ cup chopped fresh chives

12 cups mesclun

2 cups torn Italian parsley

2 cups torn basil

4 teaspoons fresh thyme

THE CROÛTES

16 (¼-inch) slices French baguette

1 tablespoon extra-virgin olive oil

1 large clove garlic, crushed

8 ounces crumbled goat cheese

3 plum tomatoes, seeded and diced small

Kosher salt

4 roasted red peppers, peeled, seeded, halved lengthwise, and cut across into
     2-inch pieces

1. To make the zucchini, combine the water, vinegar, sugar, garlic, jalapeño, peppercorns, and salt in a small saucepan. Bring to a boil, lower the heat, and simmer 5 minutes. Put the zucchini in a medium bowl and pour the hot liquid over. Let stand at least 2 hours. Drain.

2. Meanwhile, blanch the sugar snaps in boiling, lightly salted water for 1 minute. Drain and refresh under cold running water. Toss with the lemon juice, oil, salt, and mint. Set aside.

3. To make the greens, whisk together the lemon juice and mustard. Slowly whisk in the olive oil. Add the salt, pepper, and chives. Toss together the mesclun, parsley, basil, and thyme. Set aside the dressing and greens.

4. To make the croûtes, preheat the oven to 350° F. Place the bread on a baking sheet and drizzle with olive oil. Bake until toasted, about 5 to 7 minutes. Rub each piece with the garlic clove. Top with goat cheese and diced tomato. Sprinkle lightly with salt.

5. Toss the greens with the dressing and mound in the center of each of 8 plates. Surround with the zucchini, sugar snaps, and roasted pepper. Top the greens with 2 croûtes and serve.

Serves 8

Blackberry-Lemon Tart
with Champagne-Mint Granité

The tart can be made a day before a dinner party and should be kept cool and wrapped but not refrigerated. The champagne-mint granité is a marvelous match for the tart, but the time-pressed host or hostess could substitute a high-quality vanilla ice cream, or even a mango sorbet.

THE GRANITÉ

1 cup water

1 cup sugar

2 cups lightly packed fresh mint leaves and stems, coarsely chopped

3 tablespoons fresh lemon juice

1 bottle chilled champagne or sparkling wine

¼ cup chopped fresh mint leaves

THE CRUST

½ cup blanched slivered almonds, lightly toasted

2½ tablespoons sugar

¾ cup all-purpose flour, plus more for rolling

½ teaspoon kosher salt

6 tablespoons cold unsalted butter, cut into ½-inch pieces

1 large egg yolk

1 tablespoon water

¼ teaspoon almond extract

THE FILLING

4 large eggs

1¼ cups plus 2 tablespoons sugar

2 teaspoons grated lemon zest

¾ cup fresh lemon juice

2 tablespoons unsalted butter

½ cup heavy cream

4 half-pints fresh blackberries

136

A Program
for Rational
Entertaining
in an
Irrational
Age

Confectioners' sugar, for garnish
8 sprigs fresh mint, for garnish

1. To make the granité, combine the water, the sugar, and the 2 cups mint leaves in a saucepan and bring to a boil. Lower heat and simmer 5 minutes. Remove from heat and let stand 15 minutes. Strain and let cool completely. Add the lemon juice, champagne, and the ¼ cup chopped mint leaves and pour into a shallow, nonreactive dish. Freeze for several hours or overnight, until firm throughout, stirring occasionally.

2. To make the tart, pulse the almonds and sugar in a food processor until coarsely ground. Add the flour and salt and pulse to combine. Add the butter and pulse until the mixture resembles coarse meal. Whisk together the egg yolk, water, and almond extract. Add to the flour mixture and process just until the mixture starts to come together. Press into a bowl, flatten into a disk, wrap in plastic wrap, and refrigerate for 30 minutes.

3. To make the filling, place the eggs and 1 cup plus 2 tablespoons sugar in a medium nonreactive saucepan and whisk until thickened and light in color. Whisk in the lemon zest and lemon juice. Place over low heat and cook, whisking constantly, until thick, about 10 minutes; do not let the mixture come to a simmer. Remove from heat and whisk in the butter. Let cool. Refrigerate until cold.

4. Preheat the oven to 350° F. Roll out the dough and fit into a 10-inch quiche dish. Line with foil and fill with pie weights or dried beans. Bake for 20 minutes. Remove the foil and weights and bake until the crust is lightly browned, about 5 minutes longer. Let cool.

5. Whip the cream until it holds firm peaks and fold it into the lemon mixture. Spoon into the tart shell and refrigerate for several hours. About 1 hour before serving, gently toss the blackberries with the remaining ¼ cup of sugar. Just before serving, drain the blackberries and arrange them over the filling. Sift a little confectioners' sugar over the top. Place a slice of the tart on each of 8 plates. Scrape the granité into balls with a spoon, place a ball on each plate, and garnish with a sprig of mint. Serve immediately.

Serves 8

A Beckoning Warmth: Autumn Entertaining

There is an exhilaration and a sense of renewal in the breezes that stir late-summer nights, an intimation of autumn, or perhaps just an anticipation as old as the first day of school. In either case, as the heat of summer subsides, a purposeful sense of possibility flickers. There is something intrinsically intimate in the social mood of September and October.

Family-style meals, for the immediate or the extended family, seem to fit that mood. Likewise, the sorts of simple dishes that one wishes were everyday cooking, but rarely are, form a gentle symmetry between the physiological appetite, the comfort that one seeks in cooler weather, and the social appetite, the yen to reaffirm familial ties.

Three homey courses can be a metaphor for the connection people seek among home, work, and leisure, among love, obligation, and adventure, among body, mind, and soul. Of course a first course, followed by a main course with vegetables and some sort of starch, followed by a dessert, does constitute three courses, though it can require five recipes! No matter, three homey courses have a certain nostalgic value, and maybe, in the end, that's all it takes to lend a feeling of coherence to modern life. This basic paradigm, three courses, recalling three square meals as well as other triangles and trinities, provides a sturdy and appealing structure for fancier parties as well.

The ingredients of early fall can go either way—they can comfort, they can surprise. The possibility of comfort seems more potent, even as fall advances into the pre-holiday entertaining season and small gatherings grow larger, hungrier, and more about community than about the family unit. As gatherings grow, the nature of the menus served necessarily changes. The kitchen that can produce a glorious chicken, roasted with tarragon and lemon, perhaps, for eight, can't physically accommodate chicken for twelve or twenty.

Buffets composed of dishes that can be made well in advance—the fixings for a warm salad, for instance, or a generous array of antipasti—as well as family-style variations on the one-pot theme can once again rescue the hostess whose yen to knit together the people in her life slightly exceeds the limits of her oven space and the time and skill and budget she has available.

The flavor of the dishes is informed by the yearning, bittersweet feeling of autumn, its particular sort of hunger and hope. The character of the menus and the dishes, however, reflects the realities that remain unchanged by weather and its ambient moods. It seems that a certain need for convenience won't go away.

Nan Hankers for an Old-fashioned Family Dinner

Nan was emboldened, and it wasn't merely the evening breeze. Usually, wind along her collar-length hair, still damp from an evening swim, would make Nan shiver, and the shiver, in turn, would make her worry about something. It is inconceivable to Nan that an involuntary twitch not be accompanied by some fear or pressing concern. But there she was, wet hair on a clear, early-September night, feeling eager and uncharacteristically reckless.

"Wouldn't it be good to have your parents and my mother for dinner next week?" she asked Ted, who was as startled by the lightness in his wife's voice as he had been by her suggestion of a quick skinny-dip in the backyard pool—the children's pool at that, the blowup kind. He was not used to taking risks with Nan, particularly not at her suggestion. He didn't mean to, but he became Nan, just for the sake of the conversation.

"Your mother's on a diet," he said.

"So?" said Nan.

"Next weekend is really soon, I mean, it's almost next weekend already, and it's a busy week. . . ."

"So?"

So it was that the Bromleys put together a sumptuous, homey meal, and so it was, because his bedroom curtain flickered as they dashed from the wading pool to their back door, that they also ended up inviting Mr. Edwards, who lived next door.

"I guess he's family," said Nan philosophically. She had, in Ted's view, a nearly wanton disregard of fat grams and so forth as she suggested dishes they might serve. And she was also cavalier about plotting where they would find the time to shop, to cook, to set the table.

From the start, Ted knew that getting the children dressed up as well as washing the cooking dishes would end up on his list of things to do. His wife, it seemed, was approaching the family dinner party as if it were so many contemplative and solitary tasks. Maybe the hostessing group wasn't as benign as he'd thought. For a moment he regretted encouraging his wife in the free-of-charge, self-help direction, rather than toward the pricey cooking class she'd wanted to take.

"I'll do all the shopping Thursday night, and if you feed the kids and get them to bed, I can do the soup then, too," she said. Ted inhaled deeply, the way people whose suspicions are proven tend to do. But he found her excitement contagious, or at least very, very interesting in a distinctly un-Nan sort of way.

"Friday night I'll make the cornbread madeleines and the potato puree," she said thoughtfully. "Don't you want to take the kids to the movies? I could clean the broccoli and dress the chickens, too. I could make the apple crisp, but wouldn't it smell good if it were in the oven when everybody got here? Did you know that real estate agents tell their clients to bake apple pies so that prospective buyers will fall in love with their houses?"

Being a realtor, Ted was indeed aware of the trick; he was equally aware of how rarely it is actually employed.

"On the other hand, you could let me make the crisp on Saturday morning when you take the kids swimming and we could use a little apple and cinnamon potpourri to smell up the house," he said.

"No, no. I'm doing this for *you*," his wife objected. "You always say you miss the sight of a family gathered around the table. You said you sometimes missed the way we used to eat. I wanted to . . ."

"Become Betty Crocker?" offered Ted.

Just for today, thought Nan. Just for dinner, for the memories they both kept meaning to rekindle and to create.

141

Nan Hankers
for an
Old-fashioned
Family
Dinner

Sweet Potato Soup

This rich, soulful soup can be made up to three days before it is served. For those minding their diets, skim milk can be used in place of the heavy cream. Served with the Cornbread Madeleines (opposite), the soup can become a light supper with the addition of a green salad and a light fruit dessert.

1 tablespoon unsalted butter
3 large cloves garlic, minced
1 large onion, peeled and chopped
4 large sweet potatoes (about 2½ pounds), peeled and cut into 1½-inch
    chunks
7 cups chicken broth, homemade or low-sodium canned
¾ cup heavy cream
1 tablespoon kosher salt
1 teaspoon freshly ground pepper
½ cup shelled pecans, toasted and chopped
2 tablespoons chopped fresh sage
1 tablespoon chopped fresh rosemary

1. Melt the butter in a large pot over medium-high heat. Add the garlic and sauté for 15 seconds. Add the onion and sauté until softened, about 5 minutes.

2. Add the sweet potatoes and chicken broth, cover, and bring to a boil. Lower the heat and simmer, covered, until the potatoes are soft, about 20 minutes.

3. Working in 2 batches, puree the soup in a blender or food processor until smooth. Return to the pot and stir in the cream, salt, and pepper. Warm over low heat.

4. Mix the pecans, sage, and rosemary. Ladle the soup into 8 bowls and garnish with the pecan mixture. Serve with cornbread madeleines.

Serves 8

142

A Program
for Rational
Entertaining
in an
Irrational
Age

Cornbread Madeleines

These fancifully shaped cornbreads are light and savory. Their nutty flavor makes them a fine accompaniment to any squash soup or meaty stew. They can be made up to three days in advance of serving if they are cooled completely and stored at room temperature in an airtight container.

1 tablespoon melted butter, allowed to cool, plus more for greasing pans
½ cup yellow cornmeal
½ cup cake flour (not self-rising)
2 teaspoons baking powder
½ teaspoon kosher salt
2 teaspoons sugar
1 large egg
½ cup milk

1. Preheat the oven to 350° F. Butter 2 madeleine pans with medium-size shells (you will need 16 of the shells).

2. Sift together the cornmeal, flour, baking powder, salt, and sugar. Whisk together the egg and milk. Whisk in the butter. Gently stir in the cornmeal mixture.

3. Spoon the batter into the madeleine pans and bake until lightly browned, about 12 minutes. Serve warm or at room temperature.

Serves 8

143
Nan Hankers
for an
Old-fashioned
Family
Dinner

Tarragon Roast Chicken

The flavor of the herb will become more pronounced if the chicken is seasoned and prepared for roasting a day ahead of time, wrapped, and stored in the refrigerator. It is best to allow the chicken to rest at room temperature after roasting and before carving and serving. Leftovers make a fine chicken salad.

2 chickens, about 4 pounds each
1 medium onion, peeled and cut into large chunks
1 lemon, quartered
4 sprigs fresh tarragon
1 tablespoon unsalted butter, softened
Kosher salt and freshly ground pepper to taste

1. Preheat the oven to 425° F. Place the chickens on a rack in a large roasting pan. Stuff the cavities with the onion, lemon, and tarragon. Rub the butter all over the skin of both chickens and season them with salt and pepper.

2. Roast the chickens for 15 minutes. Lower the oven temperature to 375° F. Continue roasting until the juices run clear when the chicken is pricked with a fork in the thickest part of the thigh, about 1 hour 15 minutes longer. Let stand for 10 minutes. Carve the chicken and place on a platter.

Serves 8

144

A Program
for Rational
Entertaining
in an
Irrational
Age

Curried Broccoli and Carrots

While the broccoli and carrots can be prepared well in advance of serving, this dish tastes best when served directly from the sauté pan. In addition to complementing a mildly seasoned chicken, Curried Broccoli and Carrots is tasty with steamed couscous or stuffed inside baked potatoes with yogurt or sour cream.

3 large stalks broccoli (about 1½ pounds)
5 large carrots, peeled and cut into ½-inch dice
1½ tablespoons unsalted butter
1 teaspoon curry powder
1½ teaspoons kosher salt
½ teaspoon freshly ground pepper

1. Separate the broccoli florets from the stalks. Cut the florets into small pieces and cut the stalks into ½-inch dice.

2. Bring a large pot of water to a boil. Salt the water, add the broccoli and carrots, and blanch until tender, about 6 minutes. Drain.

3. Melt the butter in a large pot over low heat. Stir in the curry powder and cook, stirring constantly, for 2 minutes. Gently toss in the vegetables and stir in the salt and pepper. Divide among 8 plates and serve.

Serves 8

Nan Hankers
for an
Old-fashioned
Family
Dinner

Celery Root and Potato Puree

This puree, which makes a delicious companion for any roasted bird, can be made up to two days before serving, wrapped, and stored in the refrigerator. It should be reheated gently, preferably in a double boiler over lower heat. Leftovers can be patted into cakes, fried, and served with seafood or chicken, or surrounded by a simple green salad for lunch.

2 medium celery roots (about 2 pounds) trimmed, peeled, and cut into
    1-inch cubes
4 large baking potatoes, peeled and cut into 1-inch cubes
4 tablespoons unsalted butter
½ cup milk
Kosher salt and freshly ground pepper to taste

1. Place the celery root and potatoes in a large saucepan and cover with cold water. Cover and bring to a boil. Lower the heat and simmer until tender, about 20 minutes. Drain.

2. Press the mixture through a ricer or use a potato masher. Return to the pan and place over low heat. Add the butter and milk and stir until melted and heated through. Season with salt and pepper.

Serves 8

146

A Program
for Rational
Entertaining
in an
Irrational
Age

Apple Crisp

This homey dessert can be assembled up to a day ahead of serving, though it is at its best served directly from the oven when the topping is crisp and sweet and the fruit is bubbling and soft and slightly tart. It is difficult to imagine any simple meal that wouldn't lend itself to this crunchy apple dessert. The decadent may choose to serve it with vanilla ice cream, lightly sweetened cream whipped to soft peaks, or a dollop of crème fraîche.

½ cup all-purpose flour
1 cup old-fashioned oats
1 cup light brown sugar
2 teaspoons ground cinnamon
½ teaspoon kosher salt
½ cup cold unsalted butter, cut into ½-inch pieces
8 large Granny Smith apples, peeled, cored, and cut into ¼-inch slices
Juice of ½ lemon
1 tablespoon sugar

1. Preheat the oven to 350° F. Combine the flour, oats, brown sugar, cinnamon, and salt in a large bowl. Rub in the butter until well mixed.

2. Place the apples in a large, shallow baking dish and toss with the lemon juice and sugar. Cover with the oat mixture. Bake until the top is nicely browned and the apples are tender, about 45 minutes. Serve warm or at room temperature.

Serves 8

147

Nan Hankers
for an
Old-fashioned
Family
Dinner

The Family Spirit
in a Company Meal

In Johanna's opinion, there is much food that is simply too good for children. That is her stock response to the "yuck" duet that her twins, Max and Julia, sound in the face of some of her proudest culinary efforts, and she says it as well when the youngest, Claire, locks her jaw and refuses a second bite of something that Johanna knows to be sublime. "You're right," says Johanna efficiently, as she clears the assailed concoction. "It's too good for children."

Rarely does her reverse psychology work. Caviar and crème fraîche are quite safe in her refrigerator. So are the makings of ornate salads or anything vaguely resembling a boeuf en daube. Johanna has been sadly thwarted in passing along her adoration of slow, simmered dishes, dishes that recall the year she spent studying in Paris. No, her children want everything very clear and concise on their plates. Nothing mushy. Nothing combined.

This fact, however, has not thwarted Johanna's need to simmer and stew.

Mincing and chopping and cooking each ingredient, combining and stewing, all of this makes Johanna feel maternal in a beneficent, earth-mother sort of way. In the end, it doesn't matter if her children are repulsed by the fruits of her effort, the effort itself has a narcotic effect on their borderline–Type-A mother. She graciously makes hot dogs or pasta for them, saying in a merry voice with only the slightest hint of rue, "Stew is too good for children." She also tends to make something way cool for dessert whenever she makes a stew.

Because of the diminished audience for her efforts, Johanna frequently asks close friends or (more mature) family to share the mysteries of the pots she stews, particularly in the fall, when a stewy thing can comfort and soothe and set an intimate and informal note for a meal.

From the point of view of her recovery, Johanna can only say the obvious: stews can be made in advance—in fact, in her experience, the flavors marry and deepen with time—and are by their nature robust enough to command a light first course. Which is not to say that Johanna doesn't complicate her salads. She does, of course, but less now than before. And it is not to say that she isn't tempted to build an ornate and fragile dessert. She tries, however, to stick with a pie or a simple construction, such as a trifle, whose components, she declares to the group, "any culinary illiterate could make ahead of time and compose just before serving."

Salad Greens with Roasted Peppers and Seared Wild Mushrooms

The roasted peppers and wild mushrooms that give this salad soul and heft can be prepared ahead of time, though the final salad should be composed just before serving. This salad makes a fine first course for a full-bodied stew. Served with bread, and perhaps a little cheese, it makes a tasty fall lunch as well.

THE SALAD

3 yellow bell peppers
3 red bell peppers
¼ cup extra-virgin olive oil
30 medium-size shiitake mushrooms, stemmed
6 large portobello mushrooms, stemmed and cut into 1½-inch chunks
1 teaspoon kosher salt
¼ teaspoon freshly ground pepper
8 cups washed, assorted bite-sized salad greens such as watercress, romaine, escarole, and Belgian endive

THE VINAIGRETTE

2 shallots, finely minced
1 tablespoon fresh lemon juice
2 tablespoons sherry vinegar
1 teaspoon kosher salt
½ teaspoon freshly ground pepper
5 tablespoons walnut oil
4 tablespoons extra-virgin olive oil

1. To make the salad, place the bell peppers over a gas flame or under a broiler and roast until charred all over, about 5 minutes. Put them in a paper bag, close the top, and set aside for 15 minutes. Peel off the blackened skin and discard along with the seeds. Cut the peppers into 1-inch pieces and set aside.

2. In a large, heavy skillet (preferably cast-iron), heat 2 tablespoons of the olive oil and sear the shiitake mushrooms until softened and browned, about 2 minutes per side. Remove the shiitakes from the pan and repeat with the remaining 2 table-

150

A Program
for Rational
Entertaining
in an
Irrational
Age

spoons olive oil and the portobello mushrooms. Remove the pan from the heat and toss in the shiitakes, the salt, and the pepper. Set aside.

3. To make the vinaigrette, combine the shallots, lemon juice, vinegar, salt, and pepper in a small bowl. Whisk in the oils.

4. Just before serving, place the greens in a large serving bowl and toss with the vinaigrette. Taste and adjust seasoning with salt and pepper if needed. Divide the greens among 8 plates. Top with the mushrooms and roasted peppers and serve immediately.

Serves 6

Provençale Lamb and Gnocchi Gratin

The fact that this mélange is baked rather than simmered, that it gathers a golden crust in the oven and can be delivered directly to the table, bubbling and fragrant under a crisp layer of bread crumbs, distinguishes the dish from a standard stew and makes it a perfect candidate for a family-style meal or a buffet.

THE MARINADE AND LAMB

¼ cup fresh lemon juice
½ cup olive oil
3 large cloves garlic, crushed
¼ teaspoon freshly ground pepper
3 sprigs fresh thyme
3 sprigs fresh rosemary
2 pounds boneless leg of lamb, trimmed of excess fat and cut into 1½-inch cubes

THE GRATIN

2 tablespoons olive oil
Kosher salt and freshly ground pepper for seasoning lamb
2 medium yellow onions, peeled, halved lengthwise, and thinly sliced crosswise
3 medium fennel bulbs, trimmed, outer layers discarded, thinly sliced lengthwise
1 cup dry red wine
3 cups boxed or canned chopped tomatoes with juice
2 teaspoons salt
½ teaspoon freshly ground pepper
4 teaspoons chopped fresh rosemary
1 pound fresh or frozen potato gnocchi
1 cup Calamata olives, pitted and coarsely chopped
½ cup freshly grated Parmesan cheese
¼ cup dry bread crumbs
1 teaspoon chopped fresh thyme

152

A Program
for Rational
Entertaining
in an
Irrational
Age

1. To make the marinade, combine the lemon juice, olive oil, garlic, and pepper in a large bowl. Add the thyme, rosemary, and lamb and toss to coat well. Cover and refrigerate overnight.

2. To make the gratin, preheat the oven to 350° F. Remove the lamb from the marinade and pat it dry. Heat 1 tablespoon of the olive oil in a large, deep skillet over medium-high heat. Add half the lamb and sear until browned on all sides. Remove from the skillet and place in a bowl. Add the remaining lamb to the skillet and brown on all sides. Add to the lamb in the bowl, season lightly with salt and pepper, and set aside.

3. Add the remaining tablespoon of olive oil to the skillet. Add the onions and sauté until they begin to soften, about 3 minutes. Add the fennel, lower the heat slightly, and sauté for 5 minutes. Remove the onions and fennel from the skillet and set aside.

4. Pour the wine into the skillet, raise the heat, and simmer, scraping up any browned bits from the bottom of the skillet with a wooden spoon, until the wine is reduced to about ½ cup. Stir in the tomatoes, the 2 teaspoons salt, the ½ teaspoon pepper, and 3 teaspoons of the rosemary. Stir in the onions and fennel. Reduce the heat to very low.

5. Cook the gnocchi in boiling water just until tender; drain. Remove the tomato mixture from the heat and stir in the gnocchi, olives, and lamb, along with any juices accumulated from the lamb. Pour the mixture into a large gratin dish.

6. Combine the Parmesan, bread crumbs, thyme, and remaining teaspoon of rosemary. Sprinkle the mixture over the gratin. Bake for 25 minutes. Divide among 6 plates and serve.

Serves 6

Lemon Trifle with
Exotic Fruit Compote

The trifle must be made a day before serving. The compote can be made two hours before serving. Only the final assembly requires last-minute attention.

THE CUSTARD

1 tablespoon water
1 package powdered gelatin
6 large eggs
1½ cups sugar
1 tablespoon grated lemon zest
1 cup fresh lemon juice
4 tablespoons (½ stick) unsalted butter
1 cup heavy cream

THE SYRUP AND CAKE

1 cup water
½ cup sugar
½ vanilla bean, split lengthwise
1 tablespoon dark rum
1 (10.75-ounce) pound cake, cut into 1-inch cubes

THE TOPPING

1 cup heavy cream
2 tablespoons sugar
1 teaspoon vanilla extract

THE FRUIT

1 pineapple
2 ripe mangoes
3 oranges
¼ cup fresh mint leaves

A Program
for Rational
Entertaining
in an
Irrational
Age

1. At least 24 hours before serving, make the custard: Put the water in a small dish and sprinkle in the gelatin. Set aside. Put the eggs and the sugar in a medium-size, nonreactive saucepan and whisk until thickened and light in color. Whisk in the lemon zest and lemon juice. Place over low heat and cook, whisking constantly, until thick, about 6 minutes; do not let the mixture come to a simmer.

2. Remove from the heat and whisk in the butter and the gelatin mixture until dissolved. Let cool. Refrigerate until just chilled.

3. Meanwhile, to make the syrup, combine the water and sugar in a medium saucepan. Add the vanilla bean and bring to a boil. Lower the heat slightly and simmer for 3 minutes. Let cool. Stir in the rum and remove the vanilla bean. Set aside.

4. Whip 1 cup heavy cream until it holds firm peaks. Fold it into the lemon mixture. Lay the cake cubes out on a work surface and brush with ¼ cup of the syrup. Cover and refrigerate the remaining syrup. Assemble the trifle by spreading 1 cup of custard in the bottom of a glass trifle dish. Top with ½ of the cake. Spread with ½ of the remaining custard. Top with the remaining cake and then the remaining custard.

5. To make the topping, whip 1 cup of heavy cream to soft peaks. Add the sugar and vanilla extract and whip until firm. Spread or pipe the whipped cream over the custard. Cover with plastic wrap and refrigerate overnight.

6. At least 1 hour before serving, peel and core the pineapple and cut it into chunks. Peel and dice the mangoes. Working over a bowl to collect the juices, use a small knife to remove all peel and pith from the oranges. Cut the sections out from between the membranes. Gently combine all the fruit in the bowl with the juice and stir in the reserved syrup. Let stand until ready to serve.

7. To serve, spoon some of the trifle into the center of 8 shallow bowls. Surround with the fruit and syrup. Thinly slice the mint leaves and sprinkle over the fruit. Serve immediately.

Serves 8

A Late-Winter
Evening at Eliza J.'s

To tempt the palate is to tempt fate, particularly the fateful possibility that guests might be, shall we say, overly challenged by the bizarre," said Mrs. J. firmly.

Listening to her tone, she mused aloud at how prone to pronouncement she has become. Perhaps it's only natural. Pronouncements give one a sense of certainty. And heaven knows, she wasn't getting any younger. Mr. D. smiled indulgently—how he loved Mrs. J.! Their caterer/client relationship of nearly three decades had drifted into a sort of conspiracy. They were, the two of them, of the same vintage, facing an altered world. Like two bottles of fine Bordeaux in the land of white Zinfandel.

"The Cambodian meal was quite a success, dear," he said.

"Oh, darling, I am in no way questioning that," cried Mrs. J. "But that was a party of eight, was it not; Kenneth and I were enough ballast. The guests could confront the unfamiliar because we are, to them, so familiar and, at least at the table, at such close proximity. Here, on the other hand, we are speaking of twenty to twenty-five people, and supper in the living room and drawing rooms. No, we can't risk much exotica."

"Indeed," purred Mr. D., sounding more fatuous than he actually was. The caterer always found Mrs. J.'s instincts fascinating, and rarely had he found them to be far off base. The notion that a large party which necessarily spanned several generations begged a strong salute to tradition seemed eminently sensible to him. Mrs. J.'s genius, really, was, in his opinion, the ability to make lemonade out of lemons.

Consider, for instance, her approach to hair color. In the thirty years of their acquaintance, she had moved smoothly from honey-colored hair to something closer to platinum blond, covering the gray and accommodating the change in her complexion without a moment of unnaturalness. It really was quite something. For a moment, Mr. D. was painfully aware of the auburn rinse he himself had taken to using. It masked, but it didn't provide a vehicle for the continuous change of aging.

"It's almost as if we can choose a contemporary structure but we must conserve a sort of traditionalism in its execution," he said, "or vice versa."

"I liked Johanna's salad idea, very youthful; I wonder about adapting the notion for wintry salads and some roasted meats and such," said Mrs. J.

In this way the caterer and the hostess designed a modernistic buffet—one that appeared to be mostly salads and tasty accompaniments to those salads—whose components had traditional roots but were made with a subtle contemporary twist. It was decided that after being invited to tailor their own dinners and perch, plate in lap, on Mrs. J.'s chintz couches, they would be invited to the table for a "drop-dead dessert."

"The evening, in other words, will end in a traditional manner, at the table," said Mrs. J. with great satisfaction. "I trust you to think of some sweet that will bring them all together and make them feel coddled."

No, she wished not to even discuss dessert; "I meant what I said, Mr. D., darling." Which the caterer understood as something between a great compliment and a reassurance that his expertise was still valued and needed, albeit with slightly less frequency than before.

Sweet Potato-Apple Gratin

This bubbling, somewhat sloppy-looking gratin looks like something from a Parisian bistro but has an unabashedly American taste. It makes a fine accompaniment to roasted chicken, pork, or beef, particularly when the meat is highly seasoned, as is the pork tenderloin it is offered with here. The gratin can be assembled the day before a party and baked before guests arrive.

1 cup heavy cream
1½ cups apple cider
3 tablespoons brandy
1 medium clove garlic, minced
4 sprigs of thyme, plus 1 tablespoon coarsely chopped fresh thyme for
    garnish
1¾ teaspoons kosher salt
Freshly ground pepper
4 medium sweet potatoes (about 2½ pounds), peeled and cut across into
    ⅛-inch slices
4 medium Granny Smith apples, peeled, quartered, cored, and cut into
    ½-inch slices
2 large red onions, peeled, halved lengthwise, and thinly sliced

1. Preheat the oven to 350° F. Combine the cream, apple cider, brandy, garlic, and 4 sprigs of thyme in a medium saucepan and bring just to a boil. Lower the heat and simmer for 15 minutes. Stir in ¾ teaspoon of the salt and a dash of pepper.

2. Meanwhile, in a 13×9×2-inch glass baking dish, arrange half the sweet potato slices in overlapping layers. Season with ½ teaspoon of the remaining salt and a dash of pepper. Top with all the apples and then half of the onions. Layer the remaining sweet potatoes over the onions and season with the remaining ½ teaspoon of salt and a dash of pepper. Top with the remaining onions.

3. Strain the cream mixture and pour over the layers. Cover tightly with aluminum foil and bake until tender, about 1 hour 10 minutes. The gratin can be made a few hours ahead and reheated. Garnish with chopped thyme before serving.

Serves 8

158

A Program
for Rational
Entertaining
in an
Irrational
Age

Celery Root Salad

Traditionally, this French salad is made with a mayonnaise or rémoulade sauce, but here a dietarily judicious vinaigrette binds the grated root and gives it a sprightly, clean taste. The salad is best with grilled meat and is also best made not more than three hours before a party.

3 large celery roots, trimmed and peeled
6 tablespoons fresh lemon juice
3 tablespoons extra-virgin olive oil
2 teaspoons kosher salt
½ teaspoon freshly ground pepper
6 tablespoons coarsely chopped Italian parsley

1. Halve the celery roots lengthwise, then slice crosswise as thin as possible. Place in a bowl.

2. Whisk the lemon juice and olive oil together with the salt and pepper. Toss the celery root with the dressing, then with the parlsey.

Serves 8

Beet Crisps

These sweet crisps add color and a dash of whimsy to a buffet. They are delicious eaten with roasted meat or fish and make a pleasing counterpoint to salads as well. They can be made a day in advance but must be drained well, completely cooled, and stored in an airtight container to prevent sogginess.

4 large beets, peeled
Vegetable oil for deep frying
Kosher salt to taste

1. Using a vegetable peeler, cut the beets into thin strips as long as possible. Pour enough oil into a large, heavy pot or a heavy skillet to make a depth of about 3 inches. Heat the oil to 375° F.

2. Fry the beets in small batches until browned and crisp. Remove with a skimmer or slotted spatula and place on paper towels to drain well. Just before serving, place in a bowl and toss with salt to taste.

Serves 8

160

A Program
for Rational
Entertaining
in an
Irrational
Age

Mustard Roasted Pork Tenderloin

This pork could be served as a main course for a sit-down dinner, preceded perhaps by the Sweet Potato Soup (page 142) and accompanied by the Indian-Spiced Potato Gratin (page 52). It is delicious with the Celery Root Salad (page 159) or with the Romaine and Walnut Salad with Roasted Shallot Vinaigrette (page 162).

¼ cup grainy Dijon mustard
Kosher salt to taste
½ teaspoon freshly ground pepper
1½ pounds pork tenderloin

Preheat the oven to 375° F. Combine the mustard with the salt and pepper and rub all over the pork. Place on a baking sheet and roast until the pork is only slightly pink in the center, about 25 minutes. (If you are using a meat thermometer the internal temperature should be between 150° and 160° F.) Let stand for 10 minutes. Cut across into thin slices and place the slices on a platter to serve.

Serves 8

Romaine and Walnut Salad
with Roasted Shallot Vinaigrette

This hearty salad makes a marvelous winter lunch if served with the Pumpernickel-Sage Croutons and Stilton (opposite), after a soup such as Bean Soup (page 236) or Caribbean Sweet Potato Soup (page 238). Because the romaine is a sturdy lettuce, the salad holds up well on a buffet. While the vinaigrette can be made and the lettuce cleaned well in advance, the salad is best mixed immediately before serving.

5 large shallots, unpeeled
2 teaspoons olive oil
3 tablespoons white wine vinegar
6 tablespoons walnut oil
¾ teaspoon kosher salt
¼ teaspoon freshly ground pepper
1½ heads romaine, cored and coarsely chopped
¾ cup walnuts, toasted and coarsely chopped

1. Preheat the oven to 350° F. Place the shallots in a small casserole with a lid and drizzle with the olive oil. Cover and bake until very soft, about 1½ hours. Let cool.

2. Squeeze the shallots out of their skins and use a knife to chop into a paste. Place in a bowl and whisk in the vinegar. Slowly whisk in the walnut oil. Season with the salt and pepper.

3. Just before serving, combine the romaine and walnuts in a large bowl. Toss with the vinaigrette.

Serves 8

162

A Program
for Rational
Entertaining
in an
Irrational
Age

Pumpernickel-Sage Croutons and Stilton

These croutons can be made well in advance of a party and stored at room temperature in an airtight container. They make a delicious companion for the Romaine and Walnut Salad (opposite), give depth and panache to simple green salads, and are more intriguing than simple bread when served with a winter soup.

3 tablespoons unsalted butter
2 teaspoons chopped fresh sage
¼ teaspoon kosher salt
Dash of freshly ground pepper
4 cups cubed (½-inch) pumpernickel
¾ pound Stilton cheese, crumbled

1. Preheat the oven to 350° F. Melt the butter in a small saucepan over low heat. Add the sage and cook for 1 minute. Remove from the heat and season with the salt and pepper.

2. Place the bread cubes in a bowl, pour the butter over them, and toss to coat well. Spread on a baking sheet and bake until well toasted, about 20 minutes, stirring twice.

3. Place the croutons and Stilton in separate bowls and serve with the other salad components.

Serves 8

Mr. D.: Architect
of Desserts

Really, he embarrassed himself. At his age, to be so excited about dessert. Then again, to be his age in this age was not exactly easy. Nevertheless, few, and therefore precious, are the chances to bake with abandon. Mr. D. fairly twitched to make a little crème anglaise.

Well aware of the general appetite for chocolate, he suggested Rich Chocolate Cake with Toasted-Almond Crème Anglaise as a dessert possibility to the group. While clearly the most decadent of his suggestions, the cake was also intriguing, as it required little in the way of advanced training in pastrymaking and could be made several days in advance of a party. Elizabeth was quick to point out that the cake could be served with whipped cream or ice cream, for that matter, a point that Mr. D. conceded. Secretly, of course, the caterer knew that the sauce he envisioned provided the sort of distinction that elevates a gathering from homey to ever-so-chic.

Because meals have become lighter, or at least endeavor to appear lean,

Mr. D. felt that a sinfully rich chocolate dessert could be served with no apology—and to the delight of guests, many of whom harbor secret cravings to indulge. The Vanilla Pots de Crème with Chocolate Sauce that he suggested were along similar lines, intensely flavored and terribly rich, though in Mr. D.'s experience a slightly more difficult confection for a beginner such as Nan.

No caterer in his right mind would omit a sophisticated fruit-based dessert among the choices he offered a hostess. From his point of view, the Poached Pears, Figs, and Oranges with Clove Granité and Hazelnut-Chocolate Cookies was a brilliant winter dessert, dark and deep in flavor, wickedly contrasting in temperature and texture—sublime. Left to his own devices, he'd serve it with an assortment of cookies or pastries, to be sure.

The cerebral exercise alone was quite satisfying to the caterer. In fact, he was certain that the three desserts could transform an abstemious or informal winter meal. He grew faint just thinking about how each would taste after a grand buffet.

Desserts to Bring
Guests to Their Seats

Rich Chocolate Cake with Toasted-Almond Crème Anglaise

THE CRÈME ANGLAISE

1 cup unbleached whole almonds, coarsely chopped
2 cups whole milk
4 large egg yolks
⅔ cup sugar
1 teaspoon vanilla extract

THE CAKE

10 ounces best-quality semisweet chocolate, chopped
⅔ cup (packed) dark brown sugar
¼ pound (1 stick) unsalted butter
4 large eggs, separated
1½ teaspoons vanilla extract
½ cup slivered almonds, toasted and ground
6 tablespoons all-purpose flour
¼ teaspoon kosher salt

1. To make the crème anglaise, preheat the oven to 350° F. Place the almonds on a baking sheet and toast until nicely browned, stirring twice, about 10 minutes; watch carefully to prevent burning. Place in a saucepan with the milk and bring just to a boil. Remove from heat, cover, and let stand 15 minutes.

166
A Program
for Rational
Entertaining
in an
Irrational
Age

2. Whisk the egg yolks and sugar together until pale yellow. Bring the milk mixture back to a simmer. Whisking constantly, add the milk to the yolk mixture. Return the sauce to the pan, place over low heat, and cook, stirring constantly, until thick enough to coat the back of a spoon; do not let it simmer. Strain through a fine sieve. Let cool. Stir in the vanilla and refrigerate until cold.

3. To make the cake, preheat the oven to 350° F. Butter a 10-inch springform pan. Place the chocolate, brown sugar, and butter in a metal bowl over a pan of barely simmering water until melted. Mix well. Stir in the egg yolks and vanilla. Stir in the ground almonds, flour, and salt.

4. Whip the egg whites until firm but not dry. Stir ⅓ of the whites into the chocolate mixture. Fold in the remaining whites. Scrape the batter into the prepared pan and bake until a toothpick inserted into the center comes out only slightly wet, about 30 minutes. Let cool.

5. To serve, spoon a pool of sauce in the center of each plate and top with a slice of cake.

Serves 10

Vanilla Pots de Crème with Chocolate Sauce

These custards can be served warm, served directly from the oven, or prepared ahead of time and served cold. Either way, they are silky, rich, and delicious.

THE CHOCOLATE SAUCE

2 ounces bittersweet chocolate, finely chopped
3 tablespoons heavy cream

THE CUSTARD

1 cup whole milk
1 cup heavy cream
1 vanilla bean, split lengthwise
4 large egg yolks
⅓ cup sugar
Pinch of kosher salt

1. Preheat the oven to 325° F. To make the chocolate sauce, place the chocolate in the top of a double boiler set over barely simmering water. Heat, stirring occasionally, until melted. Remove from heat and whisk in the cream. Coat the bottom of six 6-ounce ramekins or pots de crème cups with the chocolate sauce and set aside.

168

A Program
for Rational
Entertaining
in an
Irrational
Age

2. To make the custard, place the milk and cream in a medium saucepan. Scrape the seeds from the vanilla bean into the milk and add the pod. Bring the mixture to a boil over medium heat, cover, remove from the heat, and let stand 10 minutes. Meanwhile, in a large bowl, whisk together the yolks and sugar until thick and pale yellow. Stirring constantly, whisk the warm milk into the yolks. Add a pinch of salt and strain the mixture into a bowl. Let stand for 2 to 3 minutes and skim the foam from the top.

3. Ladle the custard into the chocolate-lined molds and place them in a deep baking pan. Pour enough hot water in the pan to come halfway up the sides of the ramekins and cover the baking pan with aluminum foil. Bake until the pots de crème are just set (they will tremble slightly in the center when shaken) and a small knife inserted into the center comes out clean, about 55 minutes.

4. Remove the molds from the water and let cool. Serve the pots de crème in the molds, warm or chilled.

Serves 6

Poached Pears, Figs, and Oranges with Clove Granité and Hazelnut-Chocolate Cookies

THE FRUIT AND GRANITÉ

2 (750ml) bottles light dessert wine, like muscat canelli

1¾ cups sugar

12 cloves

10 firm Bartlett pears, peeled

2 cups dried black mission figs, stemmed

6 oranges

THE COOKIES

1 cup hazelnuts, toasted and skinned

2 cups all-purpose flour

½ teaspoon kosher salt

½ cup (packed) dark brown sugar

¾ cup (1½ sticks) cold unsalted butter, cut into ½-inch pieces

1 large egg

1 tablespoon milk

6 ounces bittersweet chocolate

1. To make the fruit, combine the wine, sugar, and cloves in a large, wide pot. Bring to a boil. Lower heat to a simmer and add the pears and figs. Simmer until the pears are soft but not falling apart, about 15 to 30 minutes. Meanwhile, use a paring knife to remove all peel and pith from the oranges. Cut the sections out from between the membranes. Add the sections and simmer 1 minute. Remove the fruit from the liquid with a slotted spoon, place in a bowl, and let cool. Cover and refrigerate.

2. Let the syrup stand until cool and strain into a shallow, nonreactive pan. Place in the freezer until firm throughout, stirring from time to time. (The granité can be made a day ahead.)

3. To make the cookies, pulse the hazelnuts in a food processor until coarsely chopped. Add the flour, salt, and sugar and process until the nuts are ground and the mixture is well combined. Add the butter and pulse to combine. Add the egg and milk and process just until dough begins to come together.

A Program
for Rational
Entertaining
in an
Irrational
Age

4. Press the dough together and divide it in half. Shape into cylinders about 1¾ inches in diameter. Wrap in plastic and refrigerate at least 2 hours or up to 3 days. Preheat the oven to 350° F. Line 2 baking sheets with baking parchment. If the dough is very cold, let stand at room temperature until firm but not too hard. Cut the dough across into ⅛-inch slices and place on the baking sheets about 1 inch apart (cookies must be baked in batches). Bake until lightly browned, about 10 minutes. Let cool.

5. Melt the chocolate and dip half of each cookie in the chocolate. Set aside and let dry completely.

6. To serve, arrange the pears, figs, and oranges in 10 shallow bowls. Use a spoon to scrape the granité into mounds and place a mound in each bowl. Serve immediately, passing the cookies separately.

Serves 10

A Pick-and-Choose Buffet

The generous spirit intrinsic to cooking for guests grows frantically in the late fall. Smaller, more personal dinner parties sprout in the slender cracks of time between the grand fêtes that Thanksgiving and Christmas command. Invitations abound. Before she realized what was happening, Johanna was, once again, bitten by the entertaining bug.

She was tempted to lay this phenomenon at the weather's doorstep. Cool breezes breed an appetite for human company and comfort; shorter days leave more evening hours to fill. But the slight insanity of planning a dinner party during a season already bloated with social and family obligations did not escape Johanna. She persuaded herself that hers was a public-service impulse. She wanted to create an antidote to the predictable and mandatory holiday soirées.

Ah, but the need to overwhelm and seduce her guests lurked beneath the surface of Johanna's seemingly selfless civic spirit. The stretch between Thanksgiving and December is thin ice for the woman who would wow. Decorating the house was definitely a trigger. Johanna had a difficult time resisting the urge to haul in a forest's worth of boughs and spend hours tying tiny bows. The truth is, she didn't resist. Her house looked divine.

And as Elizabeth pointed out, she would actually be amortizing the cost and time of the decorating she had already done if she were to give another party. Not a sit-down party. Granted there is a certain reassurance about gathering together around a well-set table—to say nothing of the satisfying challenge of setting a holiday table—but Johanna had already obligated herself to giving two rather large sit-down business dinners.

For her party-without-a-purpose, she envisioned a less structured meal—a buffet, for instance, or a prolonged cocktail hour in which hearty food is passed in canapé guise by waiters. Such a party, Johanna thought, would engender a casual ambience, allowing guests to take a deep breath, tell a good story, and luxuriate in a holiday-free zone.

Johanna designed the following procession of dishes to be served as guests mingled in her living room. It would also make a fine buffet. In either case, the menu allows guests to eat what appeals to them, when the spirit moves them. She rationalized the expansive menu by telling herself that most of the dishes could be prepared ahead of time, which is true, and all can be served either warm or at room temperature. So the meal can be leisurely, even languorous. It can be eaten in the living room or at the dining-room table.

While the flavors of each dish are exotic and distinct, they complement one another. The Curried Beef Skewers, for instance, are delicious nibbled along with the Afghani Breads with Fennel and Orange or eaten along with the Chickpea-Lamb Cakes with Red Pepper Sauce. At the same time, the beef skewers provide an alluring counterpoint to the Wild Mushroom Pie with Polenta Crust. Guests can either create a meal or sample the individual dishes like so many appetizers. Either way, the flavors are a dramatic contrast to those normally found on the holiday dinner circuit.

She added a simple green salad, and uncorked bottles of California Zinfandel as well as a spicy white Alsatian wine, and encouraged guests to serve themselves the night of the "cocktail" party.

For the first party, Johanna chose the waiter route. Other evenings, when entertaining a large group of business associates, she and Mark opted for buffets. The first featured Bacon-Roasted Pork with Prunes, a garlicky salad of broccoli rabe, and a roasted-tomato bread salad, in addition to peasant bread and a big green salad tossed with shaved Parmesan cheese. The other featured Stilton-Walnut Rice Balls served with a green salad, and Lobster Shepherd's Pie.

The peasant nature of all the meals she served in the holiday season seemed to Johanna to ask for a hint of formality. Therefore, she borrowed a page from Mrs. J.'s book and served a complex dessert, as well as coffee, at the dining-room table. The pears, figs, and oranges poached in dessert wine and served with clove granité and hazelnut-chocolate cookies proposed by Mr. D. was complicated to make—and a dazzling success—on three successive occasions.

So when the best holiday sagas had unfolded and the latest installments on family dramas had been repeated, her gathering moved to, yes, she couldn't resist, her very well set table and was served dessert by candlelight on freshly starched linen. It made for a cohesive party, in Johanna's opinion.

The formal dessert service left her guests feeling coddled, temporarily relieved of holiday burdens, reminded that the "families" we choose in our friends are usually less freighted with emotional entanglements than the ones we are born into, as Johanna remarked to her husband. Hastening to add, "At least around the holidays."

174

A Program
for Rational
Entertaining
in an
Irrational
Age

Curried Beef Skewers

To save more time on the day your guests are coming, the beef can be threaded onto skewers before marinating, then broiled—or, even better, char-grilled—an hour before guests arrive. It can be served at room temperature, as well as hot, and is easily eaten right from its skewer. The spicy beef can also be served as a first course, with a green salad or bread—delicious in any season.

¼ cup curry powder
½ cup peanut oil
2 pounds beef fillet, cut into 1-inch cubes
Kosher salt to taste

1. Place the curry powder in a small, heavy skillet over very low heat. Stir constantly until toasted and fragrant, being careful not to burn it, about 10 minutes. Place in a large bowl and let cool. Stir in the oil. Add the beef and toss to coat well. Refrigerate overnight.

2. Bring the beef to room temperature. Preheat a grill or broiler. Thread the beef onto 6-inch skewers, using 3 cubes for each. Grill or broil until medium-rare, about 1 minute per side. Sprinkle with salt and place on a platter to serve.

Serves 10

Chickpea-Lamb Cakes
with Red Pepper Sauce

The tangy sauce as well as the mixture for the cakes can be made a day before a party, but the cakes themselves should be prepared no more than several hours before guests are to arrive. They are tasty served hot or at room temperature and are small enough to be managed as a canapé—provided cocktail napkins abound.

These cakes can also be surrounded by a green salad and served as an appetizer for a sit-down meal.

THE SAUCE

1½ cups plain low-fat yogurt
2 ancho chilies
6 red bell peppers, roasted and peeled (see page 150)
1½ teaspoons fresh lemon juice
1 teaspoon kosher salt
½ teaspoon freshly ground pepper

THE CAKES

2 tablespoons plus 2 teaspoons olive oil
1 pound boneless leg of lamb
4 (15-ounce) cans chickpeas, drained and rinsed
2 large eggs
1 tablespoon ground cumin
2 teaspoons fresh lemon juice
1 cup cooked bulgur
4 scallions, chopped
2 tablespoons chopped fresh mint
6 tablespoons chopped Italian parsley
1 tablespoon kosher salt
1 teaspoon freshly ground pepper

176

A Program
for Rational
Entertaining
in an
Irrational
Age

1. To make the sauce, place the yogurt in a paper-towel-lined sieve over a bowl and refrigerate several hours, until the liquid drains out. Meanwhile, simmer the chilies in water until softened, about 5 minutes. Drain, stem, and seed. Place the yogurt cheese, chilies, roasted peppers, lemon juice, salt, and pepper in a blender and puree until smooth. Taste and adjust the seasoning. Set aside in the refrigerator.

2. To make the cakes, heat 2 teaspoons of the oil in a large nonstick skillet over medium-high heat. Add the lamb and cook, turning so that each side cooks evenly and the lamb is medium-rare, about 6 minutes per side. Let cool and then cut into small dice. Set aside.

3. Place the chickpeas and eggs in a food processor and process until smooth. Add the cumin and lemon juice. Scrape into a bowl and stir in the lamb, bulgur, scallions, mint, parsley, salt, and pepper.

4. With moistened hands, shape the chickpea mixture into patties, using ¼ cup for each. Heat the remaining 2 tablespoons oil in a large nonstick skillet over medium heat. Working in batches, sauté the cakes until well browned, about 3 minutes per side. Serve warm with the cold pepper sauce.

Serves 10

Wild Mushroom Pie with Polenta Crust

This pie, which makes a filling and satisfying one-dish meal for an informal winter dinner, also works well on a buffet: it holds together nicely and can be served at room temperature as well as warm. The pie can be completely assembled the day before a party and baked just before guests arrive.

THE CRUST

4 cups water
1 cup yellow cornmeal
2 teaspoons kosher salt
½ teaspoon freshly ground pepper
⅓ cup mascarpone (see Mail-Order Sources, page 275)

THE MUSHROOMS

1 ounce dried porcini (see Mail-Order Sources, page 275)
4 cups water
¼ cup olive oil, plus more for greasing pan
3 shallots, peeled and minced
3 pounds mixed wild mushrooms (like portobello, shiitake, and cremini), cut into large dice, stems reserved
1 cup sherry
2 teaspoons kosher salt
½ teaspoon freshly ground pepper
2 large eggs
⅓ cup chopped Italian parsley

1. To make the crust, bring the water to a boil in a medium saucepan. Whisking constantly, add the cornmeal, along with the salt and pepper, in a very thin, steady stream. Turn the heat as low as possible. Cook for 1 hour, stirring vigorously every 10 minutes.

2. Meanwhile, prepare the mushrooms: Combine the porcini and water in a large saucepan. Simmer for 30 minutes. Drain, reserving the mushrooms and broth. Coarsely chop the porcini and set aside. Return the broth to the pan, add the mushroom stems, and simmer slowly until reduced to 1 cup, about 25 minutes. Strain and set aside.

178

A Program
for Rational
Entertaining
in an
Irrational
Age

3. Heat 1 tablespoon of the oil in a large skillet over medium heat. Add the shallots and sauté 2 minutes. Add another tablespoon of oil and ⅓ of the mixed mushrooms and sauté until browned and softened, about 5 minutes. Place the shallots and mushrooms in a bowl. Repeat until the remaining oil and mushrooms are used.

4. With no mushrooms in the skillet, add the sherry and simmer, scraping the bottom of the skillet with a wooden spoon, until reduced to ½ cup. Add the mushroom broth, all the mushrooms, the salt, and the pepper. Bring to a simmer, cover, and cook for 20 minutes. Taste and adjust seasoning. Whisk the eggs in a bowl and whisk in 1 cup of the mushroom mixture. Stir the egg mixture into the skillet. Set aside.

5. Preheat the oven to 350° F. While the cornmeal mixture is hot, stir in the mascarpone. Generously brush a 10-inch springform pan with olive oil. Place the polenta in the pan, cover with a sheet of plastic wrap, and press the polenta evenly over the bottom and ¾ of the way up the sides of the pan. Discard the plastic. Spoon the mushrooms into the pan.

6. Bake the pie for 1 hour. Garnish with the parsley. Either serve hot, letting it cool only slightly before cutting, or, for neater slices and extra convenience, serve at room temperature.

Serves 10

Afghani Breads
with Fennel and Orange

While high-quality flat breads are now available in many gourmet markets, the fennel and orange that scent this version make it a worthwhile investment of time. For large parties, one would want to double or triple the recipe. The bread can be made the day before a party, provided that it is cooled completely, wrapped tightly, and stored at room temperature. It can be warmed in the oven before serving.

Afghani flat bread makes a fine companion to a luncheon soup, such as Wild Herb Soup (page 74), or to the Everything-Under-the-Sun Salad (page 134), as well as to the Curried Beef Skewers (page 175).

1 package active dry yeast
2½ cups lukewarm water
1½ cups whole wheat flour
4 to 4½ cups all-purpose flour
4½ teaspoons kosher salt
1 tablespoon grated orange zest
1 tablespoon fennel seeds, cracked
1 large egg, lightly beaten

1. Stir the yeast in the water in a large bowl until dissolved. Stir in the whole wheat flour and 1 cup of the all-purpose flour. Stir for 1 minute. Cover with plastic wrap and let stand 1 hour.

2. Stir in another cup of all-purpose flour, 3 teaspoons of the salt, and the orange zest. Continue adding flour a little at a time until the dough is stiff. Turn out onto a floured surface and knead until smooth, about 10 minutes. Place in a lightly oiled bowl (use olive oil or any vegetable oil), cover with plastic wrap, and let rise until doubled in bulk, about 1½ hours.

3. Preheat the oven to 475° F. Punch the dough down and divide into 4 pieces. Roll each piece into an oval about 5½×10 inches. Cover and let stand 20 minutes. Place baking stones or a heavy baking sheet, turned upside down, on a rack in the oven. Mix the fennel seeds with the remaining 1½ teaspoons salt.

A Program
for Rational
Entertaining
in an
Irrational
Age

4. Roll and stretch 1 piece of the dough into an oval about 8×18 inches. Press the tips of your fingers all over the dough to crimp it well. Place the dough directly on the baking stones or baking sheet, brush with a little of the egg, and sprinkle with ¼ of the fennel mixture. Bake until browned and crisp, about 8 to 10 minutes. Repeat with the remaining dough.

Makes 4

Menu for a Midwinter Buffet

Bacon-Roasted Pork with Prunes

This pork can be prepared the day before the party, wrapped well, stored in the refrigerator overnight, and baked just before the guests are due to arrive. It is wonderful on a buffet, as it is pretty and its flavor is interesting yet subtle, so it is flattered by a wide range of other dishes. It also makes a terrific main course, preceded, perhaps, by the Butternut Squash Soup with Spiced Shrimp and Cilantro (page 269) and accompanied by the Celery Root Salad (page 159) or a green salad, as well as the Indian-Spiced Potato Gratin (page 52).

4 pounds boned, rolled, and tied pork loin, halved crosswise
1 cup pitted prunes, quartered
¼ cup Dijon mustard
Freshly ground pepper to taste
16 slices bacon

1. Preheat the oven to 350° F. Run a skewer lengthwise through the center of 1 piece of pork. Remove the skewer and insert the handle of a fork into one end of the pork, in the hole created by the skewer. Twist the fork around to enlarge the hole enough to insert the prunes. Repeat at the other end. Push the prunes into the hole until you have a line of prunes running the length of the pork. Repeat with the other piece of pork.

2. Rub the mustard all over the pork and season generously with the pepper. Wrap the bacon around the pork and place in a large roasting pan. Roast until the pork reaches an internal temperature of 160° F., about 1½ hours. Let stand for 10 minutes before slicing. Serve warm or at room temperature.

Serves 10

182

A Program
for Rational
Entertaining
in an
Irrational
Age

Broccoli Rabe Salad with Roasted Garlic Vinaigrette

This salad can be made the day before a party and is wonderful served with the Bacon-Roasted Pork with Prunes (opposite) on a buffet. It needs plates and forks, so it's not ideal for a cocktail party. At a sit-down dinner, it makes a fine accompaniment to almost any meat dish.

4 pounds broccoli rabe, stalks trimmed and cut into 2-inch lengths, leaves
    cut across into thirds
12 cloves roasted garlic, peeled
6 tablespoons fresh lemon juice
½ cup extra-virgin olive oil
3 teaspoons kosher salt
¾ teaspoon freshly ground pepper
⅛ teaspoon cayenne

1. Bring a large pot of water to a boil. Salt the water, add the broccoli rabe, and blanch until just tender, about 8 minutes. Drain, refresh under cold running water, and drain well again.

2. In a large bowl, whisk together the roasted garlic and the lemon juice. Slowly whisk in the olive oil. Whisk in the salt, the pepper, and the cayenne. Add the broccoli rabe and toss to coat with the dressing. Taste and adjust seasoning if needed. Serve at room temperature.

Serves 10

Oven-Dried Tomato and Bread Salad

13 tablespoons olive oil

36 plum tomatoes, cored and halved lengthwise

3 cloves garlic, peeled

12 cups bread cubes (1½-inch), made from good-quality rustic Italian bread

3 tablespoons balsamic vinegar

2 teaspoons kosher salt

½ teaspoon freshly ground pepper

1½ cups chopped fresh basil

1. Preheat the oven to 200° F. Using a pastry brush and 1 tablespoon of the olive oil, lightly coat the skin side of each tomato half with oil. Place skin side down on a large baking sheet. Bake until the tomatoes shrink to about ¼ of their original size, about 4 to 6 hours; they should remain soft and juicy. Let cool, halve crosswise, and set aside.

2. Heat 1 tablespoon of the remaining olive oil in a large cast-iron skillet over medium heat. Add 1 clove garlic and stir for 30 seconds. Remove the garlic and discard. Add 2 cups of the bread and turn the pieces until well toasted on all sides. Place in a bowl and add 2 more cups of bread to the skillet and toast. Repeat until all of the bread is toasted, adding 1 tablespoon of oil after every other batch, flavoring it with 1 clove garlic as above. Set aside.

3. Whisk together the vinegar and the remaining 6 tablespoons of oil. Season with 1 teaspoon of the salt and the pepper. Just before serving, toss the tomatoes with the bread. Add the dressing and coat well. Toss with the remaining salt, pepper, and basil.

Serves 10

184

A Program
for Rational
Entertaining
in an
Irrational
Age

Another Menu for a Midwinter Buffet

Stilton-Walnut Rice Balls

These rice balls can be served as canapés or can be served on a buffet to be eaten with a large green salad, preferably one made with bitter greens such as watercress and arugula or endive and radicchio. They can be prepared and shaped the day before the party, and actually hold their shape best when they are, but they should be cooked just before serving and should be served warm.

4 cups water
2 cups Arborio rice
4 teaspoons kosher salt
4 large eggs, beaten
Freshly ground pepper to taste
1¼ cups dry bread crumbs
⅔ cup walnuts, toasted and broken into ½-inch pieces
½ pound cold Stilton cheese, cut into ½-inch cubes
Vegetable oil, for deep frying

1. Bring the water to a boil in a large saucepan. Add the rice and 2 teaspoons of the salt, return to a boil, lower the heat, cover, and simmer until the water is absorbed, about 15 minutes. Place in a bowl and let cool completely.

2. Add the eggs, the remaining 2 teaspoons salt, the pepper, and ¾ cup of the bread crumbs to the rice and mix well. Moisten your hands with water and form the rice mixture into 1½-inch balls. Press 1 piece of walnut and 1 piece of Stilton into the center of each one and reshape into a ball. Coat with the remaining bread crumbs.

3. Working in batches, deep-fry the rice balls until nicely browned. Drain on paper towels. Serve hot.

Serves 10

Lobster Shepherd's Pie

This rich variation on the old London pub dish makes a wonderful holiday meal, particularly if served after caviar—or other, less precious hors d'oeuvres. The pie can be made ahead of time and baked just before the guests arrive. It should be followed by a green salad, and if hearty hors d'oeuvres are not on the menu, the salad should be served with baked cheese croutons or with the Stilton-Walnut Rice Balls (page 185).

5 lobsters, about 1½ pounds each
6 large baking potatoes
7 tablespoons unsalted butter
4 large shallots, peeled and minced
4 large leeks, white and light green parts only, julienned
1½ cups finely diced carrots
8 cups shiitake mushrooms, stemmed and cut into large dice
1 cup dry white wine
1 cup heavy cream
1 cup frozen baby peas, defrosted
5 teaspoons kosher salt
1½ teaspoons freshly ground pepper
1 cup half-and-half
¼ cup chopped fresh chives

1. Steam the lobsters until slightly underdone, about 9 minutes. Let cool. Shell the meat, cut into large chunks, and set aside.

2. Meanwhile, peel the potatoes and cut into 1-inch pieces. Boil until soft, drain, and pass through a ricer. Set aside.

3. Heat 1 tablespoon of the butter in a large skillet over medium heat. Add the shallots and sauté 1 minute. Add the leeks and carrots and sauté 10 minutes. Add the mushrooms and cook for 10 minutes more. Add the wine and simmer 5 minutes. Stir in the cream and the peas and simmer 5 minutes. Stir in 2 teaspoons of the salt and ½ teaspoon of the pepper and set aside.

A Program
for Rational
Entertaining
in an
Irrational
Age

4. Preheat the oven to 350° F. Place the potatoes in a large saucepan over medium heat. Add the remaining 6 tablespoons butter and the half-and-half and stir until the butter is melted and the potatoes are smooth. Stir in the remaining 3 teaspoons salt and the remaining 1 teaspoon pepper. Stir the lobster into the vegetable mixture. Spoon the mixture into a large, shallow oval casserole. Spread the potatoes over the top. Bake just until heated through, about 25 minutes. Garnish with chives and serve hot.

Serves 10

Mr. D. Reclaims the Quiche

The canapé circuit made Mr. D. rather misty in regard to quiche. Yes, yes, nostalgia is ultimately boring, he'd be the first to say so. By the same token, he felt that fate had been unkind to the savory custard studded with bacon and baked in a crust. Quiche Lorraine, and the hundreds of variations that followed in the wake of its success, was an eminently sociable pie.

Quiche was, in fact, quite brilliant. Both peasant-like and elegant, crumbly yet soft, sweet yet pungent. The pie could be made in fluted tart pans and sliced. It could be made in individual tins and served with a flourish for lunch or for dinner's first course. It could be baked in little muffin tins for cocktail parties. It held up well.

And then along comes the cholesterol hubbub, and bye-bye quiche. Late in the fall, Mr. D. embarked on a little crusade all of his own. His mission, this time, was to resurrect quiche. Of course, no one would suspect his true motivation. They would be too smitten by his culinary wiles.

The latter-day dietary worries that had damned the pie that Julia Child helped America fall in love with, the pie that a generation came of culinary age with, the pie that helped make his fortunes, could be eradicated, of that the caterer was quite sure. Likewise, a cold look at what had yanked the crown away from quiche—designer pizza—would enable him to recast the blighted savory pie of the sixties in an eminently millennial guise.

The butter in the quiche crust was a problem. Ah, but what about using a bread? They love bread. (Bread—why is it the holy communion of the contemporary table?) If using bread, one had to exaggerate its peasant propensity, not disguise it. In a flash, Mr. D. saw free-form bread pies, stuffed with inventive and wildly varied concoctions. Bread that formed enough of a container to hold a deep filling, bread that baked to golden crusts, bread, glorious bread.

He served the pies cautiously at first, simply baking them and adding them to various buffets or slipping them onto tables as a surprise to the hostess. Within weeks, of course, they were calling and ordering Mr. D.'s savory pies. Tiny ones for canapés. Hand-sized ones, slightly misshapen and adorable on the luncheon plate. Large ones bubbling and oozing on buffets up and down the East Side.

"As if to reinvent pizza," remarked Mrs. J. "And how cleverly! You've preserved the rustic look while elevating the toppings to something more elegant, more substantial. Actually, what is the word I'm looking for, D.?"

The caterer shook his head, appeared to be mystified, and felt a part of himself taking wing, rising like a phoenix. He felt like a young man, and the world seemed, oh, no mere oyster, but an ocean to Mr. D.

Mr. D. Reclaims
the Quiche

Free-Form Crusts for Savory Pies

This basic recipe can be used to create a free-form shell for all the fillings suggested below. The dough itself can be made, wrapped in plastic wrap, and stored for one month in the freezer. It should be thawed overnight in the refrigerator before use.

1 cup warm water
1 package (¼ ounce) active dry yeast
2½ to 3 cups all-purpose flour
1 teaspoon kosher salt
1 teaspoon olive oil
1 filling (see following recipes)
1 large egg beaten with 1 tablespoon water

1. Combine the water and yeast in a mixing bowl and stir until the yeast dissolves. Stir in 1 cup of the flour. Stir in the salt and a second cup of flour. Sprinkle some of the remaining flour over a work surface and your hands. Scrape the dough out of the bowl and onto the work surface. Gradually knead in additional flour, until the dough no longer feels sticky.

2. Coat a large bowl with the olive oil. Shape the dough into a ball and rotate it in the bowl to coat it with oil. Cover the bowl tightly with plastic wrap and set in a warm, draft-free place until doubled in bulk, about 1 hour. Punch the dough down and knead it for about 1 minute. Return the dough to the bowl and let it rise until doubled again, about 45 minutes. Punch the dough down.

3. Preheat the oven to 400° F. Lightly flour the back of a baking sheet and place the dough on it. Roll the dough into a 12-inch circle, letting the dough rest for a few minutes when it becomes too elastic to roll. Place the filling in the center of the dough and spread it out, leaving a 2-inch border. Fold the edge of the dough in over the filling, making a pleat every 2 inches.

4. Brush the rim of the pie with the egg mixture. Bake until lightly browned and cooked through, about 25 minutes. Let cool slightly, cut into wedges, and serve.

Serves 4

190
A Program
for Rational
Entertaining
in an
Irrational
Age

Potato-Leek Filling with Canadian Bacon

This particular filling makes a meal-style pie. A light winter soup such as the Wild Mushroom Soup with Scallops and Thyme (page 260) before, and perhaps a salad with cheese afterward, could round out the meal.

Olive oil spray
3 large red potatoes, halved and thinly sliced
1 teaspoon olive oil
2 medium leeks, white and light green parts only, halved lengthwise and cut
      across into thin slices
½ onion, diced
2 cloves garlic, minced
2 cups sliced mushrooms
1 teaspoon kosher salt
½ teaspoon freshly ground pepper
¼ cup chopped Italian parsley
4 slices Canadian bacon, cut into ¼-inch-thick strips

1. Preheat the oven to 450° F. Spray 2 baking sheets with olive oil and divide the potatoes between them, in a single layer. Roast until tender, about 20 minutes.

2. Meanwhile, heat the olive oil in a large nonstick skillet over medium heat. Add the leeks and onion and cook until soft, about 7 minutes. Add the garlic and mushrooms and cook for 5 minutes longer. Remove from the heat and add the potatoes, salt, pepper, and parsley. Assemble the pie as described on page 190, sprinkling the Canadian bacon over the top before baking.

Serves 4

Winter Squash Filling with Rye, Walnut, and Rosemary Crumb Topping

This filling is deeply rustic and thrills those with adventuresome taste. It should be served before a simple green salad or even the Salad Greens with Roasted Peppers and Seared Wild Mushrooms (page 150), or the Middle Eastern Lamb-Stuffed Wontons (page 208) on a bed of lightly dressed bitter greens. This pie could also be preceded by a clear soup such as the Wild Mushroom Soup with Scallops and Thyme (page 260) or the Chicken Timbale (page 246). In any case, fresh fruit or Elizabeth's Pistachio-Pear Strudel (page 252) would round out this meal nicely.

1 teaspooon roasted garlic oil (optional)
1 butternut squash, halved lengthwise
3 teaspoons kosher salt
Freshly ground pepper to taste
½ spaghetti squash
1 tablespoon thinly sliced fresh sage leaves
2 slices stale rye bread, broken into pieces
½ cup walnuts
1 tablespoon chopped fresh rosemary
1 large clove garlic, finely chopped
½ cup chopped Italian parsley

1. Prepare the dough as on page 190, using the garlic oil in place of the olive oil, if desired. Preheat the oven to 350° F. Place both squash, cut side down, on a baking sheet and bake until soft, about 45 minutes. When cool enough to handle, scrape the insides of the butternut squash into a bowl and stir in 1 teaspoon of the salt and pepper to taste. Set aside.

2. Scrape the spaghetti squash into a sieve and let drain. Place in a bowl and stir in 1 teaspoon of the remaining salt, pepper to taste, and the sage. Set aside.

3. Place the bread, walnuts, rosemary, and garlic and the 1 teaspoon of remaining salt in a food processor and pulse until finely chopped. Stir in the parsley.

192

A Program
for Rational
Entertaining
in an
Irrational
Age

4. To assemble the pie, spread the butternut squash over the dough as directed on page 190. Top with ¾ cup of the crumb mixture. Top with the spaghetti squash and then the remaining crumbs. Bake as directed on page 190.

Serves 4

Three-Bean Chili Filling

The antecedents of this bean-stuffed pie are distinctly Tex-Mex, so a fitting companion is a chopped cucumber and tomato salad with chili peppers, cilantro, and lime. A soup such as the Butternut Squash Soup with Spiced Shrimp and Cilantro (page 269) would make a fine beginning. A simple dessert such as the Caramel Orange Fool (page 128) or the Orange-Scented Flan (page 88) would complete a fine winter meal.

¼ cup *each* red kidney beans, black beans, and pinto beans, soaked in water
    overnight and drained
3 cups water
1 bay leaf
2 large jalapeño peppers, seeded and minced
1 teaspoon ground cumin
1 teaspoon olive oil
½ large onion, diced
1 small green bell pepper, diced
1 medium carrot, diced small
1 rib celery, diced small
2 cloves garlic, minced
1 (14-ounce) can crushed tomatoes with puree
1 teaspoon dried oregano
1 teaspoon kosher salt
½ teaspoon freshly ground pepper
1 cup grated Monterey Jack cheese
⅓ cup chopped fresh cilantro

1. Place the beans, the water, the bay leaf, ⅓ of the jalapeño, and ¼ teaspoon cumin in a large saucepan and bring to a boil. Lower the heat to a simmer, cover, and cook until the beans are soft, about 2 hours. Drain well and discard the bay leaf.

2. Meanwhile, heat the olive oil in a large nonstick skillet over medium heat. Add the onion and green pepper and sauté for 5 minutes. Add the carrots and celery and cook until softened, about 10 minutes. Add the garlic and remaining jalapeño and cook for 3 minutes longer.

194
A Program
for Rational
Entertaining
in an
Irrational
Age

3. Stir in the beans, tomatoes, oregano, remaining cumin, salt, and pepper. Lower the heat slightly, cover, and cook for 20 minutes. Let cool.

4. Assemble the pie and bake as directed on page 190. Sprinkle the cheese over the top and bake for 5 minutes longer. Top with the cilantro before serving.

Serves 4

Red Cabbage, Bacon, and Stilton Filling

This filling is soulful and quite pungent. Preceded by Sweet Potato Soup (page 142) and followed by a simple green salad, as well as a rich dessert such as the Date–Pine Nut Tart (page 264), it is a wonderful winter meal for family or company.

½ medium head red cabbage, cored and thinly sliced
1 teaspoon kosher salt, plus more to taste
2 strips thick-cut bacon
½ medium red onion, chopped
1 Granny Smith apple, peeled, cored, and thinly sliced
½ cup currants
½ teaspoon caraway seeds
¼ cup dry red wine
Freshly ground pepper to taste
½ cup crumbled Stilton cheese, for topping

1. Place the cabbage in a large bowl and toss with the 1 teaspoon salt. Let stand for 15 minutes. Meanwhile, cook the bacon in a large heavy skillet over medium-low heat until crisp, about 10 minutes. Drain, reserving 1 teaspoon of fat. Crumble the bacon and set aside. Wipe out the skillet and add the reserved fat. Drain the cabbage.

2. Sauté the onion over medium heat until soft, about 5 minutes. Add the cabbage to the skillet in batches; as the cabbage wilts, more will fit in the pan. Stir in the apple, currants, and caraway seeds and cook for 10 minutes. Stir in the wine, lower the heat, cover, and cook until soft, about 30 minutes.

3. Season to taste with additional salt and pepper and add the bacon. Cover and cook for 10 minutes more. Let cool. Assemble the pie and bake as described on page 190. Sprinkle the cheese over the top and bake for 5 minutes longer.

Serves 4

196

A Program
for Rational
Entertaining
in an
Irrational
Age

Company in
Cold Weather

It is no coincidence that the holiday season, and the gatherings it mandates, lies in the coldest and darkest months of the year. Nor is it by chance that the months between November and February are generally filled with a flurry of dinner-party invitations. Rather, there is something fundamentally irresistible about the pleasure of human company when the earth is stiff and cold and the winds are unmitigated and the light seems parceled out by a parsimonious deity. Company affirms life. The ambient warmth of a crowd gathered around an evening table is more than comfort, it's a sort of fortitude.

Traditionally, the company meals of winter were quite ornate, and their ostentatious nature seemed intended as a talisman. Consider, for instance, the diversion of a finely set table: it is a mark of civilization. Or the endless parade of courses: guaranteed to extend the convivial evening, to distract from the very length of its shadows and its lack of light. While slightly less formal, hostesses of

Mrs. J.'s generation still entertained in a style like the one Edith Wharton describes in *A Backward Glance*.

When her parents "gave a dinner," she recalled in her memoir, the family cook, Mary Johnson, prepared:

> . . . terrapin and canvas-back ducks or (in their season) broiled Spanish mackerel, soft-shelled crabs with a mayonnaise of celery and peach-fed Virginia hams cooked in champagne (I am no doubt confusing all the seasons in this allegoric evocation of their riches), lima beans in cream, corn soufflés and salads of oyster and crabs poured in varied succulence from Mary Johnson's cornucopia—ah, then, the gourmet of that long lost day, when cream was cream and butter butter and coffee coffee, and meat fresh every day and game hung just for the proper number of hours, might lean back in his chair and murmur "fate cannot harm me" over his cup of moka and his glass of authentic Chartreuse.

In other words, the hostess indemnified her guests against a harsh world. This was accomplished through her menu, her table, her charm. The tradition faded, but its raison d'être hasn't. In the winter, particularly, the host or hostess is bound to comfort, to fortify, and to divert her guests. Lacking a Mary Johnson, we have to plan simpler menus—charm, after all, seems to diminish in direct proportion to a rise in elaboration.

Happily, the ingredients of winter lend themselves to simple, do-ahead dishes such as stews and tians (gratins) and casseroles. And the nature of these dishes can be the handmaiden to the social pining of the cold-weather months: they fortify.

Nevertheless, the hostess of winter walks a precarious line. The company meals most suitable to modern life are overwhelmingly sturdy, which is a nice way of saying potentially dowdy. And this is a time of year when the human soul begs for some reminder of civilization at its most deeply content, little reminders of the comfort inherent in elegance and finesse.

To provide this, a modern hostess can provide an elegant "frame" for a main course like a stew or a casserole, a meal-soup, or a roast. An ornate first course or an elaborate dessert, or both, for instance, can elevate a simple meal. So can a beautifully laid table—this is the best season to polish the silver, putter with flowers, fresh or dried, cut or potted, light the candles, or even to tie ribbons on the napkins. Any embellishment that smacks of care is a gift to guests in the coldest months.

Big crowds are not unknown in the dark months. There are, God forbid, holiday letdown and the Super Bowl. And while buffets can serve a crowd, hearty

198
A Program
for Rational
Entertaining
in an
Irrational
Age

finger food can do the same. But the social mood does seem to move to the table in the wintertime. Smaller and more intimate gatherings are a counterpoint to obligatory holiday entertaining, as well as a reaffirmation of family and of friends.

Bearing all this in mind, as well as the reality of their own lives and their own recovery, the hostesses in the group developed several concepts as well as a few menus to comfort and fortify the guests who arrived bundled and windblown at their door.

Company
in Cold Weather

Nan Does
New Year's Eve

Having finally discovered Ann Taylor and having begun regular pilgrimages to this shrine of young-professional wear, Nan is disconcerted as she begins to experience a certain sort of letdown after shopping binges. Ripples of remorse and pride, satisfaction and frustration, flow through her, and as she considers the mood among her friends before the turn of the year, she can't help wondering if the same feelings don't wend their way into the American psyche right before Christmas and, whipped by the gale force of holiday spirit, rise to tidal-wave proportion within a week.

Perhaps a mass commercial bender is society's way of channeling the emotions that accompany any ending and anticipate any beginning, suggests Mrs. J.

"The cliché crescendo," notes Nan, "is a numbing New Year's bash."

Privately, however, she wonders if, after seeing it all and buying a lot of it, humans lapse into lethargy. Nevertheless, don't underestimate the tough customer at the heart of any late-holiday gathering. Beneath the merriment, whether he appear merry or Grinch-like, the would-be New Year's reveler fundamentally resembles the weary traveler who writes in Jonathan Levi's *A Guide for the Perplexed*: "I've been traveling so long now that no land is new, no ocean fresh. I've seen every flower, every bird, every side of every issue and I have no heart left to lose."

Not an easy guy to divert. But oh, how Nan has tried to nudge like-minded people. In the past, she'd trotted out the glitz and glitter, the caviar and champagne, in a futile attempt to banish the resignation in the been-there-done-that pose.

In fact, the traveler who'd seen it all was weary in his search for the home he'd once had and eventually outlived. His particular fatigue is endemic to a mobile society that places a premium on one generation's distinguishing itself from another through achievement, status, and, most of all, motion. Nan is not a researcher for nothing. She can consider things very, very logically.

Though, of course, being restless for repose isn't something people talk about. Better to stiffen that detached and languid pose than to hint at its soft underbelly. Better to get no kick from champagne, or much of anything else, for that matter.

Having invited thirty friends and business associates to celebrate the New Year at her house, Nan was sure that nonchalance was of paramount importance. With self-effacing apology, she would capture the heart of the holiday season and dare to engage all its paradox. She would begin by serving something zippy and unusual—piping meat broth fortified with sherry, perhaps—or a little-known sparkling Prosecco.

Yes, she thought, hearing Mrs. J.'s voice in her mind, she would use her best china cups and crystal flutes as a decoy to the proletarian nature of her offerings. And she would be thankful that taste, even jaded taste, is one of the easier doors to the soul one can pry. Lacking name-brand familiarity, guests tend to find themselves strangely disinclined to resort to stock chatter. Nan was aware that a mild degree of surprise has a way of leveling social ground.

A small shock in the taste department can also be a wake-up call. Dramatic temperature changes, for instance, like combining hot and cold food, or edibles with a soft texture with those that crunch, surprises the eater into the present tense. Unfamiliar flavors, particularly those of exotic spices or chili peppers, and the acidic flavors of vinegar or mustard, lemon, grapefruit, or lime, do the same trick.

To shock the senses is to marshal attention to the moment. Surprise, after all, has a frisson of danger. For a moment, the possibility of the unknown is evident, the individual universe is reordered, the wits of survival are called to the forefront, and in the time that it takes to accept or reject a nibble, relief is palpable and even the most impassive are, at some level, flushed with a jolt of life.

For a novice like Nan, none of the recipes she chose was a snap. She had a few days off from work, however, could cook each recipe well in advance of company, and found the cooking itself a pleasing way to spend several days at home. She reasoned that had she been more pressed for time (and on several subsequent occasions she was), she could simply have given the recipes to a caterer to be prepared.

Most surprising in the recipes she prepared for her New Year's fête (and repeated several times) is that while they are not life-threateningly rich, they are real, substantial food—something the world-weary haven't seen in several decades, at least not in the more prosperous time zones.

202

A Program
for Rational
Entertaining
in an
Irrational
Age

Herb-Marinated Chicken Wings
Stuffed with Scallion Goat Cheese

These chicken wing hors d'oeuvres can be stuffed and marinated a day before the party. They must be wrapped well and stored in the refrigerator and are at their best if broiled shortly before guests arrive. They can be served sizzling hot or at room temperature.

6 ounces goat cheese, softened
2 scallions, finely chopped
24 chicken wings
3 large cloves garlic, finely chopped
2 tablespoons chopped fresh rosemary
1 teaspoon kosher salt
½ teaspoon freshly ground pepper
½ cup olive oil

1. Stir together the goat cheese and scallions. Separate the chicken wings at the joint and save the tips for another purpose, like stock. Loosen the skin over the top of the remaining portions, making a pocket between the skin and meat. Fill each pocket with about 1 teaspoon of the goat cheese mixture; do not overfill.

2. Combine the garlic, rosemary, salt, pepper, and oil in a large bowl. Add the chicken wings and turn to coat well. Refrigerate for several hours.

3. Preheat the broiler. Place the chicken wings on a broiler pan with a drip tray and broil until the skin is browned and chicken is cooked through, about 8 minutes.

Serves 12 as an hors d'oeuvre

Garlic Oil with Fennel and Parmesan

The garlic oil can be prepared the day before a party, but the fennel will discolor and the Parmesan will dry if they are prepared more than an hour before guests arrive.

1 cup olive oil
4 large cloves garlic, thinly sliced
1½ teaspoons kosher salt
6 small fennel bulbs, trimmed and thinly sliced
6 ounces Parmesan cheese, shaved

1. Heat 2 tablespoons of the oil in a medium saucepan over low heat. Add the garlic and cook, stirring constantly, for 1 minute. Add the remaining oil. Cook for 1 minute. Stir in the salt. Strain the oil into a fondue pot and keep hot.

2. Arrange the fennel on a platter. Let guests dip the fennel slices into the hot garlic oil. Pass bowls of the shaved Parmesan and baskets of Tomato-Cumin Breads (page 209).

Serves 12

204
A Program
for Rational
Entertaining
in an
Irrational
Age

Thai Crab Cakes

The mixture for these cakes can be prepared one or two days before a party, wrapped tightly, and stored in the refrigerator. The cakes can be cooked several hours in advance, drained well, laid on baking sheets, and stored in a 150° F. oven for up to one hour before serving.

1 pound lump crabmeat, picked over for shells
2 cups cooked basmati rice, cold
2 jalapeño peppers, seeded and minced
1 tablespoon grated lemon zest
¼ cup chopped fresh basil
3 tablespoons chopped fresh mint
2 teaspoons kosher salt
½ teaspoon freshly ground pepper
2 large eggs, lightly beaten
¼ cup dry bread crumbs
About 2 tablespoons olive oil

1. In a large bowl, gently combine the crabmeat, rice, jalapeños, lemon zest, basil, and mint. Carefully stir in the salt, pepper, eggs, and bread crumbs, breaking up the crabmeat as little as possible. Using 1 tablespoon of the mixture for each one, press into cakes that are a scant 2 inches in diameter.

2. Heat 1 tablespoon of oil in a large nonstick skillet over medium heat. Working in batches, cook the crab cakes until nicely browned and firm, about 1½ minutes per side. Add more oil to the skillet as needed between batches. Serve hot.

Serves 12

Spicy Shrimp, Bacon, and Date Skewers

These skewers can be assembled the day before the party, wrapped and refrigerated, and then cooked just before guests arrive. They can be stored briefly in a 150° F. oven, but the shrimp is at high risk of overcooking, so it is best to serve them immediately.

1 tablespoon ground cumin
¼ teaspoon cayenne
¼ cup fresh lemon juice
¼ cup olive oil
36 large shrimp, peeled and deveined
18 pitted dates, halved crosswise
18 strips bacon, halved crosswise

1. Place the cumin and cayenne in a small heavy skillet over low heat and stir constantly for 2 minutes. Place in a large bowl and whisk in the lemon juice and olive oil. Add the shrimp and toss to coat well. Cover and refrigerate for 2 hours.

2. Place 1 piece of date in the curve of 1 piece of shrimp, wrap a piece of bacon around the shrimp, and secure all together with a toothpick. Repeat with the remaining ingredients.

3. Preheat the broiler. Place the skewers on a broiler pan with a drip tray and broil until the shrimp are just cooked through, about 1½ minutes per side. Serve hot or at room temperature.

Serves 12 as an hors d'oeuvre

206

A Program
for Rational
Entertaining
in an
Irrational
Age

White Bean Croquettes Stuffed with Mozzarella and Tomato

These croquettes can be prepared, formed, and set on baking sheets the day before a party, wrapped well, and stored in the refrigerator. They should be cooked just before guests arrive and are best served immediately—and hot.

3 (19-ounce) cans cannellini beans, drained and rinsed
3 cloves garlic, chopped
2½ teaspoons kosher salt
½ teaspoon freshly ground pepper
9 tablespoons plus ¾ cup dry bread crumbs
About 42 (¼-inch) cubes cold fresh mozzarella
About 42 (¼-inch) pieces of sun-dried tomato
Vegetable oil for deep frying

1. Puree the beans, garlic, salt, and pepper in a food processor. Stir in 9 tablespoons of bread crumbs and refrigerate several hours, until firm.

2. Form the mixture into balls, using a slightly rounded tablespoon for each one. Press 1 piece of mozzarella and 1 piece of tomato into the center of each and reshape into a ball. Coat with the remaining bread crumbs.

3. Working in batches, deep-fry the balls until nicely browned (it is important to keep the oil around 365 degrees). Drain on paper towels. Serve hot.

Serves 12

Middle Eastern Lamb-Stuffed Wontons

Wonton skins are available in most supermarkets or by mail order from Vwajimaya (see page 275). This Middle Eastern variation on the Asian theme can be shaped and set on baking sheets the day before a party, wrapped, and stored in the refrigerator. The wontons should be cooked just before guests arrive and are best served hot.

¾ pound ground lamb
2½ teaspoons ground coriander
¾ teaspoon ground cinnamon
2¼ teaspoons kosher salt
¾ teaspoon freshly ground pepper
3 tablespoons golden raisins
3 tablespoons coarsely chopped pistachios
36 wonton skins (3×3¼ inches)
Vegetable oil for deep frying

1. Mix together the lamb, coriander, cinnamon, salt, pepper, raisins, and pistachios until well combined. Brush the edges of 1 of the wonton skins with water. Place 1½ teaspoons of the filling in the center. Bring the 4 corners of the skin together over the filling and press the edges together to seal tight. Repeat with the remaining skins and filling.

2. Working in batches, deep-fry the wontons until nicely browned. Make sure the oil is not too hot or the skins will brown before the filling is cooked through. Drain on paper towels and serve immediately.

Serves 12

A Program
for Rational
Entertaining
in an
Irrational
Age

Tomato-Cumin Breads

These breads can be made up to two days before a party if left in one piece, wrapped very, very well, and stored at room temperature. They should be warmed before serving to bring out the spice and flavor.

3¼ cups plus 2 tablespoons all-purpose flour
3 teaspoons kosher salt
1½ cups water
¼ pound (1 stick) unsalted butter, softened
6 oil-packed sun-dried tomatoes, well drained
½ teaspoon cumin seeds
Freshly ground pepper to taste

1. Combine the 3¼ cups flour and 1½ teaspoons of the salt in a mixing bowl, add the water, and stir until the mixture forms a dough. Turn out onto a lightly floured surface and knead until smooth. Place in a clean bowl, cover, and let stand 1 hour.

2. Meanwhile, puree the butter, the remaining 1½ teaspoons salt, the tomatoes, the cumin seeds, and pepper in a food processor. Set aside.

3. Divide the dough into 12 pieces. Place on a floured surface and flatten each piece with the palm of your hand. Cover all but 1 piece with plastic wrap; do not stack. Roll 1 piece of the dough into a 5½- to 6-inch circle. Spread with a rounded ½ teaspoon of the butter (leftover butter can be frozen).

4. Roll the dough up tightly, like a jelly roll, making a long rope-like strip. Starting at one end, tightly coil the strip, pressing the other end into the coil to make an even round. Gently flatten with your palm, then roll the dough back into a 5½-inch circle. Repeat with the remaining dough, refrigerating the finished ones on a baking sheet lined with baking parchment if your kitchen is warm.

5. Heat a large cast-iron skillet or griddle over medium heat. Working in batches, cook the breads until browned and cooked through, about 1½ to 2 minutes per side. Cut into quarters and serve hot.

Serves 12

Johanna Gives Casseroles Style and Verve

Johanna's compulsion to wow and woo wasn't, she realized, entirely a bad thing. Rather, the urge had gotten a little too pronounced, isolating her in the end, leaving her alone with all of her own perfection and effort, marooned from her guests. The desire to impress guests is part of the hospitable impulse; if restrained to a realistic time frame and budget, the desire to dazzle could create some magical moments. Especially in the winter.

The popularity of one-pot dishes—and all the attendant, oven-to-table cookware, ranging from glazed clay pots that are perfect for tians to enameled crocks that accommodate stews—made it easier for Johanna to accept the practicality of entertaining with stews and casseroles.

Obviously, she was no novice at elevating stew. Her deep regard for the slow process of assembling and simmering a stew, for the benefit of allowing a stew to rest and ripen, giving its flavors a chance to deepen and marry, were second nature to Johanna. So was creating an elegant ambience by surrounding a one-pot dish with other courses that exuded finesse.

As she relaxed and was more present to her guests, however, she began to notice that guests have anxiety, too. This fact had escaped her notice in the years in which she worried over the precise flicker of a candle and endeavored to make each dish she served worthy of three Michelin stars. But as she mastered the do-ahead form and found confidence in her concepts—be it a homey stew or a sophisticated salad bar—rather than in the details of her "performance," Johanna noticed occasional tics and twitches in her guests. The covert peek into the kitchen did not escape her, either.

She began to think that, especially in the winter, actual hunger prompts fidgets in a guest. For this reason she began to serve her stew first, followed by a smaller, sprightly course, and then dessert. By flouting the traditional progression, Johanna found, she curtailed the what's-for-dinner worry that guests bring to dinner parties.

In addition, guests didn't need to reserve appetite for a potentially heavier or more desirable course to come. This edginess was further softened by either announcing the course that would follow or displaying the courses to come. Some meals required an exquisite after-stew course; for others, she laid out a salad buffet. Both techniques, she found, soothed her guests and stoked an anticipation that was not rooted solely in appetite.

By allowing guests to serve themselves in the kitchen or from a buffet, the host not only is relieved of busboy duties but also provides guests a glimpse of the rest of the menu that can soothe and stoke feelings of anticipation.

Casseroles, though indicative of the time constraints of modern life, posed an aesthetic problem to Johanna. How to escape even a hint that she was serving "everyday" or "convenience" food or, God forbid, some throwback to the fifties.

Just as "stews" were redeemed in public opinion by giving them the mystique of the unfamiliar—consider, for instance, the difference between "beef stew" and "boeuf en daube"—casseroles that were surprising or unfamiliar or far-flung could evoke Ye Olde Village Baker's Oven rather than some generic macaroni and cheese. Is a lasagne just a lasagne if it contains pungent wild mushrooms and is baked in a fluted tart pan? Is chicken baked under a spoonbread crust just another chicken pot pie?

Johanna thought not. She was quite inspired by the French word *tian*, the ovenproof earthenware dish that is used to make gratins. In France, any gratin made in a tian, be it potatoes baked with cream or artichokes baked with anchovies, can be called a tian. In Corsica, a tian is a clay pot used to make

Johanna
Gives Casseroles
Style and Verve

ragouts. In either case, to Johanna's ear, the difference between a tian and a casserole was tantamount to the difference between baked beans and cassoulet.

The tian conceit fired her imagination, and she found it was not much different from the one-pot concept: by its nature, the dish is rustic and hearty. It needs an elegant flank.

An unexpected benefit to serving the main course first, she found, was that it limited the number of dirty dishes. So enchanted were Johanna and Mark with the notion of a single dishwasher load that they used as the underliner for the first course the serving plate for the second course.

Of course, different hosts and hostesses derive inner peace from different things. As a cook, Johanna is soothed by the process of creating a one-pot dish. And recently both she and Mark have been impressed by how a do-ahead meal that is sumptuous and rustic sets a casual, openhearted tone for an evening at home with guests.

Analyzing the situation, Mark, who once studied literature, though he's made his name designing delivery systems for health-maintenance organizations, and much of his money from distributing Johanna's documentary films, said that the process of cooking a one-pot meal anchors Johanna as well as himself and, in turn, their guests to the taste and mood of winter. He calls cold-weather one-pot dinners "culinary transcendentalism," an antidote to a climate-controlled world.

The couple acknowledges, however, that friends of theirs who are scared to cook or shy of time find that ordering a stew or a casserole is more pacific than puttering in the kitchen. They themselves hire someone to help serve and clear from time to time. The extra body provides a psychic cushion for some evenings.

The best hosts are those who recognize what they *like* to do and do well. Some people cook, some set a pretty table, some select arcane wine or have a genius for choreographing an evening's music. Do what you do best and minimize the rest.

212

A Program
for Rational
Entertaining
in an
Irrational
Age

Oven-Dried Tomato Tian with Creamy Limas and Goat Cheese

The tomatoes for this dish can be dried up to one week before the party, wrapped tightly and stored in the refrigerator. The tian itself, however, is best baked just before guests arrive.

This vegetable-centric main course would be well served by a sprightly salad such as the Salad Greens with Roasted Peppers and Seared Wild Mushrooms (page 150) or the Chicken Timbale (page 246) or the Chickpea-Lamb Cakes with Red Pepper Sauce (page 176). The Spicy Shrimp, Bacon, and Date Skewers (page 206) would make a wonderful accompaniment to this dish if served on a bed of lightly dressed greens.

7 tablespoons olive oil
4½ pounds plum tomatoes, cored and halved lengthwise
2½ teaspoons kosher salt
¾ teaspoon freshly ground pepper
1 teaspoon dried thyme
3 (10-ounce) packages frozen lima beans
½ cup heavy cream
8 cups 1-inch bread cubes from good country-style bread
8 ounces goat cheese
2 tablespoons coarsely chopped Italian parsley

1. Preheat the oven to 200° F. Using a pastry brush and 1 tablespoon of the olive oil, lightly coat the skin side of each tomato half. Place skin side down on 2 baking sheets. Sprinkle with 1 teaspoon of the salt and ¼ teaspoon of the pepper. Bake until the tomatoes shrink to about ¼ of their original size, about 4 to 6 hours; they should remain soft and juicy. Let cool. Sprinkle with the thyme.

2. Cook the lima beans as directed on the package; they should be quite soft. Drain and place in a food processor with 3 tablespoons of the olive oil, the cream, and the remaining 1½ teaspoons salt and ½ teaspoon pepper. Process until smooth.

3. Preheat the oven to 350° F. Place the bread cubes in the bottom of a 12×3½-inch round clay casserole dish. Toss with the remaining 3 tablespoons olive oil. Bake until the bread is toasted, tossing twice, about 20 minutes.

4. Top the bread with the dried tomatoes. Crumble the goat cheese over the tomatoes. Spread the bean puree over the goat cheese. (The tian can be prepared a few hours ahead up to this point; bring to room temperature before baking.) Cover with aluminum foil and bake until heated through, about 45 minutes. Garnish with parsley and serve immediately.

Serves 6

Stewed Lamb Shanks with White Beans and Rosemary

The Salad Greens with Roasted Peppers and Seared Wild Mushrooms (page 150) makes a wonderful second course for this husky-flavored, full-bodied stew. For a more elegant meal, Vanilla Pots de Crème with Chocolate Sauce (page 169) is a lovely complement.

8 meaty lamb shanks, about 1 pound each (have your butcher saw off most
    of the exposed bone)
4 teaspoons kosher salt, plus more to taste
1½ teaspoons freshly ground pepper
2 teaspoons olive oil
5 large cloves garlic, minced
1 large onion, diced

214

A Program
for Rational
Entertaining
in an
Irrational
Age

4 medium carrots, diced

3 celery stalks, diced

1 cup dry red wine

1 (28-ounce) can whole plum tomatoes packed in tomato puree

1 pound dried Great Northern beans, soaked in water overnight and drained

8 cups chicken broth, homemade, or low-sodium canned

3 sprigs fresh rosemary

2 bay leaves

1. Season the shanks with 1 teaspoon of the salt and ½ teaspoon of the pepper. Heat the olive oil in a heavy large skillet over medium-high heat. Add as many shanks as will fit without crowding. Brown the shanks well on all sides, about 10 minutes per batch. Set the browned shanks aside and repeat with the remaining shanks, pouring off the fat between batches.

2. Place the garlic, onion, carrots, and celery in the skillet and sauté until softened, about 10 minutes. Pour in the wine and cook for about 2 minutes, scraping the bottom of the skillet with a wooden spoon to loosen any browned bits.

3. Transfer the vegetable-and-wine mixture to a large stockpot. Add the tomatoes and use the back of a spoon to break them up into bite-size chunks. Add the remaining ingredients, including the shanks, and season with the remaining 3 teaspoons salt and remaining 1 teaspoon pepper. Bring to a boil. Reduce heat and simmer, skimming as necessary, until the lamb and beans are very tender, about 2 hours. If the lamb is done before the beans, take out the shanks and cover them with foil to keep them warm until the beans are done.

4. Skim off as much fat from the top of the liquid as possible and remove bay leaves. Use tongs to remove the shanks from the liquid, placing 1 shank on each of 8 plates. Season the bean mixture with additional salt if needed. Using a slotted spoon, arrange some of the beans and vegetables around each shank. Spoon some of the liquid over and around the shank and serve immediately.

Serves 8

Tangy Beef Stew

Elizabeth ate a stew like this at Auberge de la Madone in France, and over the years, she adapted the recipe for American ingredients. Her version uses orange oil, which underscores the winter flavor of the meal, rather than fresh orange juice. (Orange oil is available in gourmet stores or by mail order through the Williams-Sonoma Company, page 275.) The stew can be made up to three days before a party and reheated gently over very low heat before serving. It can be served with rice, potatoes, couscous, or pasta.

The Romaine and Walnut Salad with Roasted Shallot Vinaigrette (page 162) with the Pumpernickel-Sage Croutons and Stilton (page 163) is a fitting counterpoint that guests can build themselves after this stew. If, however, you wish to set a more elegant note, you might consider serving the White Bean Cakes with Goat Cheese and Wilted Chicory (page 244) as the second course. In either case, the meal is a filling one and seems best accompanied by a light dessert such as Elizabeth's Pistachio-Pear Strudel (page 252).

4 pounds stewing beef, a combination of beef round and beef chuck cut into 4-ounce chunks

4 carrots, cut into rounds

3 medium onions, coarsely chopped

2 cloves garlic

1 sprig Italian parsley

1 rib celery, chopped

3 bay leaves

1 teaspoon dried thyme

¼ cup cognac

5 cups spicy red wine, such as California Zinfandel

4 tablespoons olive oil

1 teaspoon whole black peppercorns

3 cloves

1 tablespoon tomato paste

2 tablespoons unsalted butter

1 pound shiitake mushrooms, stemmed

216

A Program
for Rational
Entertaining
in an
Irrational
Age

Kosher salt and freshly ground pepper to taste
Grated zest of 1 orange
2 tablespoons orange oil

1. Combine the meat, carrots, onions, garlic, parsley, celery, bay leaves, thyme, and cognac and half of the red wine and 1 tablespoon of the olive oil in a large bowl. Tie the peppercorns and cloves in a piece of cheesecloth, add to the bowl, and refrigerate overnight, stirring occasionally so that it marinates well.

2. Bring the meat and vegetables to room temperature. Use a slotted spoon to remove the meat from the marinade. Drain well, pat dry, and set aside. Strain the liquid into a large ovenproof casserole, add the cheesecloth bag, and set the vegetables aside.

3. Add the remaining wine to the pot and bring the liquid to a boil. Boil for 5 minutes, remove from heat, stir in the tomato paste, and set aside.

4. In a large skillet, melt 1 tablespoon of the butter in the remaining 2 tablespoons of olive oil over high heat. When hot, add the beef and sear each piece on each side in batches as space allows. Transfer the meat to the casserole when brown.

5. Add the remaining tablespoon butter and olive oil to the skillet. Add the reserved vegetables and sauté until browned, about 7 minutes. Transfer the vegetables to the casserole. Add the mushrooms to the skillet and sauté until brown, about 5 minutes; set aside.

6. Bring the liquid in the casserole to a simmer over medium heat. Reduce the heat to very low and simmer, skimming occasionally, until the meat is very tender, about 3½ to 4 hours. Stir in salt and pepper to taste. Add the mushrooms, orange zest, and orange oil.

Serves 8

Sweet Potato Tian with
Spiced Shrimp and Prosciutto

This tian can be made the day before a party, wrapped tightly, stored in the refrigerator, and gently reheated in a 200-degree oven for one hour before serving. It tastes best, however, and the shrimp remain most succulent, if the tian is assembled and stored in the refrigerator unbaked and then baked immediately before guests arrive.

The casserole could be followed with the Romaine and Walnut Salad with Roasted Shallot Vinaigrette (page 162), topped with the Pumpernickel-Sage Croutons and Stilton (page 163); with the White Bean Croquettes Stuffed with Mozzarella and Tomato (page 207), garnished with a green salad; or with the White Bean Cakes with Goat Cheese and Wilted Chicory (page 244). Any of the choices will render a satisfying meal that is deceptively light in character.

For this reason, you may want a rich dessert such as Mr. D.'s Chocolate Silk Pie (page 250) or Eliza J.'s Pecan Cake with Caramel Sauce (page 254).

¼ cup plus 1 tablespoon olive oil

6 medium sweet potatoes (about 4 pounds), peeled and cut into ⅛-inch slices

4¼ teaspoons kosher salt

freshly ground pepper

3 medium red onions, thinly sliced

1½ cups dry white wine

¼ cup dry sherry

¼ cup fresh lemon juice

1 teaspoon crushed red pepper

¼ teaspoon cayenne

2½ pounds jumbo shrimp, shelled and deveined

½ pound thinly sliced prosciutto, trimmed of excess fat, cut across into
    thirds

1 cup coarse fresh bread crumbs

1 tablespoon chopped Italian parsley

1. Preheat the oven to 350° F. Brush the 1 tablespoon olive oil over the bottom of a 12×3½-inch round clay casserole dish. Layer ⅓ of the sweet potatoes in

218

A Program
for Rational
Entertaining
in an
Irrational
Age

the dish, overlapping the slices slightly. Season with ¾ teaspoon of salt and pepper to taste. Scatter ⅓ of the onions over the sweet potatoes.

2. Repeat with the remaining sweet potatoes and onions, seasoning each layer of potatoes with ¾ teaspoon salt and pepper to taste. Combine the wine and sherry and pour over the top. Cover with aluminum foil and bake until the potatoes are tender, about 1 hour.

3. Meanwhile, in a bowl, combine the lemon juice, the ¼ cup of olive oil, 1½ teaspoons salt, pepper to taste, the crushed red pepper, and the cayenne. Add the shrimp and toss to coat. Refrigerate until ready to use.

4. Scatter the prosciutto pieces over the sweet potato mixture. Top with the shrimp. Bake, uncovered, until the shrimp are just cooked through, about 16 minutes. Combine the bread crumbs with the parsley, the remaining ½ teaspoon salt, and pepper to taste. Sprinkle the crumbs over the shrimp and place under the broiler until lightly browned, about 2 minutes. Serve immediately.

Serves 6

Pasta, Potato, and Green Bean Bake with Basil Cream and Parmesan

This tian can be made the day before entertaining, wrapped well, and stored in the refrigerator and then warmed in a 250-degree oven for 40 minutes before guests arrive.

The dish is a deconstructed pasta with pesto. For this reason, you will want to provide a cheese-dominant second course such as the White Bean Cakes with Goat Cheese and Wilted Chicory (page 244), or if you wish to change the mood from substantive to something more frivolous, serve the Herb-Marinated Chicken Wings Stuffed with Scallion Goat Cheese (page 203) on a bed of lightly dressed greens. To strike a strong vegetable note, the Stilton-Walnut Rice Balls (page 185), served on a salad of bitter greens, would make a fine intermezzo for this dish.

Any of these options will make for a hearty meal, so a light dessert seems in order. Elizabeth's Pistachio-Pear Strudel (page 252), the Panna Cotta (page 83), or the Caramel Orange Fool (page 128) all fit that bill. So does fresh exotic fruit, sliced and served with a smattering of fresh mint.

1½ pounds lasagne noodles
2 cups packed fresh basil leaves
¾ cup plus 2 tablespoons olive oil
1½ cups heavy cream
5 teaspoons kosher salt
1¼ teaspoons freshly ground pepper, plus more as needed
1½ pounds green beans, trimmed
2 pounds small red potatoes, thinly sliced
¾ cup toasted pine nuts
¾ cup freshly grated Parmesan cheese

1. Bring a large pot of water to a boil. Salt the water, add the noodles, and cook until al dente. Meanwhile, place the basil and the ¾ cup olive oil in a food processor and process until combined. Add the cream, 3 teaspoons salt and 1 teaspoon pepper and process until smooth. Drain the pasta, rinse, and drain well again. Place in a large bowl, add the basil cream, and toss well. Set aside.

220

A Program
for Rational
Entertaining
in an
Irrational
Age

2. Blanch the green beans in boiling water until crisp-tender, about 8 minutes. Drain well. Place in a bowl and toss with 1 tablespoon of olive oil, 1 teaspoon salt, and ¼ teaspoon pepper. Set aside. Blanch the potato slices in boiling water until just tender, about 4 minutes. Drain well. Place in a bowl and toss with the remaining 1 tablespoon olive oil, the remaining 1 teaspoon salt, and pepper to taste.

3. Preheat the oven to 350° F. Place ⅓ of the noodle mixture in the bottom of a 12 × 3½-inch round clay casserole dish. Top with ½ of the green beans and then ½ of the potatoes. Sprinkle with ⅓ of the pine nuts and ⅓ of the Parmesan. Repeat the layers. Top with the remaining noodles, then the nuts and Parmesan. (The tian can be prepared to this point up to a day ahead; bring to room temperature before baking.) Cover tightly with aluminum foil and bake for 1 hour. Serve immediately.

Serves 6

Provençale Vegetable Gratin with Feta and Croutons

This gratin itself can be half-baked the day before a party, wrapped well, refrigerated, and finished shortly before guests arrive. The Chicken Timbale (page 246) is a willing (and able) candidate for a first course. Seafood, as well, would provide the sort of lift that would allow this main course to soar. The Spicy Shrimp, Bacon, and Date Skewers (page 206), if served on a bed of lightly dressed greens, is another appetizing option.

While it is reminiscent of the texture of the main-course gratin, Nan's Apple Pandowdy (page 256) makes a fabulous rustic accompaniment to this dish. For a more elaborate note, you might consider Johanna's Chocolate Swirl Banana Cream Pie (page 251) or Eliza J.'s Pecan Cake with Caramel Sauce (page 254). For something lighter and more elegant, the Poached Pears, Figs, and Oranges with Clove Granité and Hazelnut-Chocolate Cookies (page 170) would complement this meal well.

6 cups large bread cubes from good, country-style bread

5 tablespoons olive oil

3 *each* red, yellow, and green bell peppers, cut into large squares

2 teaspoons kosher salt, plus more to taste

½ teaspoon freshly ground pepper, plus more to taste

8 small zucchini, cut across into ¼-inch slices

12 large plum tomatoes, cored and quartered

2 medium eggplants, cut across into ¼-inch slices

3 cups crumbled feta cheese

2 tablespoons chopped fresh thyme

1. Preheat the oven to 350° F. Place the bread cubes in the bottom of a 12×3½-inch round clay casserole dish. Toss with 2 tablespoons of the olive oil. Bake until the bread is toasted, tossing twice, about 15 minutes. Take out of the pan and set aside.

2. Place the peppers in a bowl and toss with 1 tablespoon olive oil, 1 teaspoon salt, and ¼ teaspoon pepper. Place the zucchini in a bowl and toss with 1 tablespoon

222

A Program
for Rational
Entertaining
in an
Irrational
Age

olive oil, 1 teaspoon salt, and ¼ teaspoon pepper. Place the tomatoes in a bowl and toss with 1 tablespoon olive oil, 1 teaspoon salt, and ¼ teaspoon pepper.

3. Arrange half of the eggplant in the bottom of the dish, overlapping the slices slightly. Season with salt and pepper to taste. Top with half of the peppers, half of the croutons, ¾ cup of the cheese, 1 tablespoon thyme, half of the zucchini, and then half of the tomatoes. Repeat the layers; the dish will be very full, but the vegetables will cook down.

4. Cover tightly with aluminum foil. For a crisper mixture, bake until vegetables are tender, about 2½ hours. For a very soft, melded mixture, bake for 3 hours 15 minutes. (The tian can be baked halfway the day ahead, refrigerated, and then completed before serving.) Serve, passing the remaining cheese to sprinkle on top.

Serves 6

Southwestern Chicken Pie
with Cheddar Spoonbread Crust

This dish can be made ahead of time, wrapped well, stored in the refrigerator, and warmed for 45 minutes in a 250-degree oven before guests arrive, but it is at its best if assembled and baked just before serving—the chicken remains moist and the spoonbread is delicately crisped.

In any guise, this is an American meal. Because of the richness of this pie, you might want to consider following it with a salad such as Salad Greens with Roasted Peppers and Seared Wild Mushrooms (page 150). A green salad embellished with a little color (some strips of roasted peppers, some grated carrots) would do just as well. There is an out-on-the-plains feel to this dish, a sense of the campfire. This can be underscored by a dessert such as Nan's Apple Pandowdy (page 256) or thrown into question by Mr. D.'s Chocolate Silk Pie (page 250).

To mitigate the heaviness of this dish, Panna Cotta (page 83) would do the trick.

THE FILLING

2 tablespoons olive oil

2½ pounds boneless and skinless chicken thighs, cut into 1-inch cubes

2½ teaspoons kosher salt

¾ teaspoon freshly ground pepper

2 medium onions, diced

3 cups diced carrots (¼-inch dice)

3 ribs celery, diced

2 jalapeño peppers, seeded and minced

3 cups chicken broth, homemade, or low-sodium canned

8 cups shiitake mushroom pieces (1-inch pieces)

1½ teaspoons ground cumin

½ teaspoon cayenne

2 tablespoons all-purpose flour

THE CRUST

3 cups water

2½ teaspoons kosher salt

224

A Program
for Rational
Entertaining
in an
Irrational
Age

1½ cups yellow cornmeal

3 tablespoons unsalted butter

3 large eggs, separated

1 cup milk

1½ teaspoons baking powder

Dash of freshly ground pepper

½ cup grated Cheddar cheese

2 large scallions, thinly sliced

1. To make the pie filling, heat 1 tablespoon olive oil in a large skillet over medium-high heat. Add half the chicken and sear until browned, about 5 minutes. Place in a 12×3½-inch round clay casserole dish. Add 1 teaspoon oil to the skillet and brown the remaining chicken. Place in the dish. Season the chicken with 1 teaspoon salt and ¼ teaspoon pepper.

2. Place 2 teaspoons oil in the skillet, lower the heat slightly, and add the onions, carrots, celery, and jalapeños. Sauté for 8 minutes. Add 1 cup broth and stir, scraping up any browned bits stuck to the bottom of the skillet. Stir in the mushrooms and cook for 5 minutes. Stir the vegetable mixture into the chicken. Stir in the remaining broth, the cumin, the cayenne, 1½ teaspoons salt, and ½ teaspoon pepper. Stir ¼ cup of the liquid into the flour, then stir the mixture back into the stew. Set aside.

3. Preheat the oven to 400° F. To make the spoonbread crust, bring the water to a boil in a medium saucepan. Add the 2½ teaspoons salt. Whisking constantly, pour in the cornmeal in a slow, steady stream. Whisk for 20 seconds and remove from the heat. Place in a large bowl, mix in the butter, and let cool. In another bowl, whisk together the egg yolks, milk, baking powder, and a dash of pepper. Gradually stir the egg mixture into the cornmeal mixture. Stir in the cheese and scallions. Whip the egg whites until stiff but not dry. Fold into the cornmeal mixture. Spread the spoonbread over the chicken mixture and bake until the bread is cooked through, about 45 minutes. Serve hot.

Serves 6

Nan Makes Broth,
the Guests Embellish

Nan was amazed. Without meaning to, she'd learned how to cook. No, that's not the way to phrase it. She was in the process of becoming a cook, and that process was informed by her (previous) lack of expertise and her (global, so there, she admitted it) health concerns. The fact that she works as a medical researcher and has two young children was probably the single most important factor in how she approached cooking. Circumstance forced her to cook ahead. The slender windows of leisure available to her helped her fight her chemist's tendency to follow recipes diligently, helped her to approach cooking as recreation.

Not everyday cooking, of course. It is foolhardy, she thinks, to imagine that getting the daily meal on the table is leisurely or fun. But cooking for company is something else entirely. She realized this one weekend when, on Mr. D.'s orders, she made her first beef broth. There was something soothing about tossing the ingredients in a pot and allowing heat to do its magic.

Having made and frozen vast quantities of beef broth, she conjured up a notion of a company meal in which company could be served a bowl of steaming broth and various add-ins could be passed, family-style, allowing guests to design a meal to suit their taste. Over the winter, the group tried variations of Nan's concept—always with great success.

In addition to the fact that they have become stylish lately, they found that soups, as the centerpiece of a dinner party or a family meal, have an enduring sort of logic.

It is the rare winter chill that persists in the face of a well-made soup. Obviously, warmth is a major factor. But the generous spirit that guides the hand of a soup-making cook also seems to preside over dinner parties at which soup is at the center. The perfume that lingers after hours of simmering broth, the steam that covers kitchen and dining-room windows, the calm that enters the cook's soul when dinner is something that has been built over a few days and requires warming, not last-minute panic, set a mood of easy intimacy.

The recipes they crafted, for instance, require either chicken or beef broth, which can be made in large quantities and frozen in small plastic containers for up to a month before using. For those immune to the charms of a simmering broth, low-sodium canned broth can be used, though increasingly, butcher shops, high-quality groceries, and specialty food stores sell rich, homemade chicken and beef broth that provide more body and deeper flavor than standard commercial ones.

Once the cook has established the medium—broth—most of the components of these soups can be made well before guests arrive.

With soup as a main course, interesting breads and a fabulous dessert are needed to round out the meal. These can be made ahead of time from favorite recipes, or they can be bought.

Since the soups are all designed for family-style serving, requiring guests to add garnishes to their own appetite and taste, serving an elegant dessert—slices of cake or pie, nicely garnished, for instance, or individual custards or soufflés—leaves guests with the sense that they were coddled and catered to.

The bounty—as well as the bold and alluring flavors—of the ingredients laid out on her table seemed to divert guests from recognizing that the soups she served over the winter were paragons of dietary virtue. Nan was gratified that her personality and her concerns were embodied by the meals.

"Real cooking," Mr. D. had said, "is when the food mirrors the cook; it's deeply intimate and quite seductive, my dear." Nan, who is rather shy, heard the compliment and was as pleased as she had been when her chemistry professor noted her fastidiousness. She blushed.

Beet Soup with Greens, Apple Salad, and Cilantro-Walnut Pesto

The soup and the cilantro pesto can be made up to one week before a party, wrapped tightly, and stored in the refrigerator. The beet greens can also be made several hours before guests arrive, but longer resting will affect the color of the dish, as the beets themselves will weep and the greens will turn an unappetizing brown. The apple salad should be made no more than one hour before guests arrive; otherwise, the apples will discolor. Nonfat Yogurt or Yogurt Cheese (page 117) can be substituted for the sour cream to make a lighter version of the soup.

Served with slabs of dark rye and pumpernickel bread or with the Caramelized-Onion Biscuits (page 231), this soup is hearty enough to make a full meal. For a longer and more elaborate evening, the Thai Crab Cakes (page 205) or the Spicy Shrimp, Bacon, and Date Skewers (page 206) would be lovely, though each would be best served on a bed of lightly dressed greens. The Chicken Timbale (page 246) is another dish that could round out this meal nicely.

Mr. D.'s Chocolate Silk Pie (page 250) is a rich and wonderful way to end this meal. Nan's Apple Pandowdy (page 256) is a more rustic option, and the apple flavor weaves an invisible thread that connects the meal, course to course. Eliza J.'s Pecan Cake with Caramel Sauce (page 254) could make a lovely ending to the meal as well.

THE SOUP

15 medium beets, trimmed, greens reserved
10 cups Beef Broth (page 230)
Kosher salt and freshly ground pepper to taste
1½ teaspoons fresh lemon juice

THE BEET GREENS

1 tablespoon olive oil
Beet greens (see above), stemmed and coarsely chopped
⅓ cup water
½ teaspoon kosher salt
Dash freshly ground pepper
1 teaspoon fresh lemon juice

228
A Program
for Rational
Entertaining
in an
Irrational
Age

1 tablespoon olive oil

2 medium onions, halved and thinly sliced

1 large Granny Smith apple, peeled, cored, and grated

1½ teaspoons walnut oil

1 tablespoon fresh lemon juice

¼ cup coarsely chopped Italian parsley

½ teaspoon kosher salt

Freshly ground pepper to taste

THE PESTO

3 cups cilantro leaves

¾ cup whole walnuts, toasted

½ cup olive oil

¾ teaspoon kosher salt

1½ teaspoons fresh lemon juice

Sour cream

1. To make the soup, place the beets and broth in a large pot. Bring to a boil. Reduce heat, cover, and simmer until tender, about 1 hour. Drain, reserving broth. When cool enough to handle, slip the skins off the beets. Set aside 2 beets. Place half of the remaining beets in a food processor. Measure the broth and add enough water, if necessary, to make 9 cups. Add half of the broth to the beets in the food processor and puree until smooth. Repeat with remaining beets and broth. Combine the batches and season with salt and pepper. Reheat before serving and stir in the lemon juice.

2. To make the beet greens, heat 1½ teaspoons oil in a large skillet over medium heat. Add the beet greens and sauté for 10 minutes. Add water, cover, and cook until tender, about 10 minutes more. Coarsely grate the reserved beets and stir into the greens with 1½ teaspoons oil, ½ teaspoon salt, a dash of pepper, and the lemon juice. Set aside.

3. To make the apple salad, heat the oil in a medium nonstick skillet over medium heat. Add the onions and cook, stirring often, until caramelized, about 15 minutes. Stir in the apple, walnut oil, lemon juice, parsley, salt, and pepper. Set aside.

4. To make the pesto, place the cilantro, walnuts, and olive oil in a food processor and process until smooth. Add the salt and lemon juice.

5. Place the beet-green mixture, the apple mixture, the pesto, and the sour cream in separate bowls. Ladle the soup into bowls. Serve, passing the condiments separately.

Serves 6

Beef Broth

This broth can be prepared in very large quantities, cooled, de-fatted, and frozen in quart-size containers for up to two months before serving. It makes a soulful base to a variety of soups and stews. It can also be used to breathe new life into leftover meat.

5 pounds beef short ribs
2 medium onions, chopped
2 carrots, chopped
2 ribs celery, chopped
4 quarts water
2 cloves garlic, chopped
1 cup dry red wine
1 tablespoon kosher salt

Preheat oven to 400° F. Divide the ribs, onions, carrots, and celery between 2 large roasting pans and roast, stirring twice, for 30 minutes. Transfer to a stockpot and add the water and garlic. Deglaze the roasting pan with the wine and add to the pot. Bring to a boil. Lower heat and simmer, skimming as needed, for 2 hours. Strain, reserving the ribs and discarding the vegetables. Degrease the broth and stir in the salt. When cool enough to handle, pull the meat off the bones, cut into large chunks, and save for another use, or use in soup.

Makes about 12 cups

230
A Program
for Rational
Entertaining
in an
Irrational
Age

Caramelized-Onion Biscuits

These biscuits are a lovely counterpoint to winter salads or to almost any winter soup. They are rich enough to turn a soup into a meal, and the caramelized onions lend a winter flavor as well as substance to the buttery biscuits. They can be made up to three days before serving and stored in an airtight container at room temperature, but they are most irresistible fresh from the oven, and for this reason you may want to make the batter four or five hours before, store it in the refrigerator, and bake the biscuits after the guests have arrived.

4 tablespoons cold unsalted butter, cut in ½-inch pieces
1 medium onion, halved and thinly sliced
2 cups all-purpose flour, plus more for shaping
1 tablespoon baking powder
¾ teaspoon kosher salt
¼ teaspoon freshly ground pepper
3 tablespoons vegetable shortening
½ cup milk

1. Heat 2 teaspoons of the butter in a medium skillet over medium heat. Add the onions and cook, stirring often, until caramelized, about 20 minutes. Let cool and coarsely chop.

2. Preheat the oven to 425° F. Sift the flour, baking powder, salt, and pepper into a large bowl. Stir in the onions. Rub in 3 tablespoons of cold butter and the shortening until mixture resembles coarse meal. Make a well in the center, pour the milk into the well, and gradually stir the milk into the flour mixture.

3. Turn the dough out onto a lightly floured surface, lightly knead until smooth, and pat out to a thickness of 1 inch. Using a floured 2-inch round cutter, cut out as many biscuits as possible. Gather the scraps, pat the dough back out, and cut more biscuits, repeating until all the dough is used. Place the biscuits in a greased 9-inch cake pan so they touch. Melt 1 teaspoon of butter and brush over the tops. Bake until well browned, about 20 minutes.

Makes about 12 biscuits

Moroccan-Spiced Vegetable Beef Soup

The soup itself can be made up to one week before serving, wrapped well, and stored in the refrigerator. The yogurt garnish can be made up to two days before the party, as can the carrots; both should be wrapped well and stored in the refrigerator. The potatoes, however, should be made no more than two hours before guests arrive, to prevent sogginess and discoloration.

This soup can make a meal if accompanied by French bread, Caramelized-Onion Biscuits (page 231), Tomato-Cumin Breads (page 209), or Afghani Breads with Fennel and Orange (page 180). The flavor and character of the soup are flattered when followed by Salad Greens with Roasted Peppers and Seared Wild Mushrooms (page 150).

For a heartier meal, the Spicy Shrimp, Bacon, and Date Skewers (page 206) could be served before the soup. As could the Chickpea-Lamb Cakes with Red Pepper Sauce (page 176) over the same greens.

The meal seems to beg for a fruit dessert such as Elizabeth's Pistachio-Pear Strudel (page 252) or Nan's Apple Pandowdy (page 256). The Lemon Trifle with Exotic Fruit Compote (page 154) or the Caramel Orange Fool (page 128) would provide a more elegant, though lighter, end to the meal.

THE SOUP

1 tablespoon canola oil
2 teaspoons ground coriander
2½ teaspoons ground cumin
2 teaspoons dry mustard
12 cups Beef Broth, plus reserved meat (page 230)
Kosher salt and freshly ground pepper to taste

THE CARROTS

15 shallots, peeled
12 medium carrots, cut into 1½-inch lengths
3 tablespoons unsalted butter, melted
¾ teaspoon kosher salt
¼ teaspoon freshly ground pepper

232

A Program
for Rational
Entertaining
in an
Irrational
Age

6 large red potatoes, scrubbed and cut into large chunks
1½ teaspoons kosher salt
1 tablespoon unsalted butter
1½ tablespoons chopped cilantro
¼ teaspoon freshly ground pepper

THE SPICED YOGURT

1½ cups plain low-fat yogurt
¼ cup Dijon mustard
1 tablespoon ground cumin
⅛ teaspoon cayenne
Kosher salt to taste
1 tablespoon chopped cilantro

1. To make the soup, heat the oil in a large pot over low heat. Add the coriander, cumin, and mustard and cook, stirring constantly, for 30 seconds. Add the broth, raise the heat, and simmer for 20 minutes. Reheat before serving and season to taste with salt and pepper.

2. To make the carrots, preheat the oven to 425° F. In a shallow baking pan, toss the shallots and carrots with the butter and the salt and pepper and roast, stirring occasionally, until the shallots are soft and the carrots are browned and tender, about 40 minutes. Set aside.

3. Meanwhile, place the potatoes in a saucepan with ½ teaspoon of the salt, cover with cold water, and boil until tender, about 8 minutes. Drain and toss with the butter, cilantro, the remaining 1 teaspoon salt, and the pepper. Set aside.

4. In a small bowl, mix together the yogurt, mustard, cumin, and cayenne and season to taste with salt.

5. Place the reserved meat, the carrot mixture, the potatoes, and the yogurt in separate bowls. Garnish the yogurt with the cilantro. Ladle the soup into 6 bowls to serve, passing the condiments separately.

Serves 6

Korean Hot Pot

The soup and the kimchi used in the recipe below can be made up to a week before a party, wrapped well and stored in the refrigerator. (The kimchi must be made at least one day ahead.) The cucumber salad, however, is best made not more than 2 hours before the party, as its allure lies in its freshness and crunch.

Because this soup is served with rice, it is quite filling and a meal in and of itself. If a first or second course is desired, the Chicken Timbale (page 246) would make a nice, light blast of protein; the Middle Eastern Lamb-Stuffed Wontons (page 208) served on a bed of lightly dressed greens is another. A soft custard, such as the Lemon Trifle with Exotic Fruit Compote (page 154) or the Panna Cotta (page 83), would be lovely. For a crisp, light counterpoint, Elizabeth's Pistachio-Pear Strudel (page 252) or the Poached Pears, Figs, and Oranges with Clove Granité and Hazelnut-Chocolate Cookies (page 170) are potentially wonderful choices.

THE SOUP

12 cups Beef Broth (page 230)
1 ounce dried shiitake mushrooms
½-inch piece peeled fresh ginger, sliced
2 teaspoons soy sauce

THE KIMCHI

1 medium head Napa cabbage, halved lengthwise and cut across into 1-inch
    strips
3 tablespoons kosher salt
1 teaspoon grated fresh ginger
3 cloves garlic, minced
4 scallions, minced
2 tablespoons seeded and minced hot red chilies
2 tablespoons Asian fish sauce
2 tablespoons water
1 teaspoon soy sauce

234

A Program
for Rational
Entertaining
in an
Irrational
Age

1 scallion, minced

2 small jalapeño peppers, seeded and minced

1 tablespoon cider vinegar

1½ teaspoons toasted sesame oil

¼ teaspoon kosher salt

1½ teaspoons toasted sesame seeds

3 medium cucumbers, peeled, halved lengthwise, seeded, and thinly sliced
   crosswise

THE FINISHING TOUCHES

4 cups cooked white rice

¼ cup chopped chives

8 scallions, sliced on the diagonal into ¼-inch-thick pieces

2 cups grated daikon or regular radish

½ pound beef eye round, sliced for carpaccio by your butcher

1. To make the soup, place the broth, mushrooms, and ginger in a large pot and simmer for 30 minutes. Strain. Stir in the soy sauce.

2. To make the kimchi (at least 1 day ahead), toss the cabbage with the salt in a large bowl and let stand at room temperature for 3 hours. Rinse and firmly press out the liquid. Combine the ginger, garlic, scallions, chilies, fish sauce, water, and soy sauce and toss with the cabbage until well coated. Place in a tightly sealed container and refrigerate overnight or for up to one week.

3. To make the cucumber salad, combine the scallion, jalapeños, vinegar, sesame oil, salt, and sesame seeds in a bowl, add the cucumbers, and toss well. Set aside.

4. Toss the rice with the chives. Place the kimchi, the cucumber salad, the rice, the scallions, and the radish in separate bowls. Arrange the carpaccio on a plate. Ladle the soup into bowls. Serve, passing the condiments separately.

Serves 6

Bean Soup with Parsley Salad and Bacon

The flavor of this soup deepens and improves when the soup is allowed to rest overnight in the refrigerator and is slowly reheated. The bacon, which adds both texture and flavor as a garnish, can be fried ahead of time and warmed on its serving platter in a low oven; the same is true of the croutons that give the soup additional heft. Only the parsley salad, which lends a refreshing crunch to the bean porridge, need be left for the last moment.

A varied and vivid and composed salad, such as Salad Greens with Roasted Peppers and Seared Wild Mushrooms (page 150), is wonderful either before or after this soup. The soup could be served after the Chicken Timbale (page 246) for a more elegant meal.

Because the soup is heavy, a light dessert such as the Lemon Trifle with Exotic Fruit Compote (page 154), the Panna Cotta (page 83), or Elizabeth's Pistachio-Pear Strudel (page 252) is a sweet way to finish the meal.

THE SOUP

1 tablespoon olive oil

3 cloves garlic, minced

2 medium onions, diced

3 cups dried navy beans, soaked overnight and drained

3 quarts chicken broth, homemade, or low-sodium canned

2¼ teaspoons kosher salt

½ teaspoon freshly ground pepper

1½ teaspoons chopped fresh rosemary

1½ teaspoons chopped fresh thyme

THE BACON

1 pound slab bacon, cut into ¾-inch-thick slices, cut across into
¼-inch-wide strips

THE PARSLEY SALAD

1½ cups very coarsely chopped Italian parsley

6 tablespoons fresh lemon juice

2 tablespoons olive oil

236
A Program
for Rational
Entertaining
in an
Irrational
Age

¾ teaspoon kosher salt
¼ teaspoon freshly ground pepper

THE CROUTONS

18 rounds French baguette, about ¼ inch thick and 1 inch in diameter
1½ tablespoons olive oil

THE FINISHING TOUCHES

1 large head Roast Garlic, cloves separated (page 44)
1 cup shaved Parmesan cheese

1. To make the soup, heat the oil in a large saucepan. Add the garlic and onions and sauté until soft, about 5 minutes. Stir in the beans and broth. Bring to a boil, lower the heat, and simmer until the beans are soft, about 1½ hours. Using a slotted spoon, remove 1½ cups of beans and place in a food processor with 2 cups of the cooking liquid. Puree until smooth and stir back into the soup. Stir in the salt, pepper, rosemary, and thyme and simmer for 5 minutes. Reheat before serving.

2. To make the condiments, preheat the oven to 350° F. Fry the bacon in a skillet over medium heat until well browned, pouring off the excess fat as it accumulates in the skillet. Drain on paper towels. Set aside.

3. Toss together the parsley, lemon juice, olive oil, salt, and pepper. Set aside.

4. Brush the bread rounds with the olive oil, place on a baking sheet, and bake until crisp, about 8 minutes. Pile on a plate. Place the bacon, parsley salad, roasted garlic, and Parmesan in separate bowls.

5. Ladle the soup into 6 bowls to serve, passing the condiments separately.

Serves 6

Caribbean Sweet Potato Soup
with Ginger Shrimp

With its spicy hint of the Caribbean, this soup can be made the day before a dinner party and warmed slowly over low heat before the guests arrive. The almonds that give crunch to the soup can also be toasted ahead of time and the cilantro that provides a pungent crispness can be rinsed and stored in damp paper towels in the refrigerator for up to a day before it is used.

The soup's shrimp garnish can be marinated the morning of the meal, and broiled, along with the bananas, in less than ten minutes after guests have arrived.

A simple green salad tastes good after bowls of this rich, hearty soup; for a longer and more elegant meal, the Thai Crab Cakes (page 205) or the Chickpea-Lamb Cakes with Red Pepper Sauce (page 176) could be served on bitter greens.

The soft texture of the soup seems to call for something crunchy and fruity in the dessert department. Elizabeth's Pistachio-Pear Strudel (page 252) is a likely candidate.

THE SOUP

6 small sweet potatoes (about 3½ pounds), peeled and cut into 1-inch-thick
    pieces
2¼ cups unsweetened coconut milk
6 cups chicken broth, homemade, or low-sodium canned
1 teaspoon kosher salt, or more to taste
1½ tablespoons fresh lime juice

THE CONDIMENTS

3 tablespoons minced fresh ginger
3 tablespoons fresh lemon juice
2 tablespoons canola oil
¼ teaspoon kosher salt
1½ pounds large shrimp, shelled and deveined
4 large bananas, peeled and cut across into ½-inch-thick slices
1 cup unsweetened coconut flakes, lightly toasted
1 cup sliced almonds, toasted

238
A Program
for Rational
Entertaining
in an
Irrational
Age

½ cup coarsely chopped cilantro
Tabasco

1. To make the soup, combine the sweet potatoes, 1 cup of the coconut milk, and the chicken broth in a large saucepan. Bring to a boil, lower the heat, and simmer until the sweet potatoes are soft, about 15 minutes. Place in a food processor and puree until smooth. Mix in the remaining coconut milk and the salt. Reheat before serving, and stir in the lime juice and additional salt, if needed.

2. To make the condiments, combine the ginger, lemon juice, oil, and salt in a shallow dish. Add the shrimp and toss to coat. Refrigerate for 1 hour. Remove the shrimp from the marinade and broil until cooked through, about 5 minutes. Set aside. Place the bananas on a greased baking sheet and broil until nicely browned, about 3 minutes. Place the shrimp, bananas, coconut, almonds, and cilantro in separate bowls.

3. Ladle the soup into 6 bowls. Serve, passing the condiments, including the Tabasco, separately.

Serves 6

Pasta e Fagioli

The bean soup that serves as a base for the build-your-own pasta e fagioli soup thickens and its flavor mellows when it's prepared the day before a party, cooled, and reheated slowly. The pine nuts used as a garnish can be toasted ahead of time and served at room temperature, as can the croutons.

Likewise, the various vegetable garnishes used in the soup can be readied several hours before guests arrive. A basil-flavored olive oil (available at specialty food stores or by mail order through the Williams-Sonoma company, page 275) adds a fresh flavor, as well as an indulgent and elegant gloss to the homey bean-and-pasta mélange.

This filling soup calls for nothing but a peasant bread, the Caramelized-Onion Biscuits (page 231) or Tomato-Cumin Breads (page 209). While the soup is hearty enough to ask only for a light dessert, such as the Panna Cotta (page 83), the dense Eliza J.'s Pecan Cake with Caramel Sauce (page 254) is well matched to the character of the soup, as is Nan's Apple Pandowdy (page 256). If serving one of these heftier desserts, however, the hostess may want to warn guests of the plenty to come, as the soup is very, very filling.

THE SOUP

1 tablespoon olive oil

1 medium onion, diced

1 large carrot, diced small

2 ribs celery, diced small

2¼ cups dried white beans, soaked overnight and drained

3 to 4 quarts chicken broth, homemade, or low-sodium canned

4½ cups water

1½ teaspoons kosher salt, or more to taste

½ teaspoon freshly ground pepper

¾ pound small pasta, like orecchiette or elbow macaroni

3 tablespoons chopped Italian parsley

THE SALAD

2 cups stemmed arugula, cut across into ¼-inch-wide strips

4 plum tomatoes, seeded and diced

240

A Program
for Rational
Entertaining
in an
Irrational
Age

2 teaspoons extra-virgin olive oil

2 teaspoons red wine vinegar

¼ teaspoon kosher salt

THE CROUTONS

18 rounds French baguette, about ¼ inch thick and 1 inch in diameter

1 tablespoon extra-virgin olive oil

2 tablespoons freshly grated Parmesan cheese

THE FINISHING TOUCHES

2 red and 2 yellow bell peppers, roasted (page 150) and cut into thin strips

¾ cup pine nuts, toasted

¾ cup oil-cured black olives, pitted and coarsely chopped

Basil-flavored olive oil

1. To make the soup, heat the oil in a large saucepan. Add the onion, carrot, and celery and sauté over medium heat until the onion is soft, about 5 minutes. Stir in the beans, 1 quart of the broth, and the water. Bring to a boil, lower the heat, and simmer until the beans are soft, about 1½ hours. Add 2 more quarts of broth and season with the salt and pepper. Bring the soup to a boil, add the pasta, and cook until al dente, about 8 minutes. Reheat before serving, adding more broth, if needed. Stir in the parsley and additional salt, if needed.

2. Preheat the oven to 350° F. To make the salad, toss together the arugula, tomatoes, oil, vinegar, and salt. Set aside.

3. Brush the bread rounds with the oil, sprinkle with the Parmesan, place on a baking sheet, and bake until the cheese is melted, about 5 minutes. Pile on a plate. Place the arugula salad, peppers, pine nuts, and olives in separate bowls.

4. Ladle the soup into 6 bowls to serve, passing the condiments, including the basil oil, separately.

Serves 6

The Elaborations of Winter: Group Conscience on Elegant Frames for Stews

Even for the host or hostess who has conceded to the constraints of modern life and seeks simplicity rather than elaboration for company meals, the desire to seduce and astound guests has not died. Just ask Johanna. The urge has merely been transcended in favor of creating an egalitarian evening. When the cook is freed from the confines of the kitchen and from the barriers between the hand that feeds and those who are served, intimacy—or at least an easygoing good time—is possible.

The cook, however, need not go cold-turkey on culinary grandstanding. A well-placed flourish helps to distinguish between a family meal and a special occasion. The embellishment can be as simple as the weight of good flatware or the reassuring feel of fine linen. A set piece of flowers or produce or fanciful props can also signal a table laid for company.

Choosing to make a single course a showstopper is another way of sending the special-occasion message. In the winter, when one-pot dishes make for good parties—as well as serene hostesses—the group designed several elaborate first courses and a battery of homey, though quite elegant, desserts to frame and elevate the peasant-style dinner.

After some discussion, they concluded that if one has chosen to serve a one-pot dish as a main course, one might begin the meal with a complicated composed salad that is pretty, bountiful, surprising—or with an appetizer that requires finesse and skill. From a taste point of view, the sprightly nature of such a dish contrasts nicely with the smooth sturdiness of most one-pot concoctions. A composed salad can be a way of acknowledging the importance of each guest, since it must be arranged on individual plates at the last moment.

Because an elaborate, à la carte–style first course can affirm the importance of each individual, it is an excellent way of beginning a meal among people who do not know each other well. Having been served an identical though singular first course seems to fortify strangers for the communal and convivial, noted Mrs. J. If, on the other hand, the party is composed of intimates, a variety of nibbles (several of the recipes that Nan used for New Year's Eve, for instance) and dips served with drinks can supplant the first course.

With either sort of guest list, dessert is another opportunity to dazzle a party and to bring it together. Again, contrast speaks volumes. If one has served a sophisticated starter and a simple main course, one can close the circle of the evening with an ornate, individual dessert or one can maintain the expansive note set by the one-pot main course by serving a part of a whole—slices of cake, wedges of pie.

Making one large dessert rather than many individual servings has obvious advantages for a recovering hostess-with-the-mostest.

The confections can generally be made ahead of time and require a minimum of fuss to serve. Some, like Mr. D.'s Chocolate Silk Pie with a Chocolate Crumb Crust (page 250), Johanna's Chocolate Swirl Banana Cream Pie (page 251), or Nan's Apple Pandowdy (page 256), can be served at the table. Because it requires a sharp knife, Elizabeth's Pistachio-Pear Strudel (page 252) is easier cut and plated in the kitchen.

While each of these desserts is rich enough to stand alone, certain garnishes flatter them while telegraphing "made for company." The chocolate silk pie, for instance, can be flanked with a rosette of whipped cream and showered with chocolate curls. The banana pie could be surrounded with sliced bananas dipped in chocolate. Additional pistachios can be candied and served with the strudel, or one can make a pistachio praline, chop it finely, and use it to garnish the dessert. One might choose to garnish the pandowdy with a small scoop of vanilla ice cream, drizzled, perhaps, with caramel sauce.

Making chocolate curls, dipping any sort of fruit in chocolate, candying nuts, making praline, and even making caramel sauce are relatively simple operations which are detailed in most baking books. For the cook, the larger challenge is deciding whether to embellish each plate before serving (thus hitting an elegant note) or to pass the sweets and allow guests to garnish their own desserts (setting a homier tone).

You have to be there to decide.

White Bean Cakes with Goat Cheese and Wilted Chicory

This recipe is a stylish and satisfying first course for a winter soup, or stew. It can also be served as a main course at lunch, accompanied by bread. The wilted chicory can be made up to two days before a party and warmed before serving. The bean mixture can be made a day before serving; however, the cakes are best served right from the skillet.

FOR THE CHICORY

1 tablespoon olive oil

1 onion, minced

2 cloves garlic, minced

4 heads chicory, washed and chopped

1 teaspoon kosher salt

½ teaspoon freshly ground pepper

¼ teaspoon chili pepper flakes

244

A Program
for Rational
Entertaining
in an
Irrational
Age

1 pound white Great Northern beans, soaked overnight
1 small yellow onion, chopped
2 cloves garlic
1 tablespoon minced fresh rosemary
2 tablespoons minced fresh parsley
1½ teaspoons kosher salt
½ teaspoon freshly ground pepper
Olive oil for frying
2 cups fresh bread crumbs
1 (12- to 14-ounce) log fresh goat cheese

1. To make the chicory, warm the olive oil in a heavy pot over medium heat. Add the onion and the garlic and cook until soft, about 5 minutes. Add the chicory, stirring, and adding more as it wilts. When all the chicory has been added, reduce the heat to low, and season the mixture with the salt, pepper, and chili pepper flakes. Cover the pot and continue cooking for 45 minutes, until the chicory is extremely tender. Generally it is not necessary to add water; however, should more water be needed, add in small amounts to avoid sticking. This mixture can be kept in the refrigerator for up to three days. Warm before serving with the bean cakes.

2. To make the cakes, drain the beans and place in a heavy pot with the onion and garlic. Cover with cold water and bring to a simmer over medium heat. Simmer the mixture until the beans are tender, about 40 minutes. Drain. Place the beans, with the rosemary, parsley, salt, and pepper, in the bowl of a food processor and pulse to combine. Allow the mixture to cool. Shape into 16 small, fat patties. If making ahead, place the patties on a baking sheet that has been covered with plastic wrap to avoid sticking, cover, and refrigerate.

3. Fifteen minutes before serving, preheat the broiler and warm the olive oil in a heavy skillet. Bread the cakes with the bread crumbs. When the oil is hot, fry each cake until golden on both sides, about 2 minutes. Drain the cakes on paper towels and place them on a cookie sheet or broiling pan.

4. Place a ¼-inch disk of the fresh goat cheese on top of each bean cake. Broil the cakes to melt the cheese. Place 2 cakes in the center of each of 8 serving plates, surround with the wilted chicory, and serve.

Serves 8

Chicken Timbale

This chicken mousse is simple to make and can be completely prepared a day in advance of the party. The ramekins are warmed in the microwave before serving, and then the timbales are topped with warm, toasted bread crumbs. This dish is delicious served with roasted pepper sauce. It is also tasty as the center of a lightly dressed salad.

FOR THE TIMBALE

3½ cups chicken breast, skinned and cut into cubes
6 large eggs
2 cups fresh bread crumbs
2 shallots, minced
1 teaspoon kosher salt, or more to taste
¼ teaspoon powdered ginger
¼ teaspoon white pepper, or more to taste
⅔ cup milk or heavy cream
2 tablespoons minced parsley
Butter for toasting bread crumbs and oiling ramekins

FOR THE ROASTED PEPPER SAUCE

18 sweet red peppers, cut into quarters
3 tablespoons fruity olive oil
1 tablespoon balsamic vinegar
1 teaspoon fresh lemon juice
½ teaspoon minced lemon zest
¼ teaspoon ground cumin
1 teaspoon kosher salt
Freshly ground pepper to taste
2 cups watercress leaves, for garnish

1. To make the timbales, preheat the oven to 350° F. Place the chicken and the eggs in the bowl of a food processor and pulse to combine. Add ⅔ cup of the bread crumbs, the shallots, salt, ginger, pepper, and cream and pulse to mince. The trick is to maintain an interesting texture by avoiding a puree. Fold in the parsley.

246
A Program
for Rational
Entertaining
in an
Irrational
Age

2. Butter eight 5- to 6-ounce ramekins. Use a rubber scraper to fill each ¾ full. Place the ramekins in a baking pan and add boiling water to reach halfway up their sides. Bake for 5 minutes, then reduce the oven temperature to 325° and bake 35 additional minutes. Remove from the water bath and cool.

3. While the timbales are baking, toast the remaining bread crumbs in butter, or in a nonstick skillet over high heat, until golden. Remove, season with salt and pepper to taste, and set aside.

4. To make the roasted pepper sauce, Sauté the peppers over high heat in 1 tablespoon of the olive oil until soft, about 7 minutes. Stir to avoid burning. Remove from heat and cool. Place the peppers, vinegar, lemon juice, lemon zest, cumin, salt, and pepper in the bowl of the food processor and puree. Slowly drizzle in the remaining olive oil.

5. To serve, use a sharp knife to loosen the timbales and turn each into the center of a salad plate. Top each timbale with toasted bread crumbs, surround with the pepper sauce, garnish with watercress, and serve.

Serves 8

Mushroom Mousse with Shrimp and Arugula Salad

Like the Chicken Timbale, this dish can be made ahead of time. Unlike the chicken, however, the mushroom mousse can be unmolded directly onto a serving plate and warmed in the microwave, according to the manufacturer's instructions. The shrimp is not only a sweet counterpoint to this husky mousse; it also makes the vegetable dish a filling first course, if not a complete luncheon meal.

FOR THE MUSHROOM MOUSSE

2 tablespoons butter

2 pounds shiitake mushrooms, washed, stemmed, and coarsely cut

1 pound white mushrooms, washed, stemmed, and coarsely cut

2 teaspoons dry sherry

6 large eggs

3 tablespoons minced white onion

⅔ cup fresh bread crumbs

⅔ cup milk or heavy cream

1 teaspoon kosher salt

½ teaspoon freshly ground pepper

2 large portobello mushrooms, sliced into ¼-inch strips (you will need
    24 strips)

FOR THE SHRIMP

2 slices bacon, diced

½ cup minced white onion

½ cup minced red pepper

1 pound baby shrimp, peeled and deveined

2 teaspoons fresh lemon juice

¼ cup minced prosciutto or Westphalian ham

2 cups arugula or watercress, washed, dried, and minced

Salt and freshly ground pepper to taste

1. To make the mushroom mousse, melt 1 tablespoon of the butter in a large skillet over medium heat and cook the shiitakes and the white mushrooms until they

248
A Program
for Rational
Entertaining
in an
Irrational
Age

begin to soften, about 10 minutes, stirring occasionally. Add the sherry, reduce the heat to low, and cook for 5 more minutes. Remove, cool, and then puree the mixture, along with the eggs, onion, bread crumbs, milk or heavy cream, salt, and pepper. Set aside.

2. Preheat the oven to 350° F. In a large skillet over medium heat, melt the remaining 1 tablespoon butter, add the portobello slices, and cook for 3 minutes on one side. Turn the mushrooms, reduce heat to low, cover pan, and continue cooking until tender, 5 to 7 minutes. Remove the slices and pat dry.

3. Oil eight 5- to 6-ounce ramekins with additional butter or with olive oil. Carefully press 3 portobello slices into each of the molds, pressing each strip into the bottom and up the side of each mold to create a racing-stripe pattern. Spoon the mushroom mixture into the prepared ramekins. Place the ramekins in a baking pan and add boiling water to reach halfway up the sides of the ramekins. Bake in a 350° oven for 5 minutes. Reduce the heat to 325° and bake for 30 minutes more, until the mousse has set. Cool slightly before demolding or store the ramekins in the refrigerator for up to 1 day.

4. To make the shrimp, in a large skillet over medium heat, cook the bacon until nearly crisp, about 3 minutes. Add the onion and pepper and continue cooking until the vegetables begin to soften. Add the shrimp and cook, stirring, for 20 minutes. Add the lemon juice, remove the pan from the heat, and stir in the prosciutto; then, just before serving, stir in the arugula or watercress. Season the mixture to taste with salt and pepper.

5. To serve, unmold the mousse in the center of a serving plate. Surround with the shrimp and wilted greens and serve.

Serves 8

Mr. D.'s Chocolate Silk Pie

Ingredients for Chocolate Crumb Crust (recipe follows)
³⁄₈ pound (1½ sticks) unsalted butter, softened
1¼ cups sugar
¼ teaspoon kosher salt
1 teaspoon vanilla extract
1 teaspoon brandy (optional)
4 ounces unsweetened chocolate, melted
3 large eggs

1. Combine the crust ingredients as in the following recipe. Work the dough until it barely comes together and reserve ½ cup of the mixture before pressing the rest into the pie plate. Bake as directed.

2. Using an electric mixer, cream the butter and sugar together until light and fluffy. Mix in the salt, vanilla, and brandy, if using. Add the chocolate and mix well. Add the eggs, 1 at a time, mixing well after each addition. Scrape the filling into the pie shell and sprinkle the reserved crumb mixture over the top. Refrigerate for 2 hours to set. Cut into wedges and serve.

Serves about 10

Chocolate Crumb Crust

1½ cups ground chocolate wafers (from about 30 cookies)
⅓ cup sugar
7 tablespoons unsalted butter, melted

Preheat the oven to 350° F. Combine the chocolate crumbs and sugar in a bowl. Add the butter and stir until well mixed. Press the mixture evenly over the bottom and up the sides of a 9-inch pie plate. Bake for 8 minutes. Set aside to cool.

Makes one 9-inch pie crust

250
A Program
for Rational
Entertaining
in an
Irrational
Age

Johanna's Chocolate Swirl Banana Cream Pie

4 large eggs
⅔ cup plus 2 tablespoons sugar
3 tablespoons all-purpose flour
½ teaspoon kosher salt
2 cups milk
3 teaspoons vanilla extract
2 tablespoons unsalted butter, melted
4 ounces bittersweet chocolate
1½ cups heavy cream
2 teaspoons dark rum
4 medium bananas, peeled and cut into ¼-inch slices
1 Chocolate Crumb Crust (opposite)

1. Whisk the eggs in a medium bowl. Whisk in the ⅔ cup of sugar, the flour, and the salt. Scald the milk in a medium saucepan. Whisking constantly, add the milk to the egg mixture. Pour the mixture back into the pan, place over medium heat, and stir constantly until it comes to a boil, about 8 minutes. Scrape the mixture into a bowl and stir in 2 teaspoons of the vanilla and the butter. Place a sheet of plastic wrap directly on the custard and refrigerate or place over a bowl of ice until cold.

2. Place the chocolate and ½ cup of the cream in a double boiler over hot but not simmering water. Stir often until the chocolate is melted and the mixture is smooth. Remove from the heat and stir in the rum. Set aside 3 tablespoons of the mixture.

3. Arrange half of the bananas in a single layer in the pie shell. Cover with half of the custard. Using half of the remaining chocolate mixture, dab it by spoonfuls over the custard. Use a table knife to swirl the chocolate into the custard. Top with another layer of bananas. Cover with the remaining custard and swirl the remaining chocolate mixture into it.

4. Whip the remaining 1 cup of cream to soft peaks. Add the remaining 2 tablespoons of sugar and 1 teaspoon of vanilla and whip until cream just holds a firm peak. Spread the whipped cream over the pie. Warm the reserved 3 tablespoons chocolate if necessary to get a pourable consistency. Drizzle or pipe the chocolate over the whipped cream. Refrigerate for several hours before cutting.

Serves about 10

Elizabeth's Pistachio-Pear Strudel

6 tablespoons unsalted butter, melted
6 Anjou pears, peeled, cored, and cut into large chunks
⅓ cup honey
2 tablespoons sweet sherry
¼ teaspoon ground cinnamon
¼ teaspoon ground cardamom
⅛ teaspoon kosher salt
½ cup golden raisins
1 tablespoon cornstarch
1 tablespoon water
1 teaspoon grated lemon zest
2 teaspoons fresh lemon juice
⅓ cup coarsely chopped pistachios, plus 2 tablespoons finely chopped
4 tablespoons sugar
4 sheets phyllo dough
Confectioners' sugar, for garnish

1. Combine 2 tablespoons of the butter and the pears, honey, sherry, cinnamon, cardamom, salt, and raisins in a large saucepan. Cook over medium heat, stirring often, until the pears are soft, about 12 minutes. Combine the cornstarch and water until smooth. Stir in the pear mixture and cook until thickened, about 2 minutes. Place in a bowl and stir in the lemon zest and lemon juice and the ⅓ cup of pistachios. Let cool completely.

2. Preheat the oven to 350° F. Combine the remaining pistachios and the sugar. Brush a baking sheet with butter. Place 1 sheet of phyllo on a work surface and brush lightly with butter. Sprinkle with ¼ of the sugar mixture. Repeat, using all of the phyllo and sugar mixture.

3. Starting 5 inches from the side nearest you, spread the filling lengthwise over the pastry in a 4-inch-wide mound, leaving a 2-inch border on each end. Fold the ends in over the filling. Fold the side nearest you over the filling. Flip the strudel over, causing it to roll up in the pastry like a jelly roll.

252
A Program
for Rational
Entertaining
in an
Irrational
Age

4. Slide the strudel onto the baking sheet. Cut 4 small diagonal slits in the top of the pastry. Bake until the phyllo is golden brown, about 45 minutes. Let stand until warm but not hot or serve at room temperature. Sift confectioners' sugar over the top. Cut into slices with a serrated knife and serve.

Serves 6

Eliza J.'s Pecan Cake with Caramel Sauce

THE CAKE

1½ cups pecan halves, toasted and cooled

2 cups all-purpose flour

½ teaspoon baking soda

2 teaspoons baking powder

½ teaspoon kosher salt

½ cup unsalted butter, softened

1¼ cups sugar

3 large eggs

1 teaspoon vanilla extract

1 tablespoon bourbon

1 cup sour cream

THE SAUCE

1 cup sugar

¼ cup water

1 cup heavy cream

2 tablespoons bourbon

1. To make the cake, preheat the oven to 350° F. Butter and flour a 10-inch tube pan. Place the pecans in a food processor and pulse until chopped medium-fine. Take out ¾ cup and set aside. Stir together the flour, baking soda, baking powder, and salt and add to the food processor. Pulse until pecans are ground and well mixed with the flour. Set aside.

2. Using an electric mixer, cream the butter and sugar together until very light. Add the eggs, 1 at a time, beating well after each addition. Mix in the vanilla and bourbon. Add the flour mixture alternately with the sour cream, beginning and ending with flour and mixing just to combine. Fold in the reserved pecans. Scrape the batter into the prepared pan and bake until the top springs back when touched in the center, about 1 hour 10 minutes. Let stand for 10 minutes, turn out onto a rack, re-invert, and let cool.

254

A Program
for Rational
Entertaining
in an
Irrational
Age

3. Meanwhile, to make the sauce, place the sugar in a medium saucepan and stir in the water. Use a pastry brush dipped in water to wash down any sugar crystals on the side of the pan. Place over medium heat and cook without stirring until mixture turns a deep caramel color. Remove from heat and carefully add the cream and bourbon. Return the pan to the heat and stir until all the caramel is dissolved. The sauce can be made ahead and reheated.

4. To serve, place a slice of cake on each plate and spoon some of the warm sauce beside it.

Serves 12 to 15

Nan's Apple Pandowdy

6 large Granny Smith apples, peeled, cored, and cut into eighths
2 tablespoons fresh lemon juice
1 cup toasted walnut halves
¾ cup plus ⅓ cup sugar
2 tablespoons water
1¼ cups all-purpose flour
1½ teaspoons baking powder
¼ teaspoon ground nutmeg
½ teaspoon kosher salt
½ cup unsalted butter, softened
¼ cup (packed) brown sugar
1 large egg
1 teaspoon vanilla extract
¼ cup milk

1. Preheat the oven to 375° F. Place the apples in a 2-quart shallow baking dish and toss with the lemon juice and ½ cup walnuts. Set aside.

2. Place the ¾ cup sugar in a medium saucepan and stir in the water. Use a pastry brush dipped in water to wash down any sugar crystals on the side of the pan. Place over medium heat and cook without stirring until the mixture turns a deep caramel color. Immediately pour over the apples; do not toss. Set aside.

3. Place the remaining ½ cup of walnuts and ¼ cup of the flour in a food processor and pulse until the walnuts are ground. Place in a bowl and stir in the remaining 1 cup flour and the baking powder, nutmeg, and salt.

4. Cream the butter, remaining ⅓ cup sugar, and brown sugar with an electric mixer until light. Mix in the egg and vanilla. Add the flour mixture alternately with the milk, mixing on low speed until smooth, stopping to scrape down the sides of the bowl from time to time.

5. Drop the batter over the apples, leaving a 1-inch border around the sides of the dish. Bake until the top is browned and cooked through, about 35 to 40 minutes. Let cool. Divide among 6 plates to serve.

Serves 6

A Program
for Rational
Entertaining
in an
Irrational
Age

Elizabeth Cooks a Dinner from the Heart

The group admired Elizabeth. She was so competent. She never seemed conflicted. It was months before anyone realized that she was lonely in her cool pragmatism and less than happy with the brusque, bottom-line efficiency that she brought to bear on anything she did. Particularly as it related to graciousness.

Rather than allow herself to be stretched to the breaking point between family and professional obligations, the working mother and tax lawyer had played the modern woman's dilemma like a chess game. She addressed the potentially conflicting spheres of her life—home and heart, career and ambition—assiduously and discretely. She allotted a certain number of hours a week to tend to her family and a certain number of hours to build her career. Elizabeth never, ever permitted herself to pause in the dangerous territory between the two. She was a moving target and appeared to be a model of resolve.

But after a year of discussing entertaining and cooking, she began to suspect that something was fundamentally flawed in her approach.

Initially, she was amused and more than a little supercilious when she listened to the group wrestle with their own dueling desires. "Face it," she imagined saying, but never did, at least not in so many words, "social graces are a casualty of modern life." In Elizabeth's view, one does not rail against reality. One accepts it and moves on.

But over the months, as the group devised new approaches to entertaining, she began to feel uncomfortable. She was surprised to find herself envying Nan her odyssey, how she was learning to cook and, in a way, reconciling the conflicts and pressures of her young life. She was jealous of Johanna, too. Initially, she'd seemed like an ostentatious social climber to Elizabeth. Over the months, she'd begun to appreciate the fact that Johanna simply wasn't going to allow modern life to extinguish her generous and hospitable spirit.

Elizabeth realized that the conflict between home and work was not so much about responsibility as it was about human desire, something she'd never permitted herself to indulge. Her pragmatism and scheduling, she thought, smoothed the surfaces of the conflict. Underneath, however, the heart was in bondage. At the end of the day, efficiency and competence are bloodless attributes. No wonder she found each, in the end, unsatisfying. Each was about getting it done, not about doing.

She considered how, in her lifetime, so much of intimate daily life had become professionalized. Decorators turned houses into homes. The minutiae of raising children was classified as "parenting." A walk in the park was a "workout" or it was a waste of time. Dinner was the daily crucible; a cook was judged (and, more important, rated herself) in terms of efficiency and nutritional expertise. Lacking either, she hired a cook or a caterer. In this way, thought Elizabeth, life was more a regimen than a pleasure. The form was perfect, the content almost nil.

Of course, her generation of women, the bridge between late-Victorian womanhood and careerism, felt pulled in contrary directions. And, of course, someone like Martha Stewart had a Svengali-like appeal: the woman had professionalized the sphere of life, the graciousness and prettiness and frivolity, that everyone, at some level, missed.

Who wouldn't like to believe that by *looking* stylish and bountiful and caring, one was, in fact, a stylish, generous, and caring person? With some dismay, Elizabeth realized that she had indeed assumed as much. How depressing.

Mrs. J. listened with great empathy as Elizabeth shared her thoughts. "Every generation resists becoming her mother and ultimately becomes her mother, albeit in a changed world," she said. "You were reared to live a life that is impossible to

258

A Program
for Rational
Entertaining
in an
Irrational
Age

live today. Your pragmatism was a cover for your ambivalence—you wanted to live a gracious and generous life, but you couldn't do it in the same way that the Emily Post generation did. You needed to feel highly competent to keep from feeling like a big failure."

Mrs. J. has never been one to mince words. But she did think that Elizabeth was quite brilliant in identifying *why* competence and efficiency were of such tremendous importance to women today. She considered how, by elevating those characteristics, a generation became vulnerable to what Elizabeth called "the professionalization of private life."

The more Johanna chased her Martha Stewart fantasy, the further she got from the life she thought it represented, pondered Mrs. J. The more Nan tried to please her inner Martha, the more she feared disappointing. The more competently Elizabeth, in Mrs. J.'s opinion, out-Martha-ed Martha, the less effectual she felt.

For a minute, Mrs. J. understood her own daughters, Katherine and Mottie, who were, after all, about the same age as Elizabeth and Johanna. All the rabid health concern, the food phobias, the obsession with gyms and trainers, the rigidity of their decor, the way they dressed. For years, Mrs. J. had mourned the fact that she'd raised girls with no personal style. For all of their rebellion, this was a generation of conformists, she thought, conforming to the appearance of content.

"Fantasy is a tyrant," Mrs. J. told Elizabeth. "If you spend your life creating a perfect picture, you don't have the heart and soul left to inhabit it anyway. Take it from an old lady."

Elizabeth did take it. She did not begin to calculate costs and consider time expenditure and weigh alternatives. She grabbed on to the idea that imperfection with heart was preferable to perfection without heart. In the end, this all came down to dinner in the mind of Elizabeth. She invited Nan and Ted, Johanna and Mark to a quiet Saturday-night dinner one winter evening at her house.

She cooked some things ahead, left others to the last minute. All of it was good, none of it was impeccable—her crown roast of lamb would have looked prettier had she shined and put some frills on the bones; the leeks looked more rustic than elegant; the tart didn't slice as perfectly as she would have liked. None of it mattered. For Elizabeth, cooking this meal was an exercise in seeing her time and effort and ample culinary talent as gifts of incalculable cost.

It was a daring and downright sybaritic turn of the psyche for Elizabeth. Peter noticed that she was flushed and giggly in the kitchen before the guests arrived. He noticed something warm and flirtatious about her at the table. He noticed that his wife made no attempt to justify and rationalize what she would once have regarded as an ill-spent squandering of talent and time. Frankly, it came as a bit of a relief to him.

Wild Mushroom Soup
with Scallops and Thyme

This elegant winter broth with fresh herbs and scallops is rich in taste and light in body, making it a wonderful first course for a hearty winter meal.

The broth can be made up to two weeks before a party, drained, cooled, covered well, and frozen. It will keep up to a week, covered, in the refrigerator. The soup tastes best if reheated gently and if the final mushrooms are added not more than an hour before serving; longer stays in the soup make them flabby.

If dried mushrooms are not available locally, they can be ordered through the mail (page 275).

2 ounces dried porcini mushrooms

12 cups water

2 tablespoons unsalted butter

6 shallots, peeled and minced

1 pound shiitake mushrooms, stemmed and thinly sliced

¼ cup dry sherry

4 teaspoons kosher salt, or more to taste

1 teaspoon freshly ground pepper, or more to taste

1 teaspoon balsamic vinegar

24 sea scallops, cleaned

1 tablespoon chopped fresh thyme

1. Combine the porcini and water in a large saucepan over medium-high heat. Simmer until the broth has reduced to 6 cups, about 1 hour. Strain, reserving the mushrooms and the broth. Coarsely chop the mushrooms and set both aside.

2. Heat 2 teaspoons of the butter in a large, wide pot over medium heat. Add the shallots and sauté until softened, about 30 seconds. Add 1 tablespoon of the remaining butter and the shiitakes and sauté until softened, about 8 minutes.

3. Stir in the sherry, mushroom broth, porcini, salt, and pepper. Simmer slowly for 15 minutes. Stir in the vinegar and additional salt and pepper, if needed. (The soup can be made ahead up to this point.)

260

A Program
for Rational
Entertaining
in an
Irrational
Age

4. Heat the remaining 1 teaspoon of butter in a large nonstick skillet over medium-high heat. Add the scallops and sear until just cooked through, about 45 seconds per side. Slice the scallops in half horizontally and season lightly with salt and pepper.

5. Ladle the soup into 8 shallow bowls and top each with 6 scallop slices. Sprinkle with the thyme and serve immediately.

Serves 8

Parmesan-Sage Crown Roast of Lamb

A crown roast of lamb—loin chops on the bone that are trimmed and shaped into a turban—is a festive and relatively simple roast for company. Most butchers will trim, shape, and tie the roast, leaving only the seasoning and baking to the cook.

The lamb can be seasoned the morning of the party and stored in the refrigerator until one hour before cooking time. It should be brought to room temperature before roasting and should be allowed to rest for 10 to 15 minutes after roasting and before carving so that the juices have time to settle into the meat and the slices will be rosy and clean.

1 crown roast of lamb, prepared by your butcher
2 teaspoons minced fresh sage
2 tablespoons freshly grated Parmesan cheese
2 tablespoons dry bread crumbs
2 cloves garlic, minced
¼ teaspoon kosher salt
Dash of freshly ground pepper

1. Preheat the oven to 425° F. Place the roast, with the ends of the bones down, in a roasting pan. Bake for 55 minutes. Meanwhile, combine the sage, Parmesan, bread crumbs, garlic, salt, and pepper in a small bowl. Remove the roast from the oven and pat the sage mixture over the outside of the roast. Bake for 5 minutes more.

2. Turn the roast over and place on a serving platter. Decorate each rib bone with a cutlet frill, if desired. Serve immediately.

Serves 8

262

A Program
for Rational
Entertaining
in an
Irrational
Age

Leek Gratin

Like most gratins, this one can be assembled ahead of time, stored in the refrigerator, and then baked just before company arrives. It is a delicious dish and a wonderful complement to almost any roast. It is, however, sloppy to serve and therefore a good candidate for being passed around the table family-style—its bubbling, golden crust helps divert attention from the messy look of the baked leeks.

16 medium leeks, white and light green parts only, trimmed and cleaned
Kosher salt and freshly ground pepper to taste
2 tablespoons unsalted butter, cut into ½-inch pieces
1 cup heavy cream

1. Preheat the oven to 350° F. Bring a large pot of water to a boil. Add the leeks and blanch until tender, about 15 minutes. Drain.

2. Place the leeks in a shallow baking dish just large enough to hold them in a single layer. Season with salt and pepper and dot with butter. Pour the cream over the top. Bake for 25 minutes.

3. Just before serving, preheat the broiler. Broil the gratin just until the tops of the leeks begin to brown. Divide among 8 plates, spooning a little of the cream over the top, or pass in the baking dish, family-style. Serve immediately.

Serves 8

Date-Pine Nut Tart

This is a rich but not overwhelmingly sweet winter dessert. It can be prepared the day before a party, but should be wrapped well and stored at room temperature. The pie should be warmed for 30 minutes in a 150-degree oven before serving. It can be served alone or with a dollop of mascarpone cheese, a bit of crème fraîche, a scoop of vanilla ice cream, or some heavy cream, lightly sweetened and whipped to soft peaks.

THE PASTRY

1 cup all-purpose flour
½ teaspoon kosher salt
¼ pound (1 stick) cold unsalted butter, cut into ½-inch pieces
1 large egg yolk
1 tablespoon water

THE FILLING

1½ cups pine nuts, toasted
½ cup unsalted butter, softened
2 teaspoons grated orange zest
⅓ cup (packed) light brown sugar
1 large egg
1 tablespoon Armagnac
¼ cup all-purpose flour
½ teaspoon baking powder
½ teaspoon kosher salt
⅓ cup pitted dates, finely chopped

1. To make the pastry, combine the flour and salt in a food processor. Add the butter and pulse until mixture resembles coarse meal. Whisk together the egg yolk and water. Add to the flour mixture and pulse until dough just comes together. Flatten into a disk, wrap in plastic wrap, and refrigerate for 30 minutes.

2. Preheat the oven to 350° F. On a lightly floured surface, roll out the dough and fit it into a 10-inch quiche dish. Set aside.

A Program
for Rational
Entertaining
in an
Irrational
Age

3. To make the filling, place ½ cup of the pine nuts in a food processor and pulse until chopped. Add the butter and orange zest and process until smooth. Add the brown sugar and egg and process until smooth, stopping to scrape down the sides of the bowl. Mix in the Armagnac. Add the flour, baking powder, and salt and pulse just until combined.

4. Scrape the mixture into a bowl and stir in the remaining pine nuts and the dates. Place the batter in the tart shell and bake until set, about 35 minutes. Place on a rack to cool slightly. Cut into 8 wedges and serve warm.

Serves 8

Saturday Night at Home with Mrs. J.

Mrs. J. had new respect for the women of her daughters' generation. She had, in her way, been rather condescending about the manias that shaped their lives. She'd been harsh in her disdain for their tastes, the studied casualness of their wardrobes, the stoutly proletarian personality of the menus they served, on the rare occasions they entertained at all.

Previously, she had regarded her daughters' devotion to pizza and pasta and what she herself called "blue plate dinners" as egg on the face of their formal rearing. Lately, she'd begun to wonder if their tastes were not a yearning for a simpler life than the harried ones they conducted—work, health club, play group, dancing lessons, the quick and healthful dinners they boasted serving their families, the midnight oil they burned—working, of course, always working.

She also suspected that women of her daughters' generation were trying to recapture the innocence of an era that never really was as innocent, or soft, as it seems when viewed in retrospect, through rose-colored glasses.

The thought behind her own proprieties had always been kindness and dignity and well-being. To the extent that she was a slave to her proprieties, she mused, kindness, dignity, and well-being are lost. And so her daughters are slaves to conventions of another sort. Mrs. J. realized one afternoon, while sipping tea in her parlor with Mr. D., that her daughters had not rejected her as much as they had embraced the world she'd brought them into. Tenderness always made Mrs. J. feel old.

"I'd like to introduce Elizabeth and Johanna to Katherine and Mottie," she said to Mr. D. "They have much in common, I think, but my motivation is selfish, actually. I have the feeling that Elizabeth and Johanna might help declaw the beast." Mr. D. nodded conspiratorially, and she added sharply, "I'm referring, of course, to the beast of my daughters' mother."

Oddly, she mused, traditional dishes could pose more of a hazard than a comfort. Indeed, the unfamiliar probably stood a better chance of establishing a common ground. Given the brutal weather, she said—it was, after all, snowing outside, in March, if you will—consolation was paramount in the first course. In keeping with the current public mood, to say nothing of the tastes of her daughters, she requested something essentially rustic, such as a squash bisque. But she warned that such a dish should be garnished in a surprising manner, perhaps employing exotic seasonings.

Pointing out that nostalgia for the sort of homey food that was never served in their own homes now informed the appetite of an entire generation, Mrs. J. suggested some variation on pork and greens for a main course. "I think here we need to continue working from an exotic palate, flavor-wise," she told Mr. D., "though it's been so long since I ate pork that I quite frankly can't imagine what you'll come up with."

Considering dessert, Mrs. J. was, in Mr. D.'s opinion, quite brilliant. "I think people miss the cheese course, D., darling. It was the first thing to go. People don't want to fritter away their fat grams and, frankly, no one wants a four-hour dinner anymore. At the same time, I think it might be nice if we could figure out a way to serve them a nice bit of cheese with something bready, and a taste of something sweet, along with a nice big red wine, and call it dessert."

Mr. D. felt positively exhilarated as he walked from Mrs. J.'s building at the corner of Park Avenue and Sixty-third Street and back toward his well-chintzed and overstuffed office nearby. It was as if, by loosening the bonds of dietary restrictions ever so slightly, Mrs. J. had given him, as a caterer, a new lease on life.

So delighted was he to have the meat and cream portion of his culinary vocabulary restored that he applied himself wholeheartedly to the task of moderating additional fat in the menu. So taken was he with the concept of a dessert of bread and cheese that he allowed his baker a few days to develop some savory rolls that, along with showy little bowls of honey for dipping and handsome wedges of Stilton, soon became *the* dessert of Le Tout New York.

"It's grown-up pizza," explained Mr. D. "It bridges the bias of two generations. It's homey and it's elegant. It's familiar food in an unfamiliar position in the menu. Sometimes I wish I could patent recipes."

His exhilaration, of course, transcended the creation of a single dish. It was the zesty feeling of having navigated the choppy waters that result when different aspects of life converge—health and time constraints, class signals, and changing tastes—and threaten the livelihood and reputation of a caterer.

He knew that Saturday night at Mrs. J.'s would be magical. It wasn't an "important" crowd. But the evening was a blueprint for the future. The menu was an inspired synthesis. He couldn't have done it without Mrs. J., or Johanna, or Elizabeth, or even little Nan, bless her soul. He'd send around flowers on Monday.

Holding his Hermès scarf over his mouth, Mr. D. huddled in his sheared nutria coat against the wind on Park Avenue, knowing that he'd weathered a tougher storm, feeling positively puckish, young, agile, and satisfied, to say nothing of greatly relieved.

268

A Program
for Rational
Entertaining
in an
Irrational
Age

Butternut Squash Soup with Spiced Shrimp and Cilantro

The soft, comforting texture of this soup contrasts with the spicy and sprightly garnish. It is filling and a wonderful way to begin a winter meal. The soup can be made several days before a party, covered well, refrigerated, and reheated gently. The shrimp and cilantro, on the other hand, should be added immediately before serving.

THE SHRIMP

2 tablesoons fresh lime juice
6 tablespoons fresh orange juice
½ teaspoon ground coriander
¼ teaspoon crushed red pepper
¼ teaspoon kosher salt
Dash of freshly ground pepper
2 teaspoons olive oil
½ pound large shrimp, peeled, deveined, and halved lengthwise

THE SOUP

2 medium butternut squash, quartered, seeds and fibers scooped out
4 cups chicken broth, homemade, or low-sodium canned
1 cup heavy cream
2 teaspoons grated orange zest
1 teaspoon ground coriander
Kosher salt and freshly ground pepper to taste
4 teaspoons chopped fresh cilantro

1. To make the shrimp, whisk together the lime juice, orange juice, coriander, crushed red pepper, salt, pepper, and 1 teaspoon of the olive oil. Add the shrimp and toss to coat well. Cover and refrigerate for 2 hours.

2. Meanwhile, to make the soup, preheat the oven to 425° F. Place the squash in a large roasting pan with enough water to make a depth of ⅛ inch. Cover loosely with aluminum foil and roast until soft, about 50 minutes.

3. When cool enough to handle, pull the skin from the squash. Place half of the squash in a blender with half of the chicken broth and puree until smooth. Pour into a large saucepan and repeat with the remaining squash and broth.

4. Stir in the cream, orange zest, coriander, salt, and pepper. Reheat just before serving.

5. To finish the shrimp, heat the remaining teaspoon of oil in a large nonstick skillet over medium-high heat. Drain the shrimp and add to the skillet. Sauté until just cooked through, about 30 seconds per side.

6. Ladle the soup into 8 shallow bowls. Garnish with the shrimp and sprinkle with cilantro. Serve immediately.

Serves 8

Spiced Roast Pork with Wilted Chicory and Warm Potato-Bacon Salad

This hearty, full-flavored dish makes a complete meal, even without the potato salad. The pork can be spiced, wrapped, and stored in the refrigerator the day before a party, but it should be brought to room temperature before roasting. The potato salad can also be made ahead and warmed before serving. The chicory, on the other hand, is best prepared immediately before serving.

THE PORK

4 slices bacon

1 teaspoon ground cinnamon

1 teaspoon ground mace

½ teaspoon freshly ground pepper

1 boneless loin of pork, about 3 pounds

270

A Program
for Rational
Entertaining
in an
Irrational
Age

3 tablespoons Dijon mustard

3 tablespoons white wine vinegar

½ cup olive oil

1 teaspoon kosher salt, plus more to taste

¼ teaspoon freshly ground pepper, plus more to taste

12 small red potatoes, cut into ⅛-inch rounds

4 scallions, thinly sliced

8 small heads chicory, stemmed, washed, and well dried

1. Cook the bacon in a large skillet until crisp. Drain on a paper towel, crumble, and set aside. Pour 2 tablespoons of bacon fat into a small dish and place in the freezer just until solid. Leave the remaining fat in the skillet and set aside.

2. Preheat the oven to 350° F. Combine the cinnamon, mace, and pepper. Place the pork in a roasting pan and rub the spice mixture all over it. Rub the solid bacon fat over the pork. Roast until the pork reaches an internal temperature of 150° to 160° F., about 1 hour.

3. About 25 minutes before the pork is done, whisk together the mustard and vinegar. Whisking constantly, add the olive oil in a slow, steady stream. Season with the salt and pepper. Place in a medium saucepan and set aside.

4. Place the potatoes in a saucepan, cover with water, and simmer, covered, until tender but firm, about 6 minutes. Drain well, cover, and keep warm. Place the dressing over low heat until hot, stirring constantly with a whisk. Place the potatoes in a bowl and gently mix in the hot dressing, the scallions, and the bacon. Cover and keep warm.

5. Heat the bacon fat in the skillet over medium-high heat. Add the chicory in batches, tossing until wilted and bright green. Place in a mixing bowl as each batch is done. Toss with salt and pepper to taste.

6. Slice the pork into ¼-inch slices and season lightly with salt. Mound the chicory in the center of 8 plates and drape 3 slices of pork over each mound. Surround with the potato salad and serve immediately.

Serves 8

Mr. D.'s Savory Bread, Stilton, and Honey

These rolls can be baked the day before a party and stored in an airtight container at room temperature, but they are best served fresh from the oven, warm and redolent of the coriander and cumin seeds. The dough can be prepared ahead of time, wrapped well, and frozen for up to two weeks. Allow it to thaw in the refrigerator overnight before use. It will rise slightly when it thaws and must be punched down and kneaded briefly before being shaped into knots and baked.

⅔ cup walnuts
¾ teaspoon coriander seeds
¾ teaspoon cumin seeds
1 package active dry yeast
1 cup warm water
½ teaspoon sugar
2⅓ cups all-purpose flour, plus more for kneading dough
1¼ teaspoons kosher salt
2 tablespoons walnut oil, plus more for oiling bowl
1 cup honey
1 pound Stilton cheese

1. Heat a large, heavy skillet over medium heat. Add the walnuts and toss frequently until toasted, about 8 minutes. Remove from the skillet and set aside. Place the coriander and cumin seeds in the skillet and stir constantly until toasted, about 1½ to 2 minutes. Place the seeds on a work surface, cover with plastic wrap, and crush with a rolling pin. Set aside. Chop the walnuts and set aside.

2. Whisk together the yeast and water in a large bowl until the yeast is dissolved. Add the sugar and let stand for 5 minutes. Stir in 1⅓ cups of the flour and the salt. Stir in the walnut oil, walnuts, and spices. Gradually stir in the remaining flour.

3. Turn the dough out onto a floured surface and knead until smooth, about 10 minutes. While kneading the dough, add as much additional flour as needed to keep the dough from sticking to your hands and the work surface.

272
A Program
for Rational
Entertaining
in an
Irrational
Age

4. Lightly oil a large, clean bowl. Shape the dough into a smooth ball and place it in the bowl, turning it once to coat the top with oil. Cover with a clean kitchen towel and let stand in a warm place until dough has doubled in bulk, about 1 hour. Punch the dough down and reshape into a ball. Cover and let double again, about 1 hour.

5. Preheat the oven to 350° F. Punch the dough down and divide it into 16 equal pieces, using a scant ¼ cup of dough for each. On a barely floured surface, roll each piece into a ball. Use your fingers to roll each ball into a rope about 9 inches long. Tie the ropes loosely into knots and place on 2 baking sheets lined with baking parchment. Cover each sheet with a towel and let stand until the rolls are doubled, about 25 minutes.

6. Bake until the rolls are golden brown, about 25 minutes. (Rolls can be made ahead and reheated.) Heat the honey in a small saucepan until hot and pour into a serving bowl or pitcher. Place 2 rolls on each of 8 plates and serve, passing the Stilton and honey separately.

Serves 8

Mail-Order Sources

Asian ingredients:
Vwajimaya, 519 Sixth Avenue South, Seattle, WA 98104, (800) 889-1928.

Basil-flavored olive oil and orange oil:
Williams-Sonoma Company, 100 North Point Street, San Francisco, CA 94133,
    (800) 541-2233 or (415) 421-4242.

Duck-and-veal demi-glace:
Dartagnan, Jersey City, NJ 07306, (800)-DARTAGNAN.

Mascarpone:
Dean and DeLuca, 560 Broadway, New York, NY 10012, (800) 221-7714 or
    (212) 226-6800.
Vermont Butter & Cheese Company, Pitman Road, P.O. Box 95, Websterville,
    VT 05678, (800) 884-6287 or (802) 479-9371.

Wild and dried mushrooms:
Earthly Delights, 4180 Keller Road, Suite B, Holt, MI 48842, (800) 367-4709
    or (517) 699-1530.
Aux Delices des Bois, 14 Leonard Street, New York, NY 10013, (800) 666-1232
    or (212) 334-1230.

Index